THE LAND

OVERTURES TO BIBLICAL THEOLOGY

THE LAND

Place as Gift, Promise, and Challenge in Biblical Faith

Second Edition

Walter Brueggemann

FORTRESS PRESS
MINNEAPOLIS

Cover photograph by Philippe Colombi © 2002 Photodisc, Inc.

Library of Congress Cataloging-in-Publication Data

Brueggemann, Walter.
    The land : place as gift, promise, and challenge in biblical faith / Walter Brueggemann—2nd ed.
        p.   cm. — (Overtures to biblical theology)
    Includes bibliographical references and index.
    ISBN 0-8006-3462-4 (pbk. : alk. paper)
     1. Bible—Theology. 2. Religion and geography. I. Title. II. Series.
BS543.B68 2003
220.6'4—dc21

                                        20020743234

Manufactured in the U.S.A.

06   05   04   03   02   1   2   3   4   5   6   7   8   9   10

To my father and mother
who lived from the land
who taught us promises they never doubted

CONTENTS

ABBREVIATIONS

AB	Anchor Bible
AnBib	Analecta biblica
ATANT	Abhandlungen zur Theologie des Alten und Neuen Testaments
BA	*Biblical Archaeologist*
BARead	*Biblical Archaeologist Reader*
BASOR	*Bulletin of the American Schools of Oriental Research*
BHT	Beiträge zur historischen Theologie
BKAT	Biblischer Kommentar Altes Testament
BWANT	Beiträge zur Wissenschaft vom Alten und Neuen Testament
CBOT	Coniectanea Biblica: Old Testament Series
CBQ	*Catholic Biblical Quarterly*
CC	Continental Commentaries
ChrCent	*Christian Century*
CJT	*Canadian Journal of Theology*
EvT	*Evangelische Theologie*
Dtr	Deuteronomist
GS	*Gesammelte Studien*
GTS	Gettysburg Theological Studies
Int	*Interpretation*
JAAR	*Journal of the American Academy of Religion*
JBL	*Journal of Biblical Literature*
JNES	*Journal of Near Eastern Studies*
JR	*Journal of Religion*
JSOT	*Journal for the Study of the Old Testament*
JSOTSup	Journal for the Study of the Old Testament: Supplement Series
KJV	King James Version (Authorized Version)
LXX	Septuagint
NEB	New English Bible
NKZ	*Neue kirchliche Zeitschrift*
NRSV	New Revised Standard Version
OBT	Overtures to Biblical Theology

OTL	Old Testament Library
PsychT	*Psychology Today*
PTMS	Pittsburgh Theological Monograph Series
RB	*Revue biblique*
RSV	Revised Standard Version
RHPR	*Revue d'histoire et de philosophie religieuses*
SBL	Society of Biblical Literature
SBLDS	Society of Biblical Literature Dissertation Series
SBS	Stuttgarter Bibelstudien
SBT	Studies in Biblical Theology
SR	*Saturday Review*
SWBA	Social World of Biblical Antiquity
TEH	Theologische Existenz Heute
ThB	Theologische Bücherei
USQR	*Union Seminary Quarterly Review*
VT	*Vetus Testamentum*
VTSup	Vetus Testamentum Supplements
WBC	Word Biblical Commentary
ZAW	*Zeitschift für die alttestamentliche Wissenschaft*
ZTK	*Zeitschrift für Theologie und Kirche*

PREFACE TO THE
SECOND EDITION

I AM DELIGHTED THAT FORTRESS PRESS HAS DECIDED TO PUBLISH A NEW, revised edition of *The Land*. I am, moreover, profoundly grateful to K. C. Hanson, who has given immense effort to the new edition, most especially in preparing a current bibliography on the topic.

The initial publication of *The Land* came at an important point in my own reflection on the Old Testament, my own reflection in a rather characteristic way alongside more general changes and developments in Old Testament studies at the time. As I have indicated elsewhere, the 1970s in Old Testament studies was a time when the major shape of Old Testament study, largely accomplished by Gerhard von Rad and G. Ernest Wright in the wake of Karl Barth, began to unravel.[1] While the upheavals in the discipline were complex and a result of complex contextual factors, in general it is fair to say that it meant, in a most important way, the diminishment of the accent on "God's Mighty Deeds in History." This diminishment entailed as well the end of the old dichotomies that had been so prominent in the field between "history and nature," "time and space."

It was in that context that I begin to see that the Old Testament, in its theological articulation, was not all about "deeds," but was concerned with *place*, specific real estate that was invested with powerful *promises* and with strategic arrangements for presence in the place as well. Once I had seen that much, then it was a ready development to see the dialectic in Israel's fortunes between *landlessness* (wilderness, exile) and *landedness*, the latter either as possession of the land, as anticipation of the land, or as grief about loss of the land; it was on that basis that my argument in

---

1. Walter Brueggemann, *Theology of the Old Testament: Testimony, Dispute, Advocacy* (Minneapolis: Fortress Press, 1997) 15–42.

the book took shape, all aspects of land being referred to the God of covenant Torah.

The categories and methodologies that now dominate Old Testament studies were then scarcely on the horizon, as Norman K. Gottwald's decisive study, *The Tribes of Yahweh*, was published only in 1979.[2] My own approach, reflected in the book, was not yet well informed or self-conscious about such emerging methodologies. As a result I offered what was still rather a study of a "biblical theme" after the manner of the older, more innocent so-called biblical theology movement. It is fair to say, I believe, that that perspective has been continued in the more recent book by Norman Habel, *The Land Is Mine: Six Biblical Land Ideologies*.[3] His book is an important advance upon my own but is I believe in general congruent with it. I estimate that my book merits reissuance because, for all its innocence, the book represents a responsible harbinger of what was to come in the field, largely through the impetus of Gottwald and the scholars who have been informed by his work.[4]

I may identify five major developments in Old Testament studies that now need to be taken into account that were not on my horizon at the time of my initial writing:

1. The *recovery of creation* as a major motif in Old Testament tradition. As I have elsewhere indicated, it is largely due to an essay of Gerhard von Rad in the wake of the "Blood and Soil" religion of German national socialism, with a strong second from G. Ernest Wright, that had turned Old Testament study away from creation to "history."[5] Articulations by many scholars in more recent time have contributed to the recovery of the theme of creation. First among them is Claus Westermann who offered a series of studies that arose in the preparation of his magisterial Genesis commentary.[6] Westermann has worked

2. Norman K. Gottwald, *The Tribes of Yahweh: A Sociology of the Religion of Liberated Israel, 1250–1050 B.C.* (Maryknoll, N.Y.: Orbis, 1979).

3. Norman C. Habel, *The Land Is Mine: Six Biblical Land Ideologies,* OBT (Minneapolis: Fortress Press, 1995).

4. See Robert B. Coote and Keith W. Whitelam, *The Emergence of Early Israel in Historical Perspective* (Sheffield: Almond, 1987); David Noel Freedman and David Frank Graf (eds.), *Palestine in Transition: The Emergence of Ancient Israel* (Sheffield: Almond, 1983); and Frank S. Frick, *The Formation of the State in Ancient Israel: A Survey of Models and Theories* (Sheffield: Almond, 1985).

5. Walter Brueggemann, "The Loss and Recovery of Creation in Old Testament Theology," *Theology Today* 53 (1996) 177–90.

6. See especially Claus Westermann, *Blessing in the Bible and the Life of the Church,* OBT (Philadelphia: Fortress Press, 1978). For reference to his other work on the theme, see Brueggemann, *Theology of the Old Testament* 161, n. 27.

at the recovery of creation as a defining theological theme in a variety of writing, but none is more important than his programmatic essay of 1971 in which the *God of deliverance* (through historical deeds) is seen to be as well the *God of blessing* who has infused creation with capacities for fruitfulness and abundance.[7] Alongside the work of Westermann I mention particularly the remarkable essay by Terence Fretheim in 1991, a thesis that is explicated in his Exodus commentary.[8] Fretheim was able to show that the Exodus narrative of Exodus 1–15 is not simply about historical deliverance, but it is about the disruption of creation by Pharaoh (reflected in the plague cycle), a disruption mastered only by Yahweh's sovereign governance of creation. Following Fretheim, I have more recently suggested that the manna narrative of Exodus 16 (placed in the final form of the text just after the conclusion of the Exodus narrative in Exodus 15) exhibits the full fruition of creation whereby even wilderness is made to be a place of nourishment by the creator God who turns every environment of chaos (= wilderness) into a place of viable life.[9]

The creation theme takes on crucial importance for Israel's faith when it is noticed that the Hebrew term *'eres* functions to refer both to "earth" and "land." In its usage as "earth," the term clearly refers to the created earth with reference to the creator God who governs "heaven and earth." The same term, however, refers to land, most specifically Israel's "land of promise" that Israel hopes for and holds from Yahweh. The important matter, however, is that the term *'eres* functions in both uses and one cannot know in any particular usage exactly which reference serves; thus it is entirely possible that Israel's land stands in for and epitomizes all land. Consequently, in the Pentateuchal traditions, the final form of the text begins in an account of "earth" (Genesis 1 and 2), but culminates with reference to the "land of promise" (Deut 34:4). In such a characteristic maneuver enhanced by the continuing interpretation of *'eres*, Israel is able to claim all the powers of the creator for its own "turf" in its theological horizon.

2. From this fundamental recognition of "creation" that was only inchoate in the Old Testament studies at the time of my book, several other important lines of interpretation are now to be noted. Among them is the recognition that the claim of "promised land" in the Old

7. Claus Westermann, "Creation and History in the Old Testament," *The Gospel and Human Destiny,* ed. Vilmos Vajta (Minneapolis: Augsburg, 1971) 11–38.

8. Terence E. Fretheim, "The Plagues as Ecological Signs of Historical Disaster," JBL 110 (1991) 385–96; Fretheim, *Exodus,* Interpretation (Louisville: Westminster John Knox, 1991).

9. Walter Brueggemann, "*Theme* Revisited: Bread Again!" (forthcoming).

Testament is not an innocent theological claim, but is *a vigorous ideological assertion* on an important political scale. This insight is a subset of ideology critique in the field that has emerged as a major enterprise only in the last decades.[10] Perhaps the most important articulation in this matter is the recognition of Jon Levenson that Israel's tradition demonizes and dismisses the Canaanites as a parallel to the anti-Semitism that is intrinsic to the New Testament.[11] That is, Israel's text proceeds on the basis of the primal promises of Genesis 12–36 to assume entitlement to the land without regard to any other inhabitants including those who may have been there prior to Israel's emergence.[12] That primary tradition in Genesis, moreover, comes to violent and concrete articulation in the Book of Joshua, whereby the land that is "promised" and "given" in the older narratives is here *taken* in a brutalizing kind of way, a brutality in which Yahweh is deeply implicated, a violence both theological and political about which the tradition itself expresses no important misgiving.[13]

It will now be generally agreed that the traditions of *land promise* and *land violence* (twin claims that are decisive for the tradition and cannot be separated out) are not given us in the final form of the text as reportage. Rather, the final form of the text is completely removed from what may have been the "happening" of land, and now function as a belated ideological rationale for the subsequent community of Israel. Thus, even though the land promises in the tradition are in purportedly old traditions, they are now to be completely understood in terms of subsequent ideological claims of important use to a later interpretive community.

Michael Prior has most fully and explicitly considered these matters.[14] Among other things, he has rightly chastened me (along with a

10. See James Barr, *History and Ideology in the Old Testament: Biblical Studies at the End of a Millennium* (Oxford: Oxford Univ. Press, 2000). Barr's own judgments seem to me not very clear, but he has gathered a useful collection of data on the current discussion.

11. Jon D. Levenson, "Is There a Counterpart in the Hebrew Bible to New Testament Antisemitism?" *Journal of Ecumenical Studies* 22 (1985) 242–60.

12. The data on the ancestral promises has been usefully summarized by Claus Westermann, *The Promises to the Fathers: Studies on the Patriarchal Narratives* (Philadelphia: Fortress Press, 1980); see also David J. A. Clines, *The Theme of the Pentateuch,* JSOTSup 10 (Sheffield: JSOT, 1978).

13. See Regina M. Schwartz, *The Curse of Cain: The Violent Legacy of Monotheism* (Chicago: Univ. of Chicago Press, 1997).

14. Michael Prior, "A Land Flowing with Milk and Honey," *Scripture Bulletin* 28 (1998) 2–17, idem, *The Bible and Colonialism: A Moral Critique* (Sheffield: Sheffield Academic, 1997). For a discussion of a derivative practice of land ideology, see Conor Cruise O'Brien, *God Land: Reflections on Religion and Nationalism* (Cambridge: Harvard Univ. Press, 1988).

number of other interpreters) for being inattentive to the ideological dimension of the land promise. This shortcoming in my book reflects my inadequate understanding at that time, but also reflects the status of most Old Testament studies at that time that were still innocently credulous about the theological importance of the land tradition in the Old Testament. Indeed, even though Gottwald has shown how the Pentateuch tradition served to fund the social experiment that was constituted by revolutionary Israel, he did not in 1979 pay attention to the ideological import of the text as it impacted other people as a necessary cost of the affirmation of Israel's land claims.[15]

More recently scholarly attention has been given to the ongoing ideological force (and cost) of the claim of "promised land." On the one hand, this ideology of land entitlement serves the contemporary state of Israel. Keith Whitelam has most frontally paid attention to the way in which land entitlement has served the ongoing territorial ambitions of the state of Israel, ambitions that, as I write, are enacted in unrestrained violence against the Palestinian population.[16] It is clear on any reading that the modern state of Israel has effectively merged old traditions of land entitlement and the most vigorous military capacity thinkable for a modern state. The outcome of that merger of old traditional claim and contemporary military capacity becomes an intolerable commitment to violence that is justified by reason of state.

On the other hand, it is clear that the same ideology of entitlement has served derivatively the Western powers that are grounded in this broad ideological claim and that have used that claim as a rationale for colonization of other parts of "the earth." That is, *land entitlement* leads to *earth occupation*. There is no doubt that such land entitlement has functioned as a warrant for European seizure of what became the United States with a brutalizing dismissal of Native Americans, who are regarded as an inconvenience for the arriving entitled Europeans. David Gunn, moreover, has explored the parallel way in which the same ideology provided an explicit ground for the British seizure of New Zealand.[17] No doubt these cases can be replicated in many other

15. Gottwald, *The Tribes of Yahweh*, 102–3 and passim, has shown the revolutionary intentionality of the traditions; while the ideological dimension of the land tradition is inchoately given in Gottwald's study, he did not go far in making it explicit.

16. Keith Whitelam, *The Invention of Ancient Israel: The Silencing of Palestinian History* (London: Routledge, 1997).

17. David M. Gunn, "Colonialism and the Vagaries of Scripture: Te Kooti in Canaan (A Story of Bible and Dispossession in Aoatearoa/New Zealand)," *God in the Fray: A Tribute to Walter Brueggemann*, ed. Tod Linafelt and Timothy K. Beal (Minneapolis: Fortress Press, 1998) 127–42.

places concerning Western colonization under the guise of an entitlement rooted in biblical tradition.

Thus land as a theological theme is never to be taken as innocent
and surely not as innocently as I had done in my book. In the Old Testament itself that strand of violence intrinsic to the theme of land is
relatively held in check by connection of land to the Torah. This connection is defining for both Deuteronomic theology and the prophetic
tradition; but of course land ideologies then as now are endlessly
imaginative and energetic in circumventing that restraint that is definitional for the text itself. A fuller attentiveness to the Torah tradition is
important in a critique of the ideology of land both as concerns the
textual tradition itself and as concerns the modern military state of
Israel and the many derivative modern uses, not least in the new wave
of military imperialism currently under way in the United States. The
tradition of Deuteronomy is repetitious and insistent in its connection
between *land possession* and *Torah obedience*.

> Do not say to yourself, "My power and the might of my own hand
> have gotten me this wealth." But remember the LORD your God, for
> it is he who gives you power to get wealth, so that he may confirm his
> covenant that he swore to your ancestors, as he is doing today. If you
> do forget the LORD your God and follow other gods to serve and
> worship them, I solemnly warn you today that you shall surely per-
> ish. Like the nations that the LORD is destroying before you, so shall
> you perish, because you would not obey the voice of the LORD your
> God. (Deut 8:17-20; NRSV)

> See, I have set before you today life and prosperity, death and adver-
> sity. If you obey the commandments of the LORD your God that I am
> commanding you today, by loving the LORD your God, walking in
> his ways, and observing his commandments, decrees, and ordi-
> nances, then you shall live and become numerous, and the LORD
> your God will bless you in the land that you are entering to possess.
> But if your heart turns away and you do not hear, but are led astray
> to bow down to other gods and serve them, I declare to you today
> that you shall perish; you shall not live long in the land that you are
> crossing the Jordan to enter and possess. I call heaven and earth to
> witness against you today that I have set before you life and death,
> blessings and curses. Choose life so that you and your descendants
> may live, loving the LORD your God, obeying him, and holding fast
> to him; for that means life to you and length of days, so that you may
> live in the land that the LORD swore to give to your ancestors, to
> Abraham, to Isaac, and to Jacob. (Deut 30:15-20; NRSV)

Military-political powers who crush opposition in order to control more land characteristically (a) forget the warning voiced by Yahweh, the ultimate land owner, (b) imagine that "the might of my power has gotten me this wealth" (Deut 8:17; my translation), and (c) therefore "choose death," both directly for those who oppose them and for themselves in less visible but in equally inescapable ways. The old story of *land gift*, *land possession*, and consequently *land loss* is a primary plot in ancient Israel's self-presentation. It is, in an elemental way, the main plot of aggressive military powers that characteristically learn too little and too late about the costliness of Torah violation.[18]

3. The way the story is told in ancient Israel about *promise-possession-loss*, the completion of the story is in loss, wherein Israel forfeits the land, is deported to Babylon, to be reconstituted as a community of exiles. Thus both the Deuteronomist (2 Kings 24–25) and the Chronicler (2 Chronicles 36) make land loss the culminating point of the narrative, offering in their respective cases only tenuous hints of life for Israel beyond loss (2 Kgs 25:27-30; 2 Chr 36:22-23). In what has become the normative telling of Israel's self-conscious narrative in the Old Testament, Joshua–Kings, the account ends with deportation and the single note on kinship-in-exile. In the alternative version of Chronicles, the ending is the same, except for the important difference that the decree of Cyrus the Persian gives a new vista of restoration and resumption of life in the land. Either way, the deportation lingers as definitional for Israel's faith.

From this rendering of reality, three observations are pertinent. First, serious critical questions have been raised about the "historicity" of exile, with a strong urging that "exile" is an ideological construct designed to serve the entitlements of the elite deported community. Against such a view, Daniel L. Smith-Christopher, among others, has made, in my judgment, a compelling case for the "historicity" of "exile." Be that as it may, there can be no doubt that "exile," as either history or as ideology, has become definitional for Israel's self-discernment.

Second, taking the lines of conventional historical criticism, it is clear that the sixth century, the time in which exile is to be situated (either historically or ideologically), became a time of immense

18. The same tension can be expressed in quite secular terms, as for example, Paul M. Kennedy, *The Rise and Fall of the Great Powers: Economic Change and Military Conflict from 1500 to 2000* (New York: Random House, 1987). A contrast is offered in the credulous affirmation of entitlement without curb by Francis Fukuyama, *The End of History and the Last Man* (New York: Free Press, 1992).

interpretive generativity in ancient Israel, no doubt because the political crisis of displacement evoked, required, and welcomed interpretive activity. Most important of such interpretive efforts are the interpretive traditions of the three great prophetic traditions of Isaiah, Jeremiah, and Ezekiel, each of which—each in a quite distinctive idiom—uttered Judah in and through exile to a new horizon of expectation:

- Isaiah in a mode of royal-Jerusalem imagery;
- Jeremiah according to covenantal and Torah traditions; and
- Ezekiel in a Priestly tradition.

It is worth noting that the three great poetic trajectories in the prophetic tradition roughly correlate to the great traditions of the Pentateuch so that (a) *the Yahwist tradition*, with its accent upon Abraham and its anticipation of David, is expressed in Isaiah; (b) *the Deuteronomic tradition*, with its accent on Torah is expressed in Jeremiah; and (c) *the Priestly tradition*, with its accent on holiness is expressed in Ezekiel. Thus, in turn, Isaiah, Jeremiah, and Ezekiel pick up the visions of J, D, and P about how the land shall be related to the Torah and how Israel shall live into "exile" and then beyond "exile."

4. Whatever may be the historical detail of the sixth-century deportation, there is no doubt that "exile" has been a defining interpretive metaphor for theological self-understanding in Judaism.[19] In the first instance, it is clear that Judaism has been nurtured as an exilic community, a stance that gives particular credence to diaspora Judaism, a conviction of Jewishness that is not necessarily defined by entitlement to "the land of Israel." Beyond that defining Jewish reality, the figure of exile serves other critical reflection as well.[20] Specifically I, along with others, have proposed that "exile" is a suggestive way in which to understand the important disestablishment of the Christian church and Christian faith in Western culture.[21] In the latter usage, it is important that "exile" be taken as a metaphor and not pressed with excessive literalness. The imagery refers to the practice of faith that is not (or no longer) supported by dominant cultural-political forces, but relies rather on freedom, courage, and imagination of the community of particularity. In Christian practice it is worth noting that in this season of cul-

---

19. See Jacob Neusner, "Exile and Return as the History of Judaism," *Exile: Old Testament, Jewish, and Christian Conceptions,* ed. James M. Scott, Supplements to the Journal for the Study of Judaism (New York: Brill, 1997) 221–38.

20. See for example, Edward W. Said, *Reflections on Exile and Other Essays* (Cambridge: Harvard University Press, 2000).

21. Walter Brueggemann, *Cadences of Home: Preaching Among Exiles* (Louisville: Westminster John Knox, 1997).

tural displacement in the Western church, the "exilic" voices of the Old Testament take on new authority and pertinence, among them the lament tradition that was never needed before in a Western church tradition that characteristically enjoyed hegemonic support and favor.[22]

5. In more recent time, we may also observe two dimensions of "land the-
ology" that have particular contemporary pertinence. This includes, first, the awareness that "land theology" readily relates to "the environmental crisis."[23] As long as Old Testament interpretation was preoccupied with ad hoc "historical events," the issue of environment could hardly be noticed. But once attention is paid to 'eres (land, earth) as God's creation and it is recognized that life in the land must be lived in conformity with the creator's intention, then the care for or abuse of creation is readily recognized as a biblical and theological concern.[24] Particular attention should be given in this connection to the initiatives of Norman Habel who is in the midst of a remarkable survey of Old Testament materials related to environmental matters.[25] Of course it is not possible to claim a direct awareness of "environment" in the Old Testament tradition, for such a claim is clearly anachronistic. Nonetheless the matter of creation as healthy environment is unavoidably implicit everywhere in the Old Testament. Particular reference might be made to the wisdom tradition that attends to "foolishness" that brings trouble and death, foolishness being the disregard for or contradiction to the intention of the creator.

6. Finally, as a subset of environmental crisis, particular attention should be called to the crisis of agribusiness whereby land-care and land

22. See Kathleen M. O'Connor, *Lamentations and the Tears of the World* (Maryknoll, N.Y.: Orbis, 2002).

23. There is now an extensive literature that finds in the Bible an accent on environment. Among the more suggestive are the following: Carol J. Dempsey and Russell A. Butkus, eds., *All Creation Is Groaning: An Interdisciplinary Vision for Life in a Sacred Universe* (Collegeville, Minn.: Liturgical, 1999); Catharina J. M. Halkes, *New Creation: Christian Feminism and the Renewal of the Earth* (Louisville: Westminster John Knox, 1991); Carol Johnston, *And the Leaves of the Tree Are for the Healing of the Nations: Biblical and Theological Foundations for Eco-Justice* (Louisville: Presbyterian Church [U.S.A.], n.d.); Sean McDonagh, *To Care for the Earth: A Call to a New Theology* (Quezon City, Philippines: Claretian, 1986); and Stephen B. Scharper and Hilary Cunningham, eds., *The Green Bible* (Maryknoll, N.Y.: Orbis, 1993).

24. See the remarkable fictional commentary by Daniel Quinn, *Ishmael: An Adventure of the Mind and Spirit* (New York: Bantam, 1995).

25. Norman C. Habel, *Readings from the Perspective of Earth* (Cleveland: Pilgrim, 2000); idem, *The Earth Story in Genesis* (Sheffield: Sheffield Academic, 2000); idem, *The Earth Story in Wisdom Tradition* (Sheffield: Sheffield Academic, 2001); idem, *The Earth Story in the Psalms and in the Prophets* (Sheffield: Sheffield Academic, 2001).

management are readily transposed into commodity without any human dimension. I mention this issue in particular because among the most consistent readers of this book have been concerned people in the upper Midwestern plains states of the United States who have watched family farms disappear and, with their loss, witnessed the demise of a viable human, social fabric.

In the Old Testament, the issues that touch the contemporary crisis of the family farm and the ominous threat of agribusiness should be focused upon the eighth-century prophets and the crisis of latifundialization. The recent book by D. N. Premnath traces the way in which the commoditization of farm land in ancient Israel is viewed by Israel's prophets as a violation of Torah and as a mocking of the covenant God.[26] The prophetic tradition leaves us with the question of a viable social alternative when the land is treated, not as commodity, but as an arena for human interaction that respects both neighbor and land. In this regard particular attention should be paid to the several writings of Wendell Berry who, in a quite distinctive and imaginative idiom, builds directly from the key urgings of biblical faith.[27]

On all these counts,
- the recovery of creation theology with 'eres as land and earth;
- the ideology of land entitlement;
- the crisis of displacement and exile;
- the environmental crises; and
- the crisis of agribusiness and the family farm,

my book recognized the key issues, though my perspective was limited to what were only my beginnings in critical awareness of these contemporary issues as they related to and were derived from and critiqued by the biblical tradition. I believe that the book will continue to be useful to those who are in the process of discovering and struggling with the fact that conventional, biblical-theological preoccupations in both church and in popular culture characteristically miss the main accent points of biblical faith.

I should add a word about method. When I wrote this book, it was clear to me that historical critical approaches to the subject of land were,

---

26. D. N. Premnath, *Eighth Century Prophets: A Social Analysis* (St. Louis: Chalice, 2002). See his earlier discussion, "Latifundialization and Isaiah 5:8-10," JSOT 40 (1988) 49–60.

27. This is articulated in both his essays and novels. For a representative essay, see Wendell Berry, *The Gift of Good Land: Further Essays Cultural and Agricultural* (San Francisco: North Point, 1981), and see his most recent novel, *Jayber Crow: A Novel: The Life Story of Jayber Crow, Barber, of the Port William Membership as Written by Himself* (Washington: Counterpoint, 2000).

by themselves, not adequate. For the intent of the book was to move beyond historical critical issues to the contemporary crisis of land, contemporary in terms of the many land disputes including that of Israel and the Palestinians, the environmental agenda, and the farm crisis at the time of my writing. It was at the time not at all clear how to move beyond historical critical perspectives, not clear for me and not generally clear in the discipline. By that time Walter Wink had uttered his famous verdict about the "bankruptcy" of historical criticism, and Brevard S. Childs had made a first run at what turned out to be "canon criticism," an attempt to remove the Bible from the control of historical judgments.[28] The moves to come later beyond historical criticism, however, at that time were less than clear, and my book is rightly critiqued as lacking theological rigor and clarity.

Since that time, of course, methodological matters have become much clearer with rhetorical criticism and social-scientific approaches now prominent alongside historical criticism, the latter newer method including ideological critique as a component of social-scientific method.[29] And, of course, a book could now be written on the land that is much more rigorous and clear about method than is my own, which is reflective of the state of the discipline at the time of writing.[30] The lack of clarity about method, of course, was reflective of a general deficit in our understanding of how to move beyond historical matters, even though a theological reading of the Bible "as Scripture" assured the legitimacy of such a move.[31]

Now, unlike then, it would be proper to consider the ideological force of land texts and to see either how such articulations served *the ideological legitimacy of land owners* or how the same text might serve *the hopes of*

28. Walter Wink, *The Bible in Human Transformation* (Philadelphia: Fortress Press, 1973) 1; Brevard S. Childs, *Biblical Theology in Crisis* (Philadelphia: Westminster, 1970).

29. On the emerging methods, see Brueggemann, *Theology of the Old Testament*, 61–89. For a clear example of the newer accent on ideology critique, see David Penchansky, *The Betrayal of God: Ideological Conflict in Job*, Literary Currents in Biblical Interpretation (Louisville: Westminster John Knox, 1990).

30. Among the more important recent titles related to the theme of land is Christopher J. H. Wright, *God's People in God's Land: Family, Land, and Property in the Old Testament* (Grand Rapids: Eerdmans, 1990).

31. Brevard Childs has been the principal figure in the move from historical studies to theological concerns that he lodges in the "canon" as an alternative to historical context. In my own way, I have sought to mediate between critical and interpretive matters in *Genesis*, Interpretation (Atlanta: John Knox, 1986); *A Commentary on Jeremiah: Exile and Homecoming* (Grand Rapids: Eerdmans, 1998); *Isaiah 1–39*, WBC (Louisville: Westminster John Knox, 1998); *Isaiah 40–66*, WBC (Louisville: Westminster John Knox, 1998); as well as *Theology of the Old Testament*.

those who anticipate receiving land but in the present moment control no land. In my analysis of Psalm 37, I have considered the way in which that Psalm can be read either as a defense of those who now hold the land or as an assurance to those who do not now hold the land but anticipate subsequent reception of the land.[32] A social-scientific approach would connect land texts more closely to the material conditions of the text-producing, text-reading community.[33] Alongside, rhetorical criticism might understand texts as acts of constructive imagination that playfully generate, entertain, and legitimate thinkable social arrangements concerning the land that are alternative to the "facts on the ground." It is my impression that in my own less clear, less rigorous way I made this interpretive turn intuitively but not in a way that was methodologically adequate.

In any case, my book is an attempt to make clear that biblical faith—and the God of the Bible—cannot be left disconnected from real public life in the world with its sociopolitical, economic dimensions. While a great deal has been done interpretively and methodologically since my book, the book nonetheless stands as a marker in the movement of scholarship, albeit a marker now in the somewhat removed past, as interpretation has taken up more systemic issues of faith and lived reality. By "systemic" I mean that Israel's embrace of land and Israel's practice of land in conformity with the will of the creator (or in defiance to the will of the creator) is quite in contrast to the notion of the more-or-less ad hoc singular intrusions of God into history. Such a "systemic" approach to land as an arena of sustained and sustainable blessing is an opportunity for further reflection about the land as nourisher and sustainer in contrast to discontinuous events that have the force of masculine intrusiveness.[34] Wendell Berry has written that any society is likely to treat its land in the same way that it treats its women.[35] While the twinning of these concerns may be a bit enigmatic and perhaps smacks of a masculine def-

32. Walter Brueggemann, "Psalm 37: Conflict of Interpretation," *Of Prophets' Visions and the Wisdom of Sages: Essays in Honour of R. Norman Whybray on His Seventieth Birthday,* ed. Heather A. McKay and David J. A. Clines, JSOTSup 162 (Sheffield: Sheffield Academic, 1993) 229–56.

33. See Ferdinand E. Deist, *The Material Culture of the Bible,* ed. Robert P. Carroll (Sheffield: Sheffield Academic, 2000) and David C. Hopkins, *The Highlands of Canaan: Agricultural Life in the Early Iron Age* (Sheffield: Almond, 1985).

34. This contrast is especially voiced by Westermann in his interface of blessing and deliverance, on which see n. 6.

35. Wendell Berry, *Recollected Essays 1965–80* (San Francisco: North Point, 1981) 215.

inition of interpretive questions, the point is worth reflection. A systems approach to the theology of the land takes land as blessed creation that evokes a particular kind of wisdom about how to live well and responsibly in the land.[36] Such a judgment now sounds rather commonplace in interpretation, but it was not so at the time of the writing of the book.

We will not finish soon with these issues and there remains much more work to be done. In the meantime, I am glad for the reissuance of this book that may continue to make its modest contribution to that urgent and difficult connection of *God*, *land*, and *Torah*, a convergence that is inescapable even in a technological era, even on the horizon of "the last superpower" that imagines its own land, power, and wealth can go uncurbed. The large witness of the Bible concerning land testifies that such uncurbed land management as legitimated in current "globalization" finally cannot succeed, even if it imagines the extension of its power "to the uttermost parts of the earth." It seems unlikely on the face of it, but entirely credible upon thoughtful reflection, that the Bible in its odd, insistent way stands as an abiding warning to and testimony against uncurbed technological exploitation in the interest of self-enhancement and self-aggrandizement, and as an abiding invitation to alternative inchoately offered in the tradition. The Bible is relentless in such testimony but, of course, that testimony requires an endless procession of interpreters who can make the connection between old texts and contemporary temptations and opportunities. This book is one voice that I am glad will continue to sound in making that connection.

Columbia Theological Seminary
April 19, 2002

---

36. Quinn, *Ishmael* has particularly appreciated the "wisdom" of creatures who have honored creation and the will of the creator long before the human creature arrived. See Walter Brueggemann, "The Creatures Know" (forthcoming).

PREFACE TO THE
FIRST EDITION

THIS STUDY ATTEMPTS TO CONTRIBUTE TO THE CURRENT REDEFINITION of categories of biblical theology. It is clear that new intersections and connections are redefining the categories. This discussion seeks to speak to (a) the interpretive questions of these categories and (b) the urgent questions of the institutions in modern society concerned with a deep sense of rootlessness.

The study is organized around three histories of the land: (a) the history of promise into the *land,* (b) the history of management into *exile,* and (c) the new history of promise that begins in exile and culminates in *kingdom.* In very general ways this division of the material parallels the scheme of Prof. Bernhard W. Anderson in his *The Unfolding Drama of the Bible.*[1] However, two factors may be noted. First, in the present discussion these are not three "mighty acts" or events as Anderson proposes. They are long historical processes that in retrospect seem respectively headed toward *land, exile,* and *kingdom,* but which in process admitted of turns, surprises, and alternatives. The recital of the three histories is not a neat scheme, but a slow tortuous process. In each case the historical sequence might have culminated differently, but it was experienced and remembered in these concrete directions. Second, my awareness of the movement of history to (a) *land,* (b) *exile,* and (c) *kingdom* came not at the beginning but only at the end of my work. This threefold pattern has grown out of the texts themselves, for that is how Israel's story was remembered and retold. Israel set out to speak and write neither about Yahweh's deeds nor about the land. Israel simply told its children what had been seen and heard. In the telling Israel discerned itself characteristically in the crunch between Yahweh and his land.

1. Bernhard W. Anderson, *The Unfolding Drama of the Bible,* 3d ed. (Philadelphia: Fortress Press, 1988).

The method utilized in this discussion is somewhat impressionistic because I have tried to engage the ripple effect of Israel's imagery about land. I have persistently been mindful of critical scholarly judgment, which I take most seriously. I have not knowingly violated any seriously established critical judgment. But my concern has been elsewhere. I have wanted, on the one hand, to avoid an arid historicism that makes the history closed, dead, and absolute, for then it is not history as the Bible embraces it. On the other hand, I have wanted to keep the imagery historical and not let it become general detached "myth" in a vacuum, a practice now much in vogue. So I have tried to do what I believe Israel itself did; tell these stories that have happened to Israel and let them influence the consciousness of the community. Perhaps even contemporary Western experience can be understood as part of that tortuous, joyous history which at the same time authorizes the contemporary faith community and calls it into question. For the believing community of the church, it is not absolute history, but it is "our" history, and probably our destiny is hidden in this history of the land and landlessness.

I have in each turn of the history of people and land tried to focus on particular texts and explore how these might permit a different reading of the whole of Israel's history. It is my hope that the story itself has provided the frame of reference and the perspective for the texts. That frame of reference I believe is shaped by the power of promise, the authority of gift, and the dis-ease with which our community has responded to gift.

I have no doubt that those of us engaged in theological study are in a crisis of categories. Simply psychologizing in either Freudian or Jungian terms or utilizing radical Marxist sociology will not finally suffice. Nor will a general "religious" approach take us far because the issue of authority finally must be faced and we cannot forever be critical and preconfessional. One grows weary of the simple dichotomy of scientific/mythological, as though historical were not an alternative, or of the parallel oversimplification of Western technology/Eastern mysticism, as though covenant did not offer a quite different perspective. It is my conviction that the Bible itself provides a perspective on human consciousness that could move us beyond the silly and exhausting antitheses that hold no promise for us. It is my hope that this study may hint at the categories of perception that will permit us to see the text differently and also permit us to discern ourselves and our history differently. The following discussion is offered in conviction that the Bible provides us with peculiar and decisively important categories for facing the crisis of the human spirit. Our intellectual history makes it difficult to engage promissory and covenantal categories without distorting them into simple-minded confessional historicism or uncommitted anthropology. But that may be the epistemological repentance to which we are now called. I believe that the biblical text provides a beginning point in envisioning a human future that if it is to matter at all must be historical, covenantal, and promissory, the very dimensions Israel peculiarly discerned in its history with the land.

I am aware that my conclusions on the relation of the Old and New Testaments are innovative. On the one hand, they do not fit our usual categories of New Testament interpretation, which are often in terms of narrowly christological doctrinal theories of atonement rather than in terms of the field of images in which the New Testament lived. I hope there is a legitimate suggestion here of fresh ways in which the intent of the text might be discerned. On the other hand, the following discussion may appear to claim the history of land in a narrowly Christian way. That is not my intention, for I hope and believe that what I have written might permit a fresh discussion between Jews and Christians about the common and peculiar promises that power our shared history of waiting for Messiah.

The literature on the subject is enormous and I have tried to acknowledge my major debts. The categories in which I have worked are parallel to those of Rolf Rendtorff, "Das Land Israel im Wandel der alttestamentlichen Geschichte,"[2] although I have dealt more fully with the themes and developed them more dialectically. I have learned much from my colleague M. Douglas Meeks and am grateful to him. I am also grateful to John R. Donahue, my editorial colleague, for his support and guidance. In working at this theme, I have become aware of how my own nurture has tilted me to value the land and to be aware of its precariousness. For that reason this book is dedicated to my parents.

---

2. Rolf Rendtorff, "Das Land Israel im Wandel der alttestamentlichen Geschichte," in *Judisches Volk—gelobtes Land,* ed. W. P. Eckert et al. (Munich: Kaiser, 1970) 153–68.

1.

LAND AS PROMISE
AND AS PROBLEM

HE SENSE OF BEING LOST, DISPLACED, AND HOMELESS IS PERVASIVE IN
contemporary culture. The yearning to belong somewhere, to have a
home, to be in a safe place, is a deep and moving pursuit. Loss of place and
yearning for place are dominant images. They may be understood in
terms of sociological displacement, as Americans have become a "nation
of strangers,"[1] highly mobile and rootless, as our entire social fabric
becomes an artifact designed for obsolescence, and the design includes
even us consumers! They may be understood in terms of psychological
dislocation,[2] as increasing numbers of persons are disoriented, characterized as possessors of "the homeless mind."[3] The despair and yearning are
expressed in the pathos of the "top forty" songs among the young, in the
fear among the old that they are forgotten, in the helplessness of the poor
in the face of "urban progress."[4] Remarkably the same sense of loss and

---

1. Compare Vance Packard, *A Nation of Strangers* (New York: McKay, 1972).

2. Compare Paul Tournier, *A Place for You: Psychology and Religion,* trans. E. Hudson
(New York: Harper & Row, 1968), which suggests the dialectic of the following discussion.
That is, one task for those not having a place is to find one, the other task for those having a
place is to leave it.

3. Compare Peter L. Berger et al., *The Homeless Mind: Modernization and Consciousness*
(New York: Random House, 1973); and especially Berger, *Pyramids of Sacrifice: Political
Ethics and Social Change* (New York: Basic, 1974) 23–24, 62, 69, 169, 175. See also Alvin W.
Gouldner, *The Coming Crisis of Western Sociology* (New York: Basic, 1970) 67, 224–25, 253–55
and *passim*; and Charles Hampden-Turner, *Radical Man: The Process of Psycho-Social Devel-
opment* (Cambridge: Schenkman, 1970) chap. 4.

4. David Shapiro, "Rediscovering a Sense of Past and Place," *SR* (April 29, 1972) 36–39;
Gustav H. Schultz, "People's Park: The Rise and Fall of a Religious Symbol," *ChrCent* (Feb-
ruary 14, 1973) 204–7; and the more extended statement of Robert Coles, *Migrants, Share-
croppers, Mountaineers,* vol. 2 of *Children of Crisis* (Boston: Little, Brown, 1971) 3–24.

the same yearning for place are much in evidence among those whom the world perceives as being well rooted and belonging, the white middle class at the peak of success and productivity. Those whom we imagine to be secure and invested with "turf" in our time experience profound dislocation, and we are, young and old, rich and poor, black and white, "as having everything, and yet possessing nothing" (see 2 Cor 6:10). We have become precisely the inversion of the life-giving One, who had nothing, yet was as though possessing everything.

This of course is not a new struggle, but it is more widespread and visible than it has ever been. Nor is this sense alien to the biblical promise of faith. The Bible itself is primarily concerned with the issue of being displaced and yearning for a place. Indeed, the Bible promises precisely what the modern world denies. It will be the premise of the following discussion that *land* is a major concern of contemporary persons.[5] In what follows, *land* will be used to refer to *actual earthly turf* where people can be safe and secure, where meaning and well-being are enjoyed without pressure or coercion. *Land* will also be used in a *symbolic* sense, as the Bible itself uses it, to express the wholeness of joy and well-being characterized by social coherence and personal ease in prosperity, security, and freedom. It will be important to recognize, both in biblical usage and in contemporary usage as well, that *land* continually moves back and forth between literal and symbolic intentions. And in any particular use it is likely that we shall not be clear on the term, simply because it is symbol-laden with dimensions of meaning that cannot be separated from each other.

A symbolic sense of the term affirms that land is never simply physical dirt but is always physical dirt freighted with social meanings derived from historical experience. A literal sense of the term will protect us from excessive spiritualization, so that we recognize that the yearning for land is always a serious historical enterprise concerned with historical power and belonging. Such a dimension is clearly played upon by the suburban and exurban real estate ads that appeal to that rapacious hunger. Land is always fully historical but always bearer of over-pluses of meaning known only to those who lose and yearn for it. The current loss of and hunger for place participate in those plus dimensions—at once a concern for actual historical placement, but at the same time a hunger for an over-plus of place meaning. This dialectic belongs to our humanness. Our humanness is always about historical placement in the earth, but that historical place-

---

5. "The New American Land Rush," *Time* (October 1, 1973) 80–99. The land rush is surely symptomatic of our sense of landlessness in American culture.

ment always includes excess meanings both rooted in and moving beyond literalism.

Land as a Prism for Biblical Faith

Land is a central, if not *the central theme* of biblical faith. Biblical faith is a pursuit of historical belonging that includes a sense of destiny derived from such belonging. In what follows I suggest that land might be a way of organizing biblical theology. The dominant categories of biblical theology have been either existentialist or formulations of "the mighty deeds of God in history."[6] The existentialist approach has been concerned with the urgent possibility of personal decision-making in which Israel's faith has clustered. In both traditions of scholarship, preoccupation with the time-space problem and the identification of time categories as peculiarly Hebraic have made interpreters insensitive to the preoccupation of the Bible for placement. Either with raw, isolated *decisions* or with identifiable decisive *events*, the major emphasis has been upon the transforming discontinuities in which God has been discerned or made himself known to his people.

Only now, with the new yearning in our culture and with the exhaustion of such motifs as fruitful lines of interpretative pursuit, is another perspective possible. No doubt the existential binge of contextless decision as a stance of interpretation has run its course, and we are forced to look again at the privatizing, ahistorical character of such an approach. No doubt fresh awareness of land as a central Jewish category in relation to the state of Israel has alerted even Christians to new interpretative possibilities.[7] But most of all it has been the failure of an urban promise that has reopened the question. That promise concerned human persons who could lead detached, unrooted lives of endless choice and no commitment.[8] It was glamorized around the virtues of mobility and anonymity

---

6. The various articulations of "the God who acts" theology tended to construct polarities of time and space, history and nature. An unintended result was a nearly total neglect of land as a central theological motif. At that particular point the Bultmannian existentialists and the "God who acts" theologians tended to make the same unfortunate stress.

7. See Hans Eberhard von Waldow, "Israel and Her Land: Some Theological Considerations," *A Light unto My Path: Old Testament Studies in Honor of Jacob M. Myers*, ed. H. N. Bream et al. (Philadelphia: Temple Univ. Press, 1974) 493–508; Jacob Neusner, *American Judaism: Adventure in Modernity* (Englewood Cliffs, N.J.: Prentice-Hall, 1972) 87–116; and Hans Ruedi Weber, "The Promise of the Land," *Study Encounter* 7 (1971) 1–16.

8. Harvey Cox lists the two major gifts of the city as anonymity and mobility, *The Secular City* (New York: Macmillan, 1965) 38–59. While Cox means to celebrate these, more sober reflection indicates they are sources of anomie and the undoing of our common humanness.

that seemed so full of promise for freedom and self-actualization. But it has failed, as chronicled in distinctive ways by Vance Packard and Peter Berger among others. It is now clear that a *sense of place* is a human hunger that the urban promise has not met. And a fresh look at the Bible suggests that a sense of place is a primary category of faith.

This discussion is an attempt to bring together that primary category of faith and that urgent hunger among us. What follows is a sober judgment that the quest for meaning as it has been interpreted is not first on our agenda, precisely because it is *rootlessness* and not *meaninglessness* that characterizes the current crisis. There are no meanings apart from roots. And such rootage is a primary concern of Israel and a central promise of God to his people. This sense of place is a primary concern of this God who refused a house and sojourned with his people (2 Sam 7:5-6) and of the crucified one who "has nowhere to lay his head" (Luke 9:58).

A sense of place is to be sharply distinguished from a sense of space as has been stressed by some scholars.[9] "Space" means an arena of freedom, without coercion or accountability, free of pressures and void of authority. Space may be imaged as weekend, holiday, avocation, and is characterized by a kind of neutrality or emptiness waiting to be filled by our choosing. Such a concern appeals to a desire to get out from under meaningless routine and subjection. But "place" is a very different matter. Place is space that has historical meanings,[10] where some things have happened that are now remembered and that provide continuity and identity across generations. Place is space in which important words have been spoken that have established identity, defined vocation, and envisioned destiny. Place is space in which vows have been exchanged, promises have been made, and demands have been issued. Place is indeed a protest against the unpromising pursuit of space. It is a declaration that our humanness cannot be found in escape, detachment, absence of commitment, and undefined freedom.[11]

Whereas pursuit of space may be a flight from history,[12] a yearning for a place is a decision to enter history with an identifiable people in an iden-

---

9. This difference is powerfully articulated by F. W. Dillistone, *Traditional Symbols and the Contemporary World*, Bampton Lectures 1968 (London: Epworth, 1973) chap. 6.

10. Compare Jonathan Z. Smith, "Earth and the Gods" *JR* 49 (1969) 108–27.

11. See the critique by Philip Rieff, *The Triumph of the Therapeutic: Uses of Faith after Freud* (New York: Harper & Row, 1966) 243–45, concerning modern values derived from living without commitment. The point of contact with the analysis of Peter Berger and the erosions of specificity of historical community are especially pertinent to our discussion.

12. See Walter H. Capps, *Time Invades the Cathedral: Tensions in the School of Hope* (Philadelphia: Fortress Press, 1972).

tifiable pilgrimage. Humanness, as biblical faith promises it, will be found in belonging to and referring to that locus in which the peculiar historicity of a community has been expressed and to which recourse is made for purposes of orientation, assurance, and empowerment. The land for which Israel yearns and which it remembers is never unclaimed space but is always *a place with Yahweh,* a place well filled with memories of life with him and promise from him and vows to him. It is land that provides the central assurance to Israel of its historicality, that it will be and always must be concerned with actual rootage in a place that is a repository for commitment and therefore identity. Biblical faith is surely about the life of a people with God as has been shown by all the current and recent emphases on covenant in a historical place. And if God has to do with Israel in a special way, as he surely does, he has to do with land as a historical place in a special way. It will no longer do to talk about Yahweh and his people but we must speak about Yahweh and his people *and his land.* Preoccupation with existentialist *decisions* and transforming *events* has distracted us from seeing that this God is committed to this land and that his promise for his people is always his land. In what follows, we will explore ways in which this focus shaped Israel's faith and ways it may speak to our own sense of displacement and our yearning to belong. Israel is that strange people who pursued a sense of place with all the hope and demands that belong to its peculiar historicality.[13]

Israel as God's Homeless People

The Bible will here be considered as Israel's reflection on what it means to belong with the land and indeed to the land before God. Israel is a landless people as we meet it earliest and most often in biblical faith. Although it is without place, it has a sense of being on the way to a promised place. Israel is a people on the way because of a promise, and the substance of all its promises from Yahweh is to be in the land, to be placed and secured where Yahweh is yet to lead it. Its whole history and life are understood in terms of that hope and in response to that promise. As landless folk, yearning for land, Israel is presented under several images derived from several experiences. Each such image presents the *land as promise* to the *landless:*

1. Israel is embodied in Abraham, Isaac, and Jacob in the earliest presentations as *sojourners* on the way to a land whose name it does not

---

13. Elie Wiesel articulates this powerfully in *The Jews of Silence: A Personal Report on Soviet Jewry,* trans. N. Kozodoy (New York: Holt, Rinehart and Winston, 1966) 78.

know. It is en route in response to the call of a God who tells it very little about himself and asks of Israel a blind trust. The Genesis narratives in a stark way present the radical demand of God that the way of
faith requires leaving a land and accepting landlessness as a posture of
faith:

> Go from your country and your kindred and your father's house. . . .
> (Gen 12:1)

> I am Yahweh who brought you out from Ur of the Chaldeans. . . .
> (Gen 15:7)

The sojourn is freely chosen, not imposed. It is a choice made by
those who could have chosen not to leave. The choice means to throw
one's self totally on Yahweh, not in order to live in some nonhistorical
relation with God but to be led to a better place, one characterized by
promises not known either in Ur or in one's father's house.

They are the people of sojourn. *Sojourner* is a technical word usually described as "resident alien." It means to be in a place, perhaps for
an extended time, to live there and take some roots, but always to be an
outsider, never belonging, always without rights, title, or voice in decisions that matter.[14] Such a one is on turf but without title to the turf,
having nothing sure but trusting in words spoken that will lead to a
place. The theme of "resident alien" is not remote from contemporary
experience. People in our time know what it means to live waiting
always for the notice of transfer, or for notice of "urban redevelop-
ment," or for any of the irresistible and unidentified forces of urban life
devoted to displacement.

In English translation, the "sojourn" is occasionally called pilgrimage (Gen 47:9; Exod 6:4 in KJV), which may sound a bit more noble and
heroic. It certainly affirms more clearly being on the way somewhere.
But the image does not change. It is being where one does not belong
and cannot settle in and having to survive there, all because of
promise. To an observer, the sojourner-pilgrim is just there, coping
and surviving. Perhaps only the insider can know that he is not just
"being there," but is on his way toward a promise. He can be observed
as placeless, but he knows of a promised place, and that changes his
sojourn.

14. See especially the detailed work on resident aliens in John H. Elliott, *A Home for the
Homeless: A Social-Scientific Criticism of 1 Peter, Its Situation and Strategy*, 2d ed. (Minneapolis: Fortress Press, 1990).

2. During the period when Israel had left the slavery of Egypt and was not yet in the land of promise (forty years' worth!) it remembered itself as *wanderer*. In wilderness traditions (Exodus 16–18; Num 10:10ff.), the buoyant faith of the fathers is much less in evidence. Now the stress is upon being without resources and at the disposal of the elements, drought and hunger, or the Amalekites. While the narrative affirms that Yahweh leads it, there is considerable evidence (forty years' worth!) that it was just there, not noticeably on its way, and without much vigor or hope toward promise.

Among the various words used for the experience, a negative term characterizes this dimension of landlessness. The very word wander *(nual)* suggests precariousness (Ps 107:27). He made them to wander in the wilderness forty years (Num 32:13). The wanderer is different from the sojourner-pilgrim because he is not on the way anywhere. He is in a situation in which survival is the key question. Israel experienced the bitterness of landlessness, being totally exposed and helpless, victimized by anything that happened to be threatening. Israel was dimly on the way in the wilderness period, but this way was mostly forgotten in the press of the moment for survival.

The traditions of the wilderness prevent us from romanticizing landlessness as a time of resourceful faith. For Israel the wilderness period provided a double image and memory. It is a route on the way to the land, but it is also a sentence of death (Num 32:13). In the wilderness, bereft of resources, faith is not easy (Deut 1:32). And when faithlessness is linked to landlessness, Israel is lost. It is destined to die the long death of the desert, on the way to nowhere. The anger and unrest of the wilderness wanderings are quite in contrast to the sojourn of the fathers and provide a very different stance toward landlessness. Here the promise is much less prominent in the literature and much less empowering in Israel's awareness.

3. Israel's third memory of landlessness is the *exile*. Although the northern tribes were exiled to Assyria in the eighth century, it is the sixth-century Jews in Babylon that provide the central image of exile for the Bible. The exiled Jews were not oppressed, abused, or imprisoned. But they were displaced, alienated from the place that gave identity and security. During the exile the Jews were alienated from all the shapes and forms that gave power to faith and life.[15]

15. Smith, "Earth and the Gods," 119, connects exile with mythic dimensions of chaos; see also Walter Brueggemann, "Kingship and Chaos (A Study in Tenth Century Theology)," *CBQ* 33 (1971) 317–32; idem, "Weariness, Exile and Chaos (A Motif in Royal Theology)," *CBQ* 34 (1972) 19–38.

For the Bible, the exile is the sharpest point of discontinuity when none of the old traditions or conventional institutions any longer seem valid or trustworthy. Exile without land or even prospect of land was indeed Israel's null point[16] when every promise seemed void. This event of landlessness evoked rage and anger (see Psalm 137) but also yearning pathos (Lam 1:2, 3, 6, 7, 21). Exile is being cut off with no way back. But strangely, this "null point" also became the context for Israel's most remarkable expression of faith, the lyrical celebration of God's faithfulness to exiles. Landlessness becomes the setting for the boldest gospel of newness (Isa 43:18-21; Jer 31:17-18; Ezek 37:5-6). Israel had a hint of the possibility of newness that perhaps could only happen there. Precisely in the context of landlessness do the promises loom large.[17] It is in the emptiness of Israel, exposed and without resources, that promises are received with power, that risks are run and hope is energizing. Yahweh's strange promise is either especially directed toward or peculiarly discerned among the landless. Faith is precisely for exiles who remember the land but see no way to it.

Israel as God's Landed People

Of course Israel's history is not all of landlessness. It had its moments of being in the land, of controlling and celebrating and exploiting the land. Having land turned out to be nearly as great a problem and temptation as not having land.

Israel's first moment of landedness is its *settlement in Egypt* under Joseph. It is given the best of the land (Gen 47:6) and made to dwell there in security and prosperity (Gen 47:27). In that land Israel did not sojourn; it *dwelt* there, securely settled in.[18] But of course the story of Israel is that being in the land soon led to slavery. Its prosperity (Exod 1:7) soon resulted in oppression (Exod 1:8-9), and the Exodus narrative is about the unbearable situation of being in land as slaves, of yearning to leave to

16. See Walther Zimmerli, "Plans for Rebuilding after the Catastrophe of 587," in *I am Yahweh*, trans. D. W. Stott, ed. W. Brueggemann (Atlanta: John Knox, 1982), on "the blessing of the nadir."

17. This abrupt discontinuity can be observed with reference to forms and traditions employed in the new situation. The exile is clearly a time when the Mosaic traditions are without power and Israel turns to the promissory traditions of Abraham and David. See the radical suggestions of John Van Seters, *Abraham in History and Tradition* (New Haven: Yale Univ. Press, 1975).

18. Note that the verb is *yashav*, "to be settled in," quite in contrast to the tentativeness of "sojourn." The use of the word itself indicates Israel's wholly new situation.

choose the freedom of the desert, of the fear of leaving the land and the oppression that kept them in the land. Land as locus of slavery posed for Israel an enormous choice, which it had to make again and again, between expulsion to the desert or continuation in slavery. Clearly the glorious promise of land, made to the fathers but then to the immediate family of Joseph, even the fleshpots of Egypt, had become a problem. Israel was left to wonder if land always led to slavery. And the question remained and remains unanswered. The promise quickly became problem.

A more significant dimension of landedness in Israel is of course the *monarchy* that runs its course from the splendor of Solomon to the frightened, pitiful days of Jehoiachin and finally his helpless son who ends in disgrace and exile. Enough has been said in recent scholarship about the novelty of monarchy in Israel. It is clear that kingship in the beginning did not grow out of theological conviction but was an accident of historical necessity. But kings will be kings and the business of kings is to stalk about and have their way in the land that sooner or later becomes their land. Mumford has shown how the introduction of absolutized, royal power radically redefines the possibilities of humanness in a political community.[19]

In Israel Solomon seems to personify the theories articulated by Mumford. Clearly the rapacious power of his state touched everything and everyone. Israel was warned early that it was in the nature of kings to covet and exploit (1 Samuel 8).[20] And of course Solomon did not disappoint. During his forty years of security and prosperity in the land, he managed to devise a bureaucratic state built upon coercion in which free citizens were enslaved for state goals. Remarkably, in one generation he managed to confiscate Israel's freedom and reduce social order to the very situation of Egyptian slavery. The king, manager of the land, made it possible to believe that the Exodus had never happened. And if the Exodus never happened history had not begun, and the promise was not visible. Could the king, manager of the land, be so effective as to remove the promise from the consciousness of Israel? And if Israel had no consciousness of promise, what could it possibly mean to be Israel? That is the question that Solomonic pretensions posed to Israel.

19. Lewis Mumford summarized the changed situation with royal power in *The Myth of the Machine*, vol. 1: *Technics and Human Development* (New York: Harcourt, Brace and World, 1966, 1967) 170. See George E. Mendenhall for a statement of the same change in Israel under David and Solomon in *The Tenth Generation: The Origins of the Biblical Tradition* (Baltimore: Johns Hopkins Univ., 1973).

20. See Isaac Mendelsohn, "Samuel's Denunciation of Kingship in the Light of the Akkadian Documents from Ugarit," *BASOR* 143 (1956) 17–22.

The rest of the long dynasty with two notable exceptions (Hezekiah and Josiah) is the less than brilliant story about getting land and keeping it and defending against losing it. The very land that promised to create space for human joy and freedom became the very source of dehumanizing exploitation and oppression. Land was indeed a problem in Israel. Time after time, Israel saw the land of promise become the land of problem. The very land that contained the sources of life drove kings to become agents of death. Society became the frantic effort of the landed to hold onto the turf, no matter what the cost. Israel finally waited for Jeremiah to bring to full expression the grief and weariness as this great landed people faced the reality that land given can become land lost. He speaks of two kings, the keepers of the land:

> They shall not lament for him, saying,
>> "Ah, my brother!" or "Ah sister!"
> They shall not lament for him, saying,
>> "Ah Lord!" or "Ah his majesty!"
> With the burial of an ass he shall be buried,
>> dragged and cast forth beyond the gates of Jerusalem.
> (Jer 22:18-19)

> Is this man Coniah a despised, broken pot,
>> a vessel no one cares for?
> Why are he and his children hurled and cast
>> into a land which they do not know?
> O land, land, land,
>> hear the word of Yahweh! (Jer 22:28-29)[21]

This is the end result of the sordid history of land management. The last of the kings is disposed of and forgotten, broken, and the land grieves for what was promised and will now not be. At the end of the dynastic period, Jeremiah's grief for the land is a particularly compelling statement of the end of the promise:

> For this the earth shall mourn,
>> and the heavens above be black;
> for I have spoken, I have purposed;
>> I have not relented nor will I turn back. (Jer 4:28)

---

21. See Hans Walter Wolff, *Anthropology of the Old Testament*, trans. M. Kohl (Philadelphia: Fortress Press, 1975) 195–96. Both uses of "cast" in our passage are the Hebrew verb *'alak*, "to be thrown out of the land." It suggests a forceful, violent action.

> How long will the land mourn,
>   and the grass of every field wither?
> For the wickedness of those who dwell in it
>   the beasts and the birds are swept away. . . . (Jer 12:4)

> For a sound of wailing is heard from Zion:
>   "How we are ruined!
>   We are utterly shamed,
> because we have left the land,
>   because they have *cast down* our dwellings." (Jer 9:19)[22]

It is all undone. Jeremiah can hardly find images to say what it means for the people of promise to exhaust all the rich possibilities. The glorious promise has become the unbearable problem, the unthinkable shame. The promise is voided. Jeremiah's images are of wilderness and drought, the terror of the land not sown (Jer 4:7, 23-26; 8:20-22; 9:10-11). The moment of the land, even four hundred years, has been lost. And the kings thought it could not happen.

Israel's final moment in the land in the biblical period was little noticed and, in contrast to the monarchy, a most modest enterprise. It is the small shabby restoration under Ezra and the organization of a *little community around Jerusalem,* probably in the fourth century. The return was under Persian approval and governance, something less than full freedom. The leadership was aware of the ambiguity of yearning for land and yet was limited by overlords who really controlled it:

> Behold, we are slaves this day; in the land that thou gavest to our fathers to enjoy its fruit and its good gifts, behold, we are slaves. And its rich yield goes to the kings whom thou hast set over us because of our sins; they have power also over our bodies and over our cattle at their pleasure, and we are in great distress. (Neh 9:36-37)

While the mood is more serene and confident, the nuance is not unlike the anticipation of 1 Samuel 8. Living in land controlled by another is to live a problematic existence.

But in that sorry situation, Israel covenanted again for land (Neh 9:38). In contrast to careless kings it resolved this time to keep the land. Now there is no brassy presumption, no careless self-indulgence in the manner of the kings. Now there is carefully, cautious, respectful intention to honor the rules of landkeeping. The Ezra community believed land could

---

22. Again the verb is *'alak.*

be kept, not by powerful bartering and wheeling-dealing, but by judicious, discreet obedience. These landholders were surely right-minded people who took no chances, who believed that land-keeping behavior could be defined, legislated, and enforced. They resolved to live lives quite in contrast to their royal fathers, whose sinful ways they confessed (Nehemiah 9; Ezra 9).

And they covenanted for the land along the lines of rigorous obedience. Evidence for consuming obedience is provided in their concern for Sabbath (Neh 13:15-22), as well as the curious passion for ending mixed marriages (Neh 13:23-27). The watchword was purity: "Thus I cleansed them from everything foreign" (Neh 13:30).

They did it consistently and convincedly. But they discovered that purity no more than power would keep the land. And so the grim holding action of morality had its day, but when it had spent itself, a succession of foreign powers came and seized the land, and Israel was again landless, aggrieved, and without power, turf, or identity.

The Bible is the story of God's people with God's land. It is the agony of trying to be fully in history but without standing ground in history. To be in history means to be in a place somewhere and answer for it and to it. But Israel's experience is of being in and belonging to a land never fully given, never quite secured. And its destiny vis-à-vis the land is always on the move toward fulfillment: from promise to the security of *slavery,* from desert to the destructive power of *kingship,* from exile to the weariness of *moral management.*

But the relation to the land changes. It is also, in reverse order, from fulfillment to emptiness: from fleshpots to *wilderness,* from control in the land to *weeping* in Babylon, from moral passion to *dislocation.* Israel is always on the move from land to landlessness, from landlessness to land, from life to death, from death to life. Its historical character derives from its questing for promises seemingly so rich and fulsome, but so burdened with ambiguity and loss.[23]

---

23. Grete Schaeder, *The Hebrew Humanism of Martin Buber,* trans. N. J. Jacobs (Detroit: Wayne State Univ. Press, 1973) 29, comments on Buber's discernment of this dynamic: "In this connection Buber has made a characteristic distinction in the history of the human spirit between epochs of *Behausung* in which man feels at home in the universe, and epochs of *Hauslosigkeit* in which man feels homeless, marooned in the universe, and inclined to regard himself as problematical." The following discussion is organized in the movement between *Behausung* and *Hauslosigkeit.* Either condition is provisional and always on the way to the other. That constitutes the central issue in biblical faith and perhaps in our own societal experience.

Israel's faith is essentially a journeying in and out of land, and its faith can be organized around these focuses. This subject is worth our attention because contemporary problems are quite parallel. We know in our time about the hunger for rootage and the yearning for turf. We know about the destructive power of coveting and the anxiety of displacement. And we know from time to time about gifts given and promises kept. In ancient Israel and now, persons and communities have been consumed by problems, most of which are about land. And so we may ask about the power of the promise, which is also mostly about land—a promise both glorious and problematic.

2.

"TO THE LAND I WILL SHOW YOU"

THE BOOK OF GENESIS PRESENTS TWO HISTORIES, BOTH CONCERNED with land. One, presented in Genesis 1–11, is about people fully rooted in land living toward expulsion and loss of land. Successively, Adam and Eve, Cain and Abel, Noah and his family, and finally the folks at Babel do everything they can to lose the land, and they eventually do.[1] That history is about presuming upon the land and as a result losing it. The Bible ponders the folly and carelessness that cause people securely landed to give it up.

The other history of Genesis is in chapters 12–50. It features Abraham and his family, and is about not having land but being on the way toward it and living in confident expectation of it.[2] The Bible considers at length that people without land have the resources and stamina to live toward a land they do not possess.

These two histories set the parameters of land theology in the Bible: presuming upon the land and being *expelled* from it; trusting toward a land not yet possessed, but empowered by *anticipation* of it. Our lives are set between expulsion and *anticipation,* of losing and expecting, of being uprooted and rerooted, of being dislocated because of impertinence and

---

1. See B. Davie Napier, *From Faith to Faith* (New York: Harper and Brothers, 1955) 23–59, Gerhard von Rad, *Old Testament Theology,* vol. 1: *The Theology of Israel's Historical Traditions,* trans. D. M. G. Stalker (New York: Harper and Brothers, 1962) 154–65, and Walter Brueggemann, "David and His Theologian," *CBQ* 30 (1968) 156–81. Gerhard von Rad, *Genesis,* rev. ed., trans. W. L. Jenkins, OTL (Philadelphia: Westminster, 1972) 159, summarizes the tragedy and pathos of these narratives concerning land loss: "What is basic for man's existence is his relation to the fertile soil (*'adamah*)."

2. Claus Westermann, *The Promises to the Fathers: Studies on the Patriarchal Narratives,* trans. D. E. Green (Philadelphia: Fortress Press, 1980).

being relocated in trust. Clearly these stories are not remote from the contemporary experience of Western culture.

The two histories are never far from each other, either in the Bible or in modern experience. The history of anticipation, as soon as it is satisfied, lives at the brink of the history of expulsion. But the Bible is clearly interested in anticipation. The Bible is not concerned with expulsion and dislocation even though theological interpreters are often preoccupied with it. Rather, the Bible focuses insistently upon anticipation and relocation. It does not look back in remorse or bitterness but it looks ahead with confident hope. In these stories of the early fathers (Genesis 12–50), the dominant themes of biblical faith are announced. The stories of Abraham and his family present a sharp break with the other history of Genesis 1–11. As Gerhard von Rad has shown, Gen 12:1 expresses a radical breaking off of the other history and a lack of sustained interest.[3] The abrupt statement of 12:1 unexpectedly seizes people out of the history of expulsion and initiates them into the history of anticipation. The human community need no longer live away from the land, always departing and being driven out, but can live toward the land, always on the way in joy.

Biblical faith begins with the radical announcement of discontinuity that intends to initiate us into a new history of anticipation. It challenges and contradicts a consciousness of land loss and expulsion as false consciousness. That is not the way life is intended to be or can finally be, because the power of anticipation rooted in the speech of God overwhelms the power of expulsion. A new history begins in that discontinuity and initiation. The remainder of biblical faith is the history of those who have broken off the old life of expulsion and have walked the risky way of anticipation.

Abraham and the History of Landlessness

The new history begins as history always begins, in a word spoken. "Now Yahweh said to Abram." How else could history begin? That is the way with individual histories when persons are addressed and called into being, into a new consciousness. Such a word spoken gives identity and personhood, and we could not have invented it. It is the voice of the prophet—or the poet if you wish—who calls a name, bestows a vision, summons a pilgrimage. This is not the detached prattle of a computer; not the empty language of a quota or a formula or a rule; but it is a word spoken that lets one not be the same again. Land-expelling history could live by coercive language

---

3. Von Rad, *Genesis*, 159; idem, *Old Testament Theology,* 1.161–65.

but land-anticipating history can only begin with One who in his speaking makes all things news. That is what Gen 12:1 does in the Bible. It makes all things new when all things had become old and weary and hopeless. Creation begins anew, as a history of anticipation of the land.

The word that begins history anew is received by Israel immediately as a voice of compelling authority: "and he went." In contrast to some other traditions in the Bible, in this one the speaker is known by name and he is immediately acknowledged. His voice is recognized as one that is authoritative, that can author a new history among us. His voice is laden with power. This is where the history of anticipation is grounded. His word, which compels, is known in its hearing to be reliable and never doubted. His voice is such a contrast to that of the serpent that was shrewd in its capacity to manipulate to death (Gen 3:1-5). Or such a contrast to the voices of the tower that wrecked the whole thing. Here there are no shrewd manipulations or destructive confusion. Here there is only the simple, clear, unambiguous invitation to begin a new history. And in the very moment of address he is acknowledged to be the One who would do what he said he would do.

Abraham entered a new history. The new history is without link to the old. The new history begins with a call to repentance, a summons to leave and go somewhere we are not, a radical breaking off and departure, to become someone whom we have not been. We know nothing about the place Abraham left.[4] The text is constructed to suggest that it also is a place of coercion and hopelessness. Abraham shared the futility of the others in that old history: "Sarah was barren" (Gen 11:30)! And Abraham and his family are invited to leave presumably secure barrenness for the sake of a risky future that promises more. But without an heir, Abraham and Sarah are to be as landless as Adam and Eve, either early or lately expelled from the land.

But this new history requires a wrenching departure, an abandonment of what is for what is not, but that is promised by the One who will do what he says. "And he went!" Yahweh spoke and he went, and in so doing a new historical alternative began, alternative to the history of expulsion and dislocation. Sarah was barren! No way to the future. No heir to receive all the riches. Nothing, future closed off, everything as good as over and done with. And he spoke and there was newness. He is the Lord of all things new, and his partners in history are pilgrims who believe he

---

4. Compare E. A. Speiser, *Genesis*, AB 1 (Garden City, N.Y.: Doubleday, 1964) 80–81. Since the Chaldeans were latecomers into Mesopotamia, "Ur" is now a theological symbol without a known historical referent. (The recent finds of Ebla suggest new historical possibilities.)

will do what he says. The barren one went on a pilgrimage with the Lord of barrenness and birth, the Ruler of hopelessness and hope. The pilgrimage was the antithesis of expulsion. The family of Abraham left the history of expulsion and began the pilgrimage of promise.

This history-beginning word is announced three times to the barren one who will embrace an alternative history. It is announced in Gen 12:1-3, with the promise, "I will make of you a great nation . . . make your name great."[5] Nobody has a great name in the history of dislocation.[6] And surely nobody is a great nation if expulsion is the order of the day. In the old history they tried for the great name and nothing happened (Gen 11:4). Surely only such an improbable announcement could energize such a radical, risky history to a land, a new land where barrenness is overcome. Nothing is known or said here of the land. No description or identification, no geographical reference. For now the land exists only as an intention of the promiser. It is a new land and that is enough, not like any of the old land, tired, sterile, unproductive, filled with thorns and thistles (Gen 3:18).

The second announcement occurs in what is regarded as an old, even primitive narrative of encounter, Gen 15:7-21.[7] Again it begins in this bald, unexplained statement, "to give you this land to possess." Here is a hint of the identity of the land, the very one Abraham is in, where he now finds himself. A new word is spoken that redefines the relation of people and the land in which they already sojourn. That is what this God does. He speaks to restructure the relation of land and people. What had been threat becomes promise. What had been coveted now becomes gifted.

The response of Abraham (15:8) is one of incredulity. He asks for assurances. It is too much to hope for after this long history of barrenness, too much to trust to newness. The reassurance is a strange one, one that could hardly penetrate our calculating consciousness. It is another word

---

5. On the structure and function of the text see Hans Walter Wolff, "The Kerygma of the Yahwist," *Int* 29 (1966) 137–47, now reprinted in Walter Brueggemann and Hans Walter Wolff, *The Vitality of the Old Testament Tradition* (Atlanta: John Knox, 1975) 41–66.

6. See "David and His Theologian," *CBQ* 30 (1968) 172, on contrasts of Gen 11:4; 12:2; 2 Sam 12:28; 1 Kgs 1:47; and Phil 2:9.

7. See Ronald E. Clements, *Abraham and David: Genesis XV and Its Meaning for Israelite Tradition*, SBT 2/5 (Naperville, Ill.: Allenson, 1967); and Norbert Lohfink, *Die Landverheissung als Eid: Eine Studie zu Gn 15*, SBS 28 (Stuttgart: Katholisches Bibelwerk, 1967), for the evidence that establishes this text as fundamental to promissory faith in the Bible; and John Van Seters, *Abraham in History and Tradition* (New Haven: Yale Univ. Press, 1975) 249–78, for an alternative view. For detailed exegesis and extensive bibliography on this passage, see Claus Westermann, *Genesis 12–36*, trans. J. J. Scullion, CC (Minneapolis: Augsburg, 1981) 209–31.

spoken by the same One, only this time it is spoken on Yahweh's turf, when Abraham is asleep. This is a heavy, nominal sleep when the Presence broods in compelling ways. The old history had been only of tense, anxious wakefulness, as if our attentiveness could make things safe. But this deep sleep is for the emergence of gifts (see 2:21-23). And the drama of the new history is presented to Abraham:

> Your descendants will be sojourners [present but not in possession]. . . .
> [They] will be slaves [at the disposal of another]. . . .
> They shall come out with great possessions [the promise will be kept]. (Gen 15:13-14)

Of course it is all unlikely. But such incredulity is the way of the new history, and it surged upon Abraham in the mysterious sleep. His defenses were down. His calculating wakefulness was overcome as it must be for such newness. In the twilight he was at the disposal of this other One and in the awe of this dream, the other One turned Israel's history in a new direction.

The drama is concluded in vv. 17-21. We do not know if Abraham is still asleep or perhaps he is for the first time really awake: "To your descendants I give this land." That is all. No bargaining, no condition, just a flat, bold, unqualified one-liner that changed everything. Thus to the husband of the barren one, to his descendants the land. The new history contradicts all the old history, the curse on Adam and Eve and their progeny (Gen 3:14-19), the universe of the destiny of Cain (Gen 4:12), the rejection of the scattering of Babel (Gen 11:1-9). Israel will be rooted! It has seemed impossible because of barrenness, always a yearning, but now a promise, not a desperate wish but his bold assurance, this One who will do what he says.

Genesis 15:1-6 is likely a subsequent reflection on this new history and there the two modalities are sharply contrasted: "I continue childless. . . . Thou hast given me no offspring. . . . A slave . . . will be my heir." That is the old history, a history in which slaves take over and there is no hopeful route to the future. It is the history of loss and expulsion and hopelessness, of having land but being sure you will lose it. That is the old history and one can see no way from it.

But in the same narrative, the new history begins right at the point of hopelessness: "Your own son shall be your heir"! His new word stands against all the data, the word that protests the history of expulsion. Destiny is not that of closed-off slaves but that of hopeful bearers of heirs. That model of slave-heir is fundamental to all of biblical faith (see Gal 4:1-7).

The old history/new history wrenching is that the heir displaces the slave. The history of expulsion invites all persons to become obedient, fearful slaves, going through the motions, hoping nothing, asking nothing, and now there is another way: barrenness transformed, the appearance of the child of promise and the way to the future.

And he believed! As Paul discerned (Rom 4:3, 9, 22; Gal 3:6), here begins the new history. He believed against the data. He trusted that history is for heirs and not for slaves. It is not the story of land possessed but the story of land promised. He trusted that God intended honorable rootage and not shameful expulsion for him and his family. His embrace of newness cannot be explained because newness explained would not be new. It is not a new doctrine or a new relation. It is a new history moving toward a radical promise—land!

The new history begins in a surprising promise and a strange act of trusting courage reckoned as righteousness. Israel is that strange people who reject the identity of the world because that is always bound to slavery. The world knows nothing of newness. And only such newness can bestow inalienable land. Without such newness the land is never held and the human community is never safe. That is the old history in Genesis 3–11. It is also the contemporary experience of affluence and a sense of dislocation and alienation. But an heir! That is the focus of the new history toward the land.

The third and most majestic, symmetrical announcement of the beginning of the new history is in Genesis 17.[8] Again the contrast is sharply drawn between the old age of Abraham and Sarah and the new promise of God. The promise is announced in a style reminiscent of the promise to Adam (Gen 1:28) and to Noah (Gen 9:1):

> I . . . will multiply you exceedingly. (Gen 17:2)

> I will make you exceedingly fruitful. (Gen 17:6)

Both formulas have the intensive, repeated adverb *me'od me'od,* "very exceedingly" (used also in v. 20 of Ishmael). There could be no stronger insistence on the firmness and forcefulness of God's intent, and this to a ninety-nine-year-old man who had borne no son toward the future. The promise, against that hopelessness of Abraham, is given futurity by God: ". . . after you throughout their generations for an everlasting covenant" (*berith 'olam,* v. 7; see v. 13).

---

8. See Samuel R. Külling, *Zur Datierung der "Genesis-P-Stücke" nämentlich des Kapitels Genesis XVII* (Kampen: Kok, 1964), for a suggestive attempt to discern the text in covenantal categories.

But the point of fruitfulness, of having a son, of entering into an enduring covenant is announced only in v. 8, an affirmation made not to either
Adam or Noah but only to father Abraham. It is delayed until now, till the
new history of Abraham, and it concerns land: "And I will give to you and
to your descendants after you, the land of your sojournings, all the land of
Canaan, for an everlasting possession; and I will be their God." This is the
focal verse of the tradition of promise history. Commonly assumed to be
exilic in its final articulation, it asks about the prospect of land. The barren
one is the one promised an heir. The verse announces a remarkable inversion of the facts. The land is referred to as the "land of sojourning," the
place where they are but do not belong and do not have rootage. It is also
called the "land of Canaan," possessed by another and not by them. But the
land of rootlessness, possessed by others, is Israel's future. It will become
'olam ahazath, everlasting possession. The *berith 'olam* leads to *ahazath*
'olam. The enduring covenant leads to enduring land. This is the new history. The rootless one is given land; the history of banishment is displaced
by the history of promise against all the circumstantial evidence.

After the announcement, vv. 9-14 concern the ritual of sealing through
circumcision and God's statement is concluded in vv. 15-16 with a promise
to the barren one: "I will bless her, indeed *(gam)* I will give you a son by her;
I will bless her" (my translation). That is the new history, the mention of the
son for the first time in this chapter, enveloped in the rhetoric of blessing.

Not until v. 17 does Abraham respond. It has all been speech by the
Lord of the new history until now. When father Abraham speaks, it is the
incredulous voice of the old history of calculation, control, and hopelessness. Verse 17 is a rejection of the promise because it is against the facts:
"Then Abraham fell on his face and laughed, and said to himself, 'Shall a
child be born to a man who is a hundred years old? Shall Sarah, who is
ninety years old, bear a child?'" And v. 18 is a desperate clinging to the old
way of Ishmael, child of the old history (see Gal 4:21-31) because there
seems no other way: "And Abraham said to God, 'O that Ishmael might
live in thy sight!'" And so the issue is joined between the Lord who makes
all things new (here to Sarah) and the believer who cannot believe in such
newness and clings to the sojourn against the land. Ishmael is remembered in the older tradition as a wilderness wanderer (Gen 21:14), and he
is the type for the old history, the only one Abraham now believes possible. He clings to Ishmael as the only possible way. He clings to a destiny of
landlessness because he does not know any other possibility.

But the text of the new history is against Abraham. It rejects his hopelessness and insists against his will that Abraham is destined for land,
because Yahweh will do what he says. And so God, as is characteristic of the
new history, has the last word, a word of assuring promise: "God said, 'No,

but Sarah your wife shall bear you a son. . . . I will establish my covenant with him as an everlasting covenant for his descendants after him'" (v. 19). The "no" of God is a powerful and strange adversative in which God radically and totally refutes the doubt of Abraham. God and not Abraham will set the future by an heir for the land. The covenant is forever and that means land forever. Ishmael will be blessed, even *me'od me'od*, but Isaac, the one whom the old history mocks, is covenanted to the land-promising God.

The radicalness of this new history is poignantly presented in Gen 18:10-15. Abruptly (the new history is always abrupt) the visitors announce a new history: "Sarah your wife shall have a son." Abraham and Sarah resist and dismiss the assurance. But the voice of the new history persists. The critical affirmation is in a rhetorical question: "Is anything too hard for Yahweh?"9 The voice, which is the voice of God, answers: "[No:] Sarah shall have a son." The Lord answers his own question, and his answer is a promise of a landed future to those still without land. The Lord does the impossible. He inverts hopeless history into land expectation. (Compare the same word, always among the hopeless landless who now can move toward turf, in Exod 3:20; 15:11; Judg 13:20; Jer 32:17, 27.)

The question of the voice is the question of the entire Bible. Can he do the hard thing? Can he bring freedom out of slavery, life out of death, fertility out of barrenness, rivers out of desert (Isa 41:18), cypress out of thorns (Isa 55:13), joy out of sorrow (John 16:20)? Can a sojourner receive an eternal possession? The issue turns on the power and fidelity of Yahweh. That is the issue for faith when this old history meets the promise of the new history.

All three announcements make the same affirmation. Genesis 15 with its primitive awesome quality, Genesis 12 as a programmatic statement, and Genesis 17 with its majestic, unilateral confidence. All declare that the history of sojourn is toward land. And only the mind-set of the old history enmeshed in rootlessness, only the harsh memories of banishment make it necessary to resist the new promise. But such doubting cannot void the promise.

The Promise and the Heirs of Abraham

Is anything too difficult for Yahweh? It is a question to be taken seriously, and the assuring answer of Yahweh seems implicit in the question. But the answer is never fully or visibly given in Genesis. There is always a waiting

9. The Hebrew term for "hard" is *pela'*: In the LXX the term is *adunat'sei*. Compare Luke 1:37; Mark 10:37; Matt 17:21, surely in intentional uses of the tradition.

and wondering and not knowing. And "the difficult things" often seem delayed or seem not to happen. The power of the old history that denies difficult things seems to have its way even among the people under promise.

In the Abraham story, the promise of heir and therefore land is underway with Isaac, child of impossibility, named "Laughter," the scandal nearly lost under God's radical demand (22:1-14). The promise of land is reasserted under the curious formula "Your descendants shall possess the gate of the enemies" (22:17; 24:60). But it is yet to come. For Abraham the land he holds consists only in enough turf in which to be buried (25:9-10), land held by clear title and securely possessed (see 23:17-20).[10] It is only a small plot. But that securely held, called *ahazath*[11] (23:20), is surely a token of the promise made but not yet fulfilled. Beyond that Abraham dies without land—but with an heir!

The narrative does not linger with Isaac, who begins also with a barren wife (25:21) and ends with an heir (27:37). It is enough that the promise is pronounced to him also (26:3-4) and that in his sojourn he can envision a luxuriant land for which his heir is destined (27:28-29). He does not believe history is closed, but believes rather that he is indeed a child of the new history.

The action is more vivid and expensive but less focused in the story of Jacob. The cult legends (Gen 28:10-22; 32:22-32; 35:9-15), undoubtedly taken from old sources, provide a way by which the impossibility of God is arrested in the narrative, for at least two of them affirm the land promise and the third reflects on the meaning of Israel:

> . . . the land on which you lie I will give to you and to your descendants; and your descendants shall be like the dust of the earth, and you shall spread abroad to the west and to the east and to the north and to the south. . . . Behold, I am with you and will keep you

10. On the nature of the title to the land, see Manfred R. Lehmann, "Abraham's Purchase of Machpelah and Hittite Laws," *BASOR* 129 (1953) 15–18; Cyrus H. Gordon, "Abraham and the Merchants of Ura," *JNES* 17 (1958) 28; Gene M. Tucker, "The Legal Background of Genesis 23," *JBL* 85 (1966) 77–84; and Van Seters, *Abraham*, 293–95.

11. On the term see Friedrich Horst, "Zwei Begriffe für Eigentum (Besitz)," in *Verbannung und Heimkehr: Beiträge zur Geschichte und Theologie Israels im 6. und 5. Jahrhundert v. Chr. Wilhelm Rudolph zum 70. Geburtstage,* ed. A. Küschke (Tübingen: Mohr/Siebeck, 1961) 153–56, where the term is contrasted with *nahalah*. Siegfried Herrmann (*A History of Israel in Old Testament Times,* rev. ed. [Philadelphia: Fortress Press, 1981] 206, 235) suggests that purchase of land is characteristically a Canaanite practice in contrast to the Israelite notion of inheritance. He cites especially the purchase by David (2 Samuel 24) and Omri (1 Kgs 16:23). Apparently it is the way of kings to purchase and possess.

> wherever you go, and will bring you back to this land; for I will not
> leave you until I have done that of which I have spoken to you.
> (Gen 28:13-15)

> Your name shall no more be called Jacob, but Israel, for you have
> striven with God and with men, and have prevailed. (Gen 32:28)

> The land which I gave to Abraham and Isaac I will give to you, and
> I will give the land to your descendants after you. (Gen 35:12)

Jacob, in the face of Laban and Esau, is most often on the run, a fugitive without right, resource, or sanctuary, not unlike Cain in the old history (Gen 4:12). But the narrative affirms that the Laban/Esau pressures are manageable, precisely because in his flights he had been encountered by the promise-maker. Finally, it is not sheep-stealing Laban, or wronged, avenging Esau who shapes his life, but it is the promise-maker whose promises endure in the face of such enmity. The story of Jacob ends with a remarkable sequence of events:[12]

1. Jacob changes his garments in an act of ritual purification (Gen 35:1-4). Jacob makes a radical break with the old history.[13]
2. Jacob is strangely protected by a "terror from God." The bearer of the new history is safe among the attackers from the old history, just as he has been safe from Laban and Esau (Gen 35:5-8).
3. The promise is again asserted that land is to be given (Gen 35:9-15).
4. Rachel, the mother of promise, the barren one (Gen 29:31), gives birth to the beloved Benjamin.[14] The history of barrenness is overcome by promise. As the child of promise appears, the mother of barrenness is removed.

In the Joseph narrative, which completes Genesis 12–50, we may note two motifs that relate to the theme of promise. One is the story about Joseph who, because Yahweh is with him (39:2, 21, 23) and because he "feared God" (42:18), begins as a hated younger brother without resource

---

12. I am, of course, aware of the problem of literary sources in this chapter as elsewhere. Verses 9-13 are likely P and so most self-consciously concerned to announce the promise. Compare von Rad, *Genesis*, 338–39. Nonetheless, the sequence of motifs in the completed text is instructive.

13. Compare Albrecht Alt, "Die Wallfahrt von Sichem nach Bethel," *Kleine Schriften*, vol. 1 (Munich: Beck, 1953) 79–88, and the process in relation to covenant making, Josh 24:23. While Gen 35:1-4 undoubtedly reports a very primitive rite, in the completed tradition the same ritual is now put in the service of the promise.

14. The overcoming of barrenness and movement to the land focused in Benjamin is telling. James Muilenburg, "The Site of Ancient Gilgal," *BASOR* 140 (1955) 11–27.

or authority and becomes the powerful, respected, and feared controller of the empire. He is the embodiment of that central conviction of Israel that God's impossible promises will come to fulfillment. He becomes the model for the land-getter and the land-manager (41:57; 42:6; see 47:6, 20, 27).[15]

There is a counter-theme to this public history. It concerns Joseph, his brothers, and his father. The whole family understands that this is not really the land anticipated since father Abraham.

This is not the land for this turf belongs finally to Pharaoh and not to Joseph. This is not the land because it is imperial and is attained by management and not as gift. It is not the land because no amount of management can ever de-Egyptianize it. No matter how well off, Israel in Egypt knew very well that it was not rooted and could not be rooted there.[16] Jacob's last wish is to affirm the line of promise and land: "If now I have found favor in your sight, put your hand under my thigh, and promise to deal loyally and truly with me. Do not bury me in Egypt, but let me lie with my fathers; carry me out of Egypt and bury me in their burying place" (47:29-30). While the conversation is in Egypt, Jacob's memory and vision (see 48:19) are all on the land of promise. Even Joseph in his success must not be deceived. The action is in the land *promised,* not in the land *possessed:* "Behold, I am about to die, but God will be with you, and will bring you again to the land of your fathers" (48:21; see 50:24). So Jacob, bearer of promise, is buried in Canaan under promise (50:5-14).

Less directly the same is true for Joseph. He is buried in Egypt by Egyptian standards and perhaps he was impressed by such possibilities (Gen 50:26). But even he knew this is not the place and finally he will be buried in his own land (v. 25; Exod 13:19). Even in death, Joseph is destined for a place of promise. But with such yearning, the question to Sarah (Gen 18:14) is only provisionally answered. The barren one continues to ask about the impossibility.

15. Compare Donald B. Redford, *A Study of the Biblical Story of Joseph (Genesis 37-50),* VTSup 20 (Leiden: Brill, 1970) 175–76.

16. Hans Eberhard von Waldow, "Israel and Her Land: Some Theological Considerations," *A Light unto My Path: Old Testament Studies in Honor of Jacob M. Myers,* ed. H. N. Bream, et al. GTS 4 (Philadelphia: Temple Univ. Press, 1974), expressed the theme well: "Either there is a people of God—Israel—related to Canaan; or there is just another powerful ethnic minority group trying to invade the territory of a foreign nation." Israel may not look to just any land, but precisely to this one.

3.

"YOU LACKED NOTHING"

A SECOND COMPONENT OF ISRAEL'S MEMORY OF LANDLESSNESS IS THAT of the wilderness.[1] This memory, expressed in Exodus 16–18 and Num 10:11ff., shares the experience of being displaced and without land with the sojourn of the fathers. It provides another angle by which Israel could discern itself as "having nothing yet lacking nothing." But the thrust of these passages is in sharp contrast to the fidelity, trust, and obedience of the patriarchs. Abraham and his family are presented in Israel's memory as models for faith. The generation of the wilderness is remembered and characterized as recalcitrant and disobedient. Landlessness does strange things to Israel.[2] In the Genesis narrative it drives Israel to radical faith. But in the wilderness tradition, Israel's experience of landlessness nearly destroys both Israel and its faith.

The wilderness wanderings are a surprise to Israel. This is not the promise of Exodus. The deliverance rhetoric of Exodus talks rather of going out of Egypt and into the land (Exod 3:7-8).[3] Clearly what happens falls short of the promise. Israel is victimized by a gross miscalculation of the post-Exodus possibility. Exodus is about freedom but it is about freedom in the good land under the good word of promise.

It turns out otherwise. The wilderness tradition is the most radical memory Israel has about landlessness. Wilderness is not simply an in-between place that makes the journey longer. It is not simply a sandy place

---

1. The basic critical study of these traditions is that of George W. Coats, *Rebellion in the Wilderness: The Murmuring Motif in the Wilderness Traditions of the Old Testament* (New York: Abingdon, 1968).

2. Coats, *Rebellion* 249–254, concludes that (a) the murmuring of Israel concerns open rebellion and (b) a strong impetus for articulation of murmuring is "to explain the tragedy of the exile." The tradition can only be understood in terms of the problem of landlessness.

3. J. Wijngaards, *The Formulas of the Deuteronomic Creed (Dt. 6/20-23: 26/5-9)* (Tilburg: Reijen, 1963) has meticulously summarized the data.

demanding more stamina. It is space far away from ordered land. It is Israel's historical entry into the arena of chaos that, like the darkness before creation, is "formless and void" and without a hovering wind (Gen 1:2). Wilderness is the historical form of chaos and is Israel's memory of how it was before it was created a people.[4] Displacement, in that time and our time, is experienced like the empty dread of primordial chaos, and so Israel testifies about itself.

Wilderness is formless and therefore lifeless. To be placed in the wilderness is to be cast into the land of the enemy—cosmic, natural, historical—without any of the props or resources that give life order and meaning. To be in the wilderness is landlessness par excellence, being not merely a resident alien, as were the fathers, but in a context hostile and destructive. Not without reason did Jeremiah call this *lo' zeru'ah,* "not sown" (Jer 2:2). Such a land is not only not sown—that is, beyond cultivation—but it is seedless. Not only is nothing growing, but nothing can grow. It is land without promise, without hope, where no newness can come. Perhaps that is a point of contact between the sojourning fathers who were without heir (*lo' nathattah zara'*) (Gen 15:3) and the wilderness folk in a land not sown (*lo' zeru'ah*) (Jer 2:2). The missing heir of Abraham and Sarah and the missing growth in the wilderness are the same *zera',* either "heir" or "seed," both without entry to the future. This is Israel's dominant memory of landlessness, to be at the disposal of an environment totally without life supports and without any visible hint that there is an opening to the future. This is the central struggle of both the patriarchs with barren women (Gen 11:30; 25:21; 29:31) and Israel in the barren land (Exodus 16–18). Interestingly, in the in-between period of landedness in Goshen, Israel prospered and knew fertility and productivity, both of sons and of crops (Gen 47:27; Exod 1:7), but that was an interval in a memory of landless barrenness.[5]

Thus much of Israel's history is placed in conditions of barrenness, staggered between oases, between promises that no longer seem operative and fulfillments that seem remote and implausible.[6] The recipients of the

---

4. Compare Walter Brueggemann, "Weariness, Exile and Chaos (A Motif in Royal Theology)," *CBQ* 34 (1972) 19–38. Ivan Engnell argues the sojourn materials must be symbolically (culturally) and not historically understood; "The Wilderness Wandering," in *A Rigid Scrutiny: Critical Essays on the Old Testament,* trans. J. T. Willis (Nashville: Vanderbilt Univ. Press, 1969) 207–14.

5. See Norman K. Gottwald, "Were the Early Israelites Pastoral Nomads?" in *Rhetorical Criticism: Essays in Honor of James Muilenburg,* ed. J. J. Jackson and M. Kessler, PTMS 1 (Pittsburgh: Pickwick, 1974) 244–47, for a powerful presentation of the problem.

6. Gottwald describes them as ". . . those whose intolerable conditions of oppression drove them in the direction of a community yet to be" ("Early Israelites," 247).

gift of the Exodus become the victims of deathly wilderness. Buoyant trust is rapidly turned to grim resentment. Faith rapidly erodes in situations of landlessness, yet Israel is called to be precisely a people of faith in precisely a situation of landlessness.[7]

Exodus 16: Nourished though Alienated

Exodus 16 is one of the focal memories of the wilderness tradition.[8] It contains the major features of the drama of existence in a context without an adequate life-support system. Israel remembers wilderness landlessness as a place of murmur, protest, quarrelsome dissatisfaction. Israel says to its leaders: "Would that we had died by the hand of Yahweh in the land of Egypt when we sat by the fleshpots and ate bread to the full; for you have brought us out of this wilderness to kill this whole assembly with hunger" (16:3). The protest is against the freedom-giving leadership of Moses.[9] The contrast is full and sharp. Egypt may have been slavery but it was filled with life-giving resources. Land always is. That is what land is. And wilderness is filled with hunger. Thus the correlation:

> Egypt : flesh/bread : fullness
> wilderness : hunger : death

That is the choice Israel had unwittingly made. In heady confidence it had chosen the freedom of deathly wilderness and found itself between oases. Israel did not know what it was choosing. But it could not believe its rightful destiny was to live between oases.

The second component is the response to the protest. That is the wonder of the narrative. Even in the forsaken (God-forsaken?) wilderness, Yahweh is there with his answer:

> Yahweh: Behold, I will rain bread from heaven. (v. 4)
> Moses: When Yahweh gives you in the evening flesh to eat and in the morning bread to the full . . . (v. 8)

---

7. See Rubem A. Alves, *Tomorrow's Child: Imagination, Creativity, and the Rebirth of Culture* (New York: Harper & Row, 1972) for an eloquent call to faith in a situation of drastic landlessness.

8. See the critical analysis of Coats, *Rebellion*, 83–96. In "Weariness, Evil and Chaos," I have dealt with the meaning of hunger/weariness and nourishment/rest as related to the Exile.

9. Gottwald, in speaking of the tradition of the death of Moses, suggests, "It is probably that they attest to dissatisfactions with his leadership so great that he was deposed, banished or killed during the intense intra-communal struggles for power" ("Early Israelites," 246).

> Yahweh: At twilight you shall eat flesh, and in the morning you shall
> be filled with bread. (v. 12)

The speech of Yahweh in v. 4 contrasts the bread of heaven and the bread of Egypt. He gives bread from a different source, heaven, not Egypt. Presumably a different quality of bread. The statement of Moses in v. 8 contains the same three members as the protest—flesh, bread, and full—and these are echoed in the speech of Yahweh in v. 12. Thus the answer is built around the same triad as the protest. But now flesh, bread, and fullness do not come from the land itself, but from heaven, from the Lord of landlessness. By the use of the same triad to promise exactly what is wanted, Israel is shown that life-giving resources do not come from land but from Yahweh. Israel is not tied to, dependent upon, or subservient to the land. The Lord of chaos gives these resources to the landless.

Israel could experience in the wilderness what it thought was only available in Egypt, discovering that in landlessness it could have what it thought only land could give. Imagine that—wanderers in wilderness satiated! Protests answered, bellies filled, needs supplied, cries heard! There are dimensions of Yahweh's wilderness that surprise the hopeless sojourners.

Interwoven with this theme of protest/answer[10] is a theme with a quite different stress. It is about Yahweh's presence in the hiddenness of glory: "At evening you shall know that it was Yahweh who brought you out of the land of Egypt, and in the morning you shall see the glory of Yahweh" (Exod 16:6-7). Where should the glory appear? Glory in its awesome inscrutability is characteristically in the serenity of cultic establishment. But strangely glory comes here in this odd place, in wilderness.[11] The narrative does not linger with description or location but his glory is seen in *making empty full.*[12]

The same theme appears in vv. 10-12: "They looked toward the wilderness, and behold, the glory of Yahweh appeared in the cloud." And again the same implication is drawn: "At twilight you shall eat flesh, and in the

10. See Walter Brueggemann, "From Hurt to Joy, from Death to Life," *Int* 28 (1974) 13–19, for an argument that this construction is constitutive for the life of Israel.

11. The glory theme in this tradition is peculiarly related to the concerns of P, and for good reason. In exile, i.e., in a new wilderness, the power and presence of Yahweh are especially in doubt. Compare Claus Westermann, "Die Herrlichkeit Gottes in der Priesterschrift," in *Forschüng am Alten Testament: Gesammelte Studien,* ThB 55 (Munich: Kaiser, 1974) 115–37.

12. The theme of "empty become full" may well be linked to landless becoming landed. See the book of Ruth; 1 Sam 2:5; Luke 1:53; and Phil 2:7-10. See D. F. Rauber, "Literary Values in the Bible: The Book of Ruth," *JBL* 89 (1970) 27–37.

morning you shall be filled with bread; then you shall know that I am Yahweh your God."[13]

The themes cluster together. There is knowing and seeing, again the triad of flesh/bread/full, and the affirmation that this leads to acknowledgment of Yahweh as Lord.[14] In the Exodus tradition just prior to this text (Exod 14:4, 18), the Egyptians also know. They know by being destroyed. Now Israel shall know, in this very different context, not by being destroyed, but by being filled. Again the contrast of landed/landless is asserted by relating the two texts:

> Egypt : landed : know : being destroyed
> Israel : landless : know : being filled

There is something about landlessness that makes the disclosure of Yahweh of a different sort. Israel reflected extensively on that in these narratives.

His glory is known, his presence discerned, and his sovereignty acknowledged in this capacity to transform the situation from emptiness to satiation, from death to life, from hunger to bread and meat. He acted decisively to make for landless Israel an environment as rich and nourishing as any landed people had ever known. Yahweh is transformer of situations. The surprise is that landlessness can become nourishing.

Verses 1-12, which express a promise, are presented according to the pattern of protest and answer. The remainder of the chapter is the actualization of what is announced in these opening verses. First comes the promised meat (quail); then comes the promised bread (manna). The narrative has little interest in the data itself, although v. 15 no doubt preserves an old etiological concern. But vv. 16-18 make an assertion about the bread from Yahweh which recognizes its peculiar character: "'Gather. . . .' And the people of Israel did so; they gathered, some more, some less. But when they measured it with an omer, he that gathered much had nothing over, and he that gathered little had no lack; each gathered according to what he could eat." That is very strange bread, certainly not the kind gathered in the land, in the place of planning and calculation and control. That is bread such as they had not known in Egypt. Egypt was the land and the

---

13. On formulas in P, see Walther Zimmerli, "I am Yahweh," in *I Am Yahweh*, trans. D. W. Stott, ed. W. Brueggemann (Atlanta: John Knox, 1982) 1–28; and idem, "The Knowledge of God according to the Book of Ezekiel," in *I Am Yahweh*, 29–98.

14. On "know" as acknowledgment of covenant, compare Herbert B. Huffmon, "The Treaty Background of Hebrew *Yada'*," *BASOR* 181 (1966) 31–37; and Huffmon and Simon B. Parker, "A Further Note on the Treaty Background of Hebrew *Yada'*," *BASOR* 184 (1966) 36–38.

land is always organized and administered, and the purpose of administration is that some shall always have too much and some shall always have too little.

A double contrast is established: (a) a contrast between expected hunger and unexpected satiation and (b) a contrast between Egyptian bread and wilderness bread. This second contrast Israel had to learn so many times. What does it mean to receive bread in wilderness, in a land without life supports? It surely means to receive bread (sustenance) that refuses to be administered and managed and therefore is not perverted by the destructive inequities of land-bread. In the wilderness before the surprising eyes of his people, Yahweh makes a protest against managed land-bread.

The announcement is radical: "No lack!" That in the very wilderness where hunger to death had seemed so real twelve verses earlier! This surely is bread from an economy Israel did not know or understand, bread given and not planned, received and not coerced, bread on someone else's terms, bread as a sacrament of glory. Israel reflected on this for a long time because this bread stood outside the limits of its understanding. It did not reflect on the mechanical details, for they never interested Israel. But hard questions came: Is such bread only given in wilderness? How could we have it in our own secure land? The land mentality, the effort at managed security, is evident in vv. 20-21, when they tried to store it. But the wilderness won't permit it: "worms, foul, melting" (my translation). What kind of place is it and what kind of bread? We don't die of starvation as we feared. But we can't store it. Never too little, but not too much. *Not lack!* Just when lack seemed most likely and inevitable.

The next section, vv. 22-30, has a curious turn to it. No doubt this was a legitimating legend for Sabbath in the first place.[15] But we may press behind that. Yahweh declares in wilderness a holy day of Sabbath rest and the people rest (desist from gathering). They stop their efforts at securing bread. They stop because they had been adequately nourished and could be full and content. The movement of the text from v. 2 to v. 30 is extraordinary— a movement from frantic anger to confident trust, from chaotic insecurity to serene security. The movement in this narrative is precisely parallel to that of Genesis 1, as it moves from chaos (Gen 1:2) to Sabbath (Gen 2:1-4a). That is a creation story. But so is this text. As Yahweh has authority to bring a world from disorder to harmonious order, so he has authority to bring a people to rest out of a frantic mob. He has transformed the wilderness, still not sown, but a place in which nourishment is now given.

---

15. Compare Niels-Erik A. Andreasen, *The Old Testament Sabbath: A Tradition-Historical Investigation*, SBLDS 7 (Missoula, Mont.: Society of Biblical Literature, 1972) 129–30.

Yahweh knew, always knows, when Israel never knows. The environment of his people is according to his purposes. Sabbath rest emerges, even in the wilderness. The place without life support becomes the place of abundance and security. Israel had misread wilderness and had miscalculated about Yahweh and so had yearned for managed land. The wilderness is not managed land. This is what makes it wilderness. But it is gifted land, and surprising meat and bread and Sabbath do come there. Always Israel is in gifted land yearning for managed land, but characteristically Israel learned that *gifted land* gives life and *managed land* does not. This moment of manna happened in the placelessness between the lands. Israel still has a yearning memory of Egypt, even though it was slavery. But the bread is given between the lands. And as v. 35 indicates, the gift bread lasted till they reached the inhabited land. Is the narrative intentional? Does it recognize knowingly that entrance into that land means the end of manna? Manna may have been welcome in a moment of desperation, but it is also hard to take. Israel is always crossing out of manna land into Canaan. There Israel could bake its own bread.

Numbers 14: The Two Histories in the Wilderness

Having rejected safe slavery, Israel found its immediate destiny to be landlessness. But even in wilderness it discovered that one may be a participant in one of two histories, surely a continuation of the two histories we have discerned in Genesis. Numbers 14 presents in rapid succession a series of images about facing the competing claims of the two histories.[16] One is driven by a sense of banishment, characterized by mistrust, expressed as quarrelsomeness, and devoted to return to Egypt. The other is the history of hope, trusting in Yahweh's promises, enduring in the face of want and need, sure that history was on its way to the new and good land.[17] Israel discerned what rootless people must each time learn over again, that in such landlessness there may be unexpected sustaining resources. Or one may discern there only darkness and abandonment. In the events of wilderness Israel wrestled like Jacob for its being and for its faith.

The first expression in this chapter of the two histories is in vv. 1-10. The issues are clearly stated. The history of banishment is articulated in

---

16. See Coats, *Rebellion,* 137–56, and Simon J. de Vries, "The Origin of the Murmuring Tradition," *JBL* 87 (1968) 51–58.

17. See Walter H. Capps, *Time Invades the Cathedral: Tension in the School of Hope* (Philadelphia: Fortress Press, 1972) chap. 6, describes "two religions." While his imagery does not correlate precisely to these two histories, the points of parallel are more than incidental.

vv. 1-4, characterized by loud cries, weeping, and murmuring. Landlessness leads to bitter accusation, here expressed as two explanations of indignation, two rhetorical questions, and a concluding appeal:

exclamations: (a) Would that we had died *in the land of Egypt!*
(b) Or would that we had died *in this wilderness!*
questions: (a) Why does Yahweh bring us *into this land* to fall by the sword?
(b) Would it not be better for us to go *back to Egypt?*
appeal: Let us choose a captain and go *back to Egypt.*

Three times there is positive appeal to Egypt and two times sharp negative contrast; this wilderness, this land, the one abandoned without resources. This history is driven by a yearning for restoration to safe slavery, always a compelling model for being in the land, but surely appealing to the landless. The two exclamations and questions form a chiasmus around the two points of reference:

land of Egypt
this wilderness
this land
Egypt

The speech itself reflects the movement anticipated by the speakers, out of and back into Egypt.

The counter-theme of this protest is represented by Moses and Aaron, but more dramatically by Joshua and Caleb. The old history led to complaint. The new history leads to repentance: they "rent their clothes." The speakers for the new history do not mention Egypt or return because they are singularly oriented to the land yet promised. They speak not of hardships but only of the richness of what is promised: "The land, which we passed through to spy it out, is an exceedingly good land" (v. 7).[18] The others had spoken only of wilderness and Egypt as though these were the only options. They framed the land-landless around the limited options of death and slavery. But Joshua and Caleb speak of yet another option; the land still in the future, the land good, exceedingly, exceedingly. Superlatives fail. The land is still conditional: "if" (v. 8). But the promise for which they left Egypt is still compelling: "a land flowing with milk and honey" (Exod 3:8). What led them here in the first place is still the main reason.

18. The double use, *me'od, me'od,* is noteworthy, reserved for especially great emphasis. compare Gen 7:19; 17:2, 6, 20; 30:43; Exod 1:7.

The promise makes an appeal: do not rebel; do not fear; do not fear—
an appeal for trust in the Promiser. What seemed formidable against them
is not, because the enemy is already defeated. The enemy is bread for them
and they shall consume them who are without a protective shadow. The
enemy is helpless before the trusters of the promise. The enemy is manna
for Israel in the new history. Two more antithetical views of landlessness
cannot be imagined. The wilderness is the *route of promise* on the way to
land, or the wilderness is *unbearable abandonment* to be avoided by
return to slavery. All the faith questions are put to Israel in wilderness.
Only a few in Israel discern what is in fact really going on and the true
character of landlessness as the route to the new land.

The antithesis is sharpened in vv. 22-24. Miraculously there is forgiveness in the wilderness, and the untrusting ones are forgiven. There is
assurance that Yahweh's presence is indeed with his people. But the power
of the two histories reasserts itself and even God's promise cannot change
that. The bearers of banishment are excluded from the future: "None of
the men who have seen my glory and my signs which I wrought in Egypt
and in the wilderness, and yet have put me to the proof these ten times and
have not hearkened to my voice, shall see the land which I swore to give to
their fathers; and none of those who despised me shall see it" (vv. 22-23).
The bearers of banishment did not listen. They despised Yahweh. They
acted in the wilderness out of cowardice and fear. What they did with
their wilderness determined their possibilities for landlessness. And they
blew it! They refused to credit their landlessness as a place for trusting,
not testing; for listening and honoring, not despising.

The contrast is again stated in v. 24, in which the new history is represented by Caleb: "But my servant Caleb, because he has a different spirit
and has followed me fully, I will bring into the land into which he went,
and his descendants shall possess it." He has followed and has not despised.
He is the one who has another spirit, contrasted with the ones choosing
death. This extraordinary expression marks Caleb as one who is positioned differently toward the promise and toward the land. The phrase
anticipates the more programmatic use of the theme "different spirit" in
Ezek 11:19; 18:31; 36:26-27; 37:14, addressed to the exiles, who are in a wilderness situation. For both the wanderers of the old tradition and the exiles of
the sixth century, for both Caleb and the contemporaries of Ezekiel, coping with a situation of landlessness is possible because of a new orientation
that permits one to trust the promises. As Ezekiel calls for repentance
(18:31), so Caleb is the one who repents (Num 14:6) and positions himself
to receive the promise. The contrast is complete and devastating, for the
bearers of one history will have the promise and the others clearly will not.

A more intense statement of the same reality is expressed in vv. 30-33, where again Caleb and Joshua are bearers of the new history. The contrasts are sharp in this unit:

> Caleb/Joshua: all the others
> the little ones: the older generation
> those who will come in: those who will fall in the wilderness

In particular, two contrasts are decisively presented. First, those who despise (*ma'as*) the land and those who know (*yada'*) the land. That is a central contrast. Those who despise cannot know. That perhaps is the new spirit of Caleb who refuses to despise what the others find it easy to ridicule and dismiss (Isa 53:3; 1 Cor 1:28). The ones who will come to the land are those who have maintained their expectancy and have grown neither weary nor cynical.

The second contrast worth noting is the one between the old and young generations. The older ones are characterized by calloused, calculated knowing, beset by quarrelsome impatience. The little ones who have no claim to power, leverage, or virtue, who are totally vulnerable, shall receive the promise. Vulnerability is a central theme in the wilderness tradition. In Exodus 16, openness to vulnerability lets Israel trust manna but calculating control brings a desire to store it. And it turns sour. Here the contrast is ironic. The land will be given not to the tough presuming ones, but to the vulnerable ones with no right to expect it. The vibrations begin about the "meek" inheriting the land, not the strident. This is a discernment that Israel would no doubt have wished to reject. The world believes that stridency inherits, but in its vulnerability Israel learns that the meek and not the strident have the future.

The contrast is sharp between the big ones who despise the land (v. 23) and the despised ones who will receive it. The very ones whom the world would not accept will indeed receive it. Already in the wilderness materials is the recognition of this strange inversion, which is fully acknowledged in Isa 52:13—53:12, the one who is despised and rejected is the one who prospers.[19] The despising ones shall die: Their dead bodies shall fall in the wilderness, because of the fornication, that is, because of the lack of singular loyalty to the one Promise of Israel. Interestingly Ezekiel especially utilizes this word to talk about how Israel got to exile (Ezek 16:15, 16; 20:22, 25, 26, 29, 34, 36; 23:7, 8, 11, 14, 18, 19, 23). Both our text and Ezekiel make the contrast: fornicators/new spirit. Ezekiel presents it sequentially.

---

19. See the double use of *bas* in 53:3.

Numbers 14 sees the old generation as *zonah* and therefore unfit, and the young possess the "other spirit." In both cases a spirit of fidelity receives land; the alternative is death. The despised get the land. The two histories are about *despisers* and *despised,* and the promise is given and withheld in ways that surprise—then and now. The wilderness is either the way to the land or the way to death. The announcement of radical alternatives produces in Israel a repentance remembered as less than authentic. The bearer of deathly history resolves at the last moment to join the others, but it is too late. Verses 39-45 report their last-ditch effort to enter the history of promise, but the history of promise requires enduring trust and no flashes of high resolve. So their last minute obedience, no substitute for enduring trust, will not hack it.[20] They confess sin but their repentance is rejected (vv. 41-43). They are condemned for turning away (*shuv*). The concluding narrative reports that they try anyway, but without the ark, without Moses, without visible sign of Yahweh's sanction. And predictably, they fail. The verb rendered "presume" is problematic, but the parallel in Deut 1:43 makes the case in other unmistakable terms: You were presumptuous (*zid*); you did not listen; you did not give ear. And so come humiliation, defeat, and a longer time in the desert. The God who rules in the wilderness also rules access to the land.

The two texts of Exodus 16 and Numbers 14 provide a polarity for our understanding of wilderness and land anticipation. Exodus 16 is a story about gifted landlessness, about surprising manna being given and received, so that wilderness is discerned as a place of surprising expectations and unexpected resources. Numbers 14 is a story about mistrust that begins in murmuring, which asserts exclusion from the land because of despising, and then finally announces death for lack of singular trust in Yahweh. It yields a presumptive effort to recover the promise by an act of stridency, sure to fail. Whereas Exodus 16 is about gifts given and received, Numbers 14 is about promises suspected and the seduction of slavery. Each text contains an echo of the other as a counter-theme. In Exodus 16, for all its amazement, there is the desperate attempt to store, and it leads to sourness and worms. And conversely, in the midst of the cynicism of Numbers 14, there is the remarkable assertion that the land will be received by the vulnerable little ones who are usually regarded as prey for stronger ones.

In the midst of wondrous manna, Israel is tempted to hoard. In the midst of stridency and death, there is an assertion of weakness that is blessed. The two together announce the possibility and limits of hope

---

20. See a similar ineffective effort in Jeremiah 34.

for wilderness. And Israel always wants less than or more than. But characteristically there is enough, but not too little and not too much (Exod 16:18).

The Crisis of Presence

Being in the wilderness is enough. Being there alone, abandoned, is unbearable. Inevitably the issue of God's presence is raised as a desperate question. Is he a god who lingers with the owners and supervisors in Egypt? Is he a god who awaits his people in the good land? And is wilderness an in-between moment without him? Or is wilderness a place that he prefers for his peculiar presence because of his peculiar character? Could it be that he is a god who most desires the interactions of the wilderness? What would it mean for the rootless in our own time to discover that he is a god peculiarly present to the landless, but in ways consistent with the experience of landlessness, which means less than sure and guaranteed? There is his vulnerability, but never to be presumed upon.

The issue is raised in Exodus 16—not by Israel but by Yahweh. Israel does not raise the issue of *presence* but of *bread*. Characteristically Yahweh transforms the question so that bread-talk has the dimension of God-talk concerned with fidelity and power: "At evening you shall know that it was Yahweh who brought you out of the land of Egypt, and in the morning you shall see the glory of Yahweh" (Exod 16:6-7). His response to the plea for food is to assert his presence as sustainer. He is there in the wilderness with Israel to transform the situation. In the reprise of v. 12 the assertion is somewhat refined: "At twilight you shall eat flesh, and in the morning you shall be filled with bread; then you shall know that I am Yahweh your God." Eating and being filled are the ways to know.

Between the two announcements, in v. 10, there is this remarkable statement: "And as Aaron spoke to the whole congregation of the people of Israel, they looked toward the wilderness, and behold, the glory of Yahweh appeared in the cloud." He is seen in a cloud and therefore not fully. He is seen in the wilderness, the sure and certain sign that he is with his people in their land of abandonment, with them in his inscrutable way to transform the situation.

The same issue of presence is raised in the remarkable prayer of Moses: "They have heard that you, O Yahweh, are in the midst of this people; for you, O Yahweh, are seen face to face, and your cloud stands over them and you go before them, in a pillar of cloud by day and in a pillar of fire by night" (Num 14:14; NRSV). Here the appeal is not on behalf of Israel but out of concern for God's reputation among the other peoples. The statement allows the central problem of God's presence to be expressed. He is hidden in the cloud, but he is seen face to face. The clarity and precision of religious formulation do not concern the text. The only form of Yahweh's presence that could possibly matter is his willingness and capacity to keep Israel alive and bring his people to the land of promise: "And now, I pray thee, let the power of Yahweh be great as thou hast promised" (Num 14:17). Do what you say! Keep your promise that just now is forgiveness but that finally is land. Clearly presence is assured as long as there are sustenance and movement toward fulfillment. Presence is for pursuit of the promise. Here there is no concern for cultic presence, but only for leadership and care on the way to the word yet to be given as land.[21] Yahweh's response to that prayer is radical. In vv. 20-25 he asserts that he is present to forgive and to do as he says. But in vv. 22-23 he denies to Israel what it most wants from him: assurance it would get to the land. He is not present to assure continuities but to work newness out of discontinuities. He will let die those who would live, but he will also evoke a new history and form a new people for himself just when the old history shamefully ends. The new people, contrasted with the old, are promise-trusters, rooted in Moses (v. 12), linked to the faith of Caleb (v. 24), and identified as the vulnerable ones (v. 31). His presence is evident in his intervention not to keep things going but to bring life out of death, to call to himself promise-trusters in the midst of promise-doubters.

Israel is not abandoned in wilderness. But it has no glory to manage or administer. It has only goodness, covenantal generosity, expressed as water, quail, and manna. These are always powerfully given to transform the wilderness, but always given at the time of extreme precariousness when Israel knows itself "prey," totally vulnerable. They are always given in response to cry, but always given with his inscrutable hiddenness.

Wilderness crisis issues for Israel revolve around Yahweh's presence. Like everything in the wilderness, it is not given in terms desired or expected. Like manna, his wilderness presence is always enough on which to survive, but not too much. Like manna, he can be graciously received but not stored or presumed upon. Like manna, it is given out of fidelity but never fully seen and controlled.

---

21. Jürgen Moltmann, *Theology of Hope: On the Ground and the Implications of a Christian Eschatology*, trans. J. W. Leitch (Minneapolis: Fortress Press, 1993) 148, is clear that the land promise keeps the Bible promissory and prevents its reduction to epiphany: "It would lose its power to give eschatological direction, and would become either gnostic talk of revelation or else preaching of morals, if it were not made clear that the gospel constitutes *on earth* and in time the promise of the future . . ." (italics mine).

Wilderness and Yahweh belong to each other. As Yahweh's presence transforms wilderness, so wilderness suggests the peculiar mode and parameters of Yahweh's presence. Facing that presence is Israel's peculiar struggle with landlessness, always toward the promised land, the land of the promiser, but always without resource.

On Lacking Nothing

Israel discerns Yahweh peculiarly in the desert. His way of being there is appropriate to the situation, present but not guaranteed. Like manna, enough but not too much. His presence in the wilderness is like all Israel's wilderness experiences, exceedingly precarious.

But he is there with Israel. He enters into the desolation with his people. He subjects himself to the same circumstances as Israel. He also sojourns without rootage, with his people, en route to the fulfilling land of promise. The ancient statement of Exodus 15 ends with Yahweh himself taking his *place* after being with his people in the sojourn (vv. 16-18), but it is only after the long sojourn.

Wilderness, landlessness for Israel, is a place without resources. But it is also the place where Yahweh is present with and to his people. Israel characteristically "looked to the wilderness" and there discerns his inscrutable presence. Wilderness, precarious as it is, is where Yahweh is present. That requires a new discernment of Yahweh. It also provides a fresh understanding of wilderness, no doubt experienced only by those who discern his presence by fully facing wilderness. Others worry about food and death. But the traditions of Israel offer a remarkably different reading of Israel's experience. They draw a bold conclusion:

> He knows your going through this great wilderness; these forty years Yahweh your God has been with you; you have lacked nothing. (Deut 2:7)

> I have led you forty years in the wilderness; your clothing has not worn out upon you and your sandals have not worn off your feet. (Deut 29:5)

Israel's reflection on that forty years of landlessness leads to a remarkable affirmation. Wilderness should have been a place of death, but life is given. Wilderness should have been a place of weariness, sickness, poverty, and disease, but Israel is sustained and kept well. Israel has no tattered clothes, no sore feet. It is subjected to the worst thinkable conditions and is kept well. The place of all lacks, because Yahweh is present, is where nothing is lacking.

Wilderness is not the place of destiny Israel or anyone else would prefer. But Israel is a people created in impossibility (Sarah) and sustained against every deathly prognosis. Israel lives only by miracle. It never decides its destiny is landlessness, but it concludes in these traditions that landlessness as a way to land is a bearable, even celebrative event because Yahweh is there with his people. And because Yahweh is there, gifts are given, healings emerge, newness governs, and nothing grows old. It is against all the wise expectations of this age, of all those who would reasonably leave Israel there to die.

In the wilderness Yahweh provides when there seems to be no available provision (see Gen 22:14). Life is rooted in impossibility. Landlessness is a condition in which the land promiser sustains his people. The surprise of manna, the unexpectedness of quail, the surging of water, all are hints of the real miracle of landlessness. There in Yahweh's presence, life-giving resources are adequate, not too much, but not too little. Israel knows life as unmerited gifts and so it can say, "Yahweh is my shepherd, I will not *lack*" (Ps 23:1). Yahweh has acted in landlessness to provide there for his people, just enough for life.

4.

REFLECTIONS
AT THE BOUNDARY

FINALLY ISRAEL COMES TO THE LAND. THE EXODUS IS ABOUT TO BE completed. The promise is about to be fulfilled. Landless sojourning is about to end. Israel comes to the Jordan and needs only to cross it and history will begin anew. The Jordan looms as a decisive boundary in the Bible. It is not simply between east and west but it is laden with symbolic power. It is the boundary between the precariousness of the wilderness and the confidence of at-homeness. The crossing of the Jordan is the most momentous experience that could happen to Israel. The Jordan crossing represents the moment of the most radical transformation of any historical person or group, the moment of empowerment or enlandment, the decisive event of being turfed and at home for the first time.[1] Nothing is more radical than this, that the sojourner becomes a possessor. The precarious sojourner has the heady new role of controller of what is promised and now given. The moment drastically redefines who Israel will be. Land entry requires of Israel that it cease to be what it had been in the wilderness and become what it has never been before. Land makes that demand. At this moment Israel does indeed become a new creation, a slave becomes an heir, a helpless child becomes a mature inheritor (see Ezek 16:1-14).

1. On the Jordan as boundary, compare 2 Sam 17:24 as boundary between wilderness and royal, ordered space (see Luke 3:3). Concerning the "conquest" and the crossing of the Jordan, I am aware of the conclusions of George E. Mendenhall, "The Hebrew Conquest of Palestine," *BA* 25 (1962) 66–87, reprinted in *Biblical Archeologist Reader 3* (Garden City, N.Y.: Doubleday, 1970) 100–120. In what follows, "wilderness" and "land" are intended primarily not as geographical but as sociological categories. On geography as an expression of theology see Willi Marxsen, *Mark the Evangelist: Studies on the Redaction History of the Gospel*, trans. J. Boyce (New York: Abingdon, 1969) 54–94.

good reason at that moment, Israel pauses to do what it does
is most characteristically Israel—it listens![2] At the moment of the
Jordan, at the boundary between landlessness and landedness—Israel listens! And Moses, covenanter and shaper of Israel, speaks and in his speaking defines the shape and character of new Israel, of Israel in the land and
for the land and over the land. Thus the tradition of Deuteronomy is precisely placed at the moment of the Jordan, where characteristically Israel
listens and Moses speaks. In that speaking/hearing moment, a new Israel
is called into being, one appropriate for the new time of the land.

More than at any other moment in Israel's history, here there is a long
reflective pause. It is as though Israel's traditionists had intuitively known
that this is the hour of destiny; as though Israel knows that hard, disciplined reflection is never more needed than at this moment, when the
new situation of land requires a new Israel with a new faith. Deuteronomy
more than anything else in the tradition provides the most radical and
bold articulation of faith.[3] The long pause of Deuteronomy is presented as
though Israel is reluctant to put its feet in the Jordan, dry though it would
be, because Israel knows that in so doing, it is walking away from the
inscrutable nourishment of wilderness. It is entering a context where all
the tasks of self-identity have to be addressed again. That moment
between Shittim and Gilgal is a moment of most difficult decision for
there is no turning back. In the land, in contrast to the wilderness, there
are no rocks to strike for water (Num 20:2-13), no manna to be received.
Israel wants to enter the land, knows that it must, knows that for this it
was called out of Egypt and away from slavery. But Israel hesitates. Perhaps the hesitation is not from fear, but in the face of an ominous recognition that life must be redefined. Moses' speech in Deuteronomy is filled
with promise and demand. It is talk about land and about Israel, about
gifts and covenant, about temptation and faith.[4]

God's faithful people in the present time linger here as did Israel to
reflect, because that moment stands as a paradigm for what is under way

2. On "listening" as constitutive for Israel, see Norbert Lohfink, *Das Hauptgebot: Eine Untersuchung literarischer Einleitungsfragen zu Dtn 5-11*, AnBib 20 (Rome: Pontifical Biblical Institute, 1963) 65–68 and *passim;* and Otto Bächli, *Israel und die Völker: Eine Studie zum Deuteronomium*, ATANT 41 (Zurich: Zwingli, 1962) 70–82.

3. The critical questions concerning Deuteronomy need not occupy us here. It is the dynamic interaction between old tradition and new situation that determines the method and intent of Deuteronomy. Compare Gerhard von Rad, *Studies in Deuteronomy*, trans. D. Stalker, SBT 1/9 (Naperville: Allenson, 1953) 60–73.

4. See the summary statement of Patrick D. Miller Jr., "The Gift of God," *Int* 23 (1969) 451–65.

at the boundary of the new land, fraught with problems and loaded with promise. The identity questions must all be addressed again. And we are only beginning that task in the newly landed America.

As Israel, we take our new identity vis-à-vis the land. It is important to be very clear about what the land is, how it addresses us, what it expects of us, and how we shall shape our faith and admit our identity in relation to it.[5]

The Land as Gift

The land to Israel is a gift. It is a gift from Yahweh and binds Israel in new ways to the giver. Israel was clear that it did not take the land either by power or stratagem, but because Yahweh had spoken a word and had acted to keep his word. The central memories of Israel were told and retold to recall this very point. Israel had always known it was a creature of his word. It lived because he called it (see Hos 11:1). Israel knew that in his speaking and Israel's hearing was its life. That is why the first word in Israel's life is "listen" (Deut 6:4)! Israel lived by a people-creating word spoken by this people-creator (Deut 8:3).

The flections at the boundary affirm that the land is a gift of his word. Israel had land because God keeps his words:

> Not one of all the good promises which Yahweh had made to the house of Israel had failed; all came to pass. (Josh 21:45)[6]

> ... And you know in your hearts and souls, all of you, that not one thing has failed of all the good things which Yahweh your God promised concerning you; all have come to pass for you, not one of them has failed. (Josh 23:14)

Israel reflects on how it is to regard the land. A land is different when it is given in speaking and received in listening. It is not just an object to be taken and occupied. It is rather a party to a relation. Because the land is

---

5. On land and wilderness as they illuminate Christian history see George H. Williams, *Wilderness and Paradise in Christian Thought: The Biblical Experience of the Desert in the History of Christianity and the Paradise Theme in the Theological Idea of the University* (New York: Harper & Row, 1962). See especially 98–131 with reference to American uses of the imagery.

6. See Gerhard von Rad on the centrality of this text, "The Problem of the Hexateuch," *The Problem of the Hexateuch and Other Essays,* trans. E. W. T. Dicken (New York: McGraw-Hill, 1966) 73–74.

the means of Yahweh's word becoming full and powerful for Israel, it is presented as a life-giving embodiment of his word:

> And when Yahweh your God brings you into the land *which he swore* to your fathers, to Abraham, to Isaac, and to Jacob, to give you, with great and goodly cities, which you did not build, and houses full of all good things, which you did not fill, and cisterns hewn out, which you did not hew, and vineyards and olive trees which you did not plant . . . (Deut 6:10-11)

The rhetoric at the boundary is that of pure gift, radical grace. There is no hint of achievement or merit or even planning. It is all given by the giver of good gifts and the speaker of faithful words. At the boundary, Israel affirms that being landed is *sola gratia:* You did not build; you did not fill; you did not hew; you did not plant. The new land is in a peculiar way like the wilderness. It wells up with life-giving power, unplanned by Israel, in inscrutable ways. Deuteronomy reflects early: Israel cannot and does not and need not secure its existence for itself. The same One who gave manna, quail, and water does it for them. Only now the gifts are enduring and not so precarious. Now it is cities and houses, cisterns, vineyards and trees. These surely are contrasted with the more provisional gifts of the wilderness. And they surely carry new temptations. Israel knows that at the boundary.

And the result—land is for satiation. You will be satisfied! Satiation is a vivid memory and firm hope for Israel. Israel remembers satiation in Egypt and is ready for satiation even if it comes with slavery (Exod 16:3). It discovered in the wilderness it could be strangely satisfied (16:8, 12), albeit unexpectedly and precariously. But at the Jordan, Israel reflects on the new dimension of satiation when the promise is kept—no longer satisfied in Egyptian slavery, no longer satisfied in the sojourn precariousness. Now Israel, the ones lacking in wilderness, the ones Pharaoh controlled in Egypt, is satisfied and given the apparatus of satiation—cities, houses, cisterns, vineyards and trees—not just food, but the instruments of production. The land is not only for satiation, it is for *guaranteed* satiation.

The boundary reflection becomes even more lyrical in Deut 8:7-10:

> For Yahweh your God is bringing you into a good land, a land of brooks of water, of fountains and springs, flowing forth in valleys and hills, a land of wheat and barley, of vines and fig trees and pomegranates, a land of olive trees and honey, a land in which you will eat bread without scarcity, in which you will lack nothing, a land

whose stones are iron, and out of whose hills you can dig copper.
And you shall eat and be full, and you shall bless Yahweh your God
for the good land he has given you.

It is a good land, the work of the good word (see Josh 23:15-16). The
land matches the word that gave it. It fulfills every anticipation of the
wilderness: water—brooks, fountains, springs; food—wheat, barley,
vines, fig trees, pomegranates, olives, honey; plenty—without scarcity
(*miskenath*), without lack (*ḥesar*); minerals—iron, copper. The water
does not need to come at the last moment, incredibly from a rock. Its
sources are visible and reliable. The food does not need to appear surpris-
ingly. It rises up from the land of gift. The minerals, without parallel in
the sojourn, are marks of guaranteed security, the stuff of which cities and
houses and security networks can be constructed, all the resources
Pharaoh had in Egypt and helpless Israel lacked.[7] Israel is given the means
to withstand historical disruptions and discontinuities and perhaps to
dare to eliminate them. Such a land makes possible the living of a less
exposed, less vulnerable life, the kind it had yearned for both in slavery
and in sojourn. Israel after Jordan is less exposed, more guaranteed.

We have already seen the wilderness remembered as a place of "no
lack" (Exod 16:18). But that is only in retrospect. It never could be counted
on in prospect. Now, in the land, "no lack" is anticipatory and such anticipation is believable. "Land" means to know that even the future is secure
and Israel in land can be without anxiety. And the culmination of it all:
satiation! "You shall be satisfied!" Israel knows that at the boundary. It
anticipates a new history of guaranteed satiation, precisely the antithesis
of the history of banishment. That is what land is all about. Obviously in
a history more guaranteed and less contingent, listening to the word of
the giver and guarantor becomes more urgent and less compelling.[8]

Israel's reflection on the land is like a continual return to the theme
because it cannot believe it. Land requires of Israel that it face its radical
newness. Its meaning cannot be extrapolated from any previous experience, because there has never been such a historical land before. That is
the power of the new history that has led to the land. This is not land such
as anybody had ever known, not the land of hostility and covetousness

7. The change is to be understood not simply in terms of geographic placement but in
terms of an alternative consciousness in which sociological and cultural possibilities were
transformed.

8. Compare Deut 32:15 and George E. Mendenhall, *The Tenth Generation: The Origins of
the Biblical Tradition* (Baltimore: Johns Hopkins Univ. Press, 1973), especially chaps. 7 and 8,
for the changes that came upon Israel in the land.

and decisiveness and fear. This is gifted-land, and people under gift are rare. And Deuteronomy knows that people under gift are even rarer who stay that way and who do not forget.

The gift land is contrasted with every land of coercion:

> For the land which you are entering to take possession of it is not like the land of Egypt, from which you have come, where you sowed your seed and watered it with your feet, like a garden of vegetables; but the land which you are going over to possess is a land of hills and valleys, which drinks water by the rain from heaven, a land which Yahweh your God cares for; the eyes of Yahweh your God are always upon it from the beginning of the year to the end of the year. (Deut 11:10-12)[9]

The old land that Israel remembered so well, the land of slavery, even of banishment, was land by effort. And it was therefore precarious, requiring effort and attention. It was *demanding land.* The new land, the land given beyond the Jordan, the land of restoration, is land by graciousness. And therefore the land shall be secure and life-giving. It is land where security does not need to be manufactured, where well-being need not come by conjuring and calculation. Here security and well-being are not from the grudging task-master, but from the benevolent rain-sender, the same one who was bread-giver. Both rain and manna come from heaven, from outside the history of coercion and demand.

This land beyond the boundary is one that Yahweh, land-giver, Exodus-causer, manna-sender, seeks perpetually and attends to faithfully. Israel need not be anxious about the land. Yahweh is preoccupied with it on Israel's behalf. He never takes his powerful eyes off it, through the whole cycle of life and nourishment from planting to harvest: he will give rain (v. 14); he will give grass (v. 15). And the result—Israel will be satiated! At the boundary Israel could not affirm it too often. This faith is contrasted not only with precarious life always lived under exposure. It is also contrasted with a life of coercion in which land is held by fearful, wearisome duty.[10]

Israel lives under gift—not gift anticipated, but gift given. That is its new consciousness, and nothing is more radical, especially to landed, empowered people, than to discover they are creatures of gift. Such a fulsome celebration of guaranteed satiation and secure existence under gift in the land warns one against misreading the text.

9. See Wilhelm Vischer, "Foi et Technique," *RHPR* 44 (1964) 102–9, on the contrast in this passage.

10. On land as coercion and anxiety, compare Matt 6:25ff. The perfectly anxious one is Solomon, the supreme holder of coerced land.

On the one hand, it protests against the existentialism that interprets the Bible only for dramatic events, finding meaning in intrusive, disruptive discontinuities. Deuteronomy, a reflection on the boundary, can believe Yahweh grants his people enduring, wholesome continuities, enjoying the span of planting and harvest, participating in the full cycle of life with the earth—and all under Yahweh's attentive, protective eye. Truly said that he is a fertility God.[11]

But on the other hand, Deuteronomy will not permit the reduction of faith to a natural fertility religion in which faith becomes possessions and land manipulation.[12] Deuteronomy is no charter for technological values of growth, production, and development, as though to secure our own existence. The situation is more dialectical. Israel's involvement is always with land and with Yahweh, never only with Yahweh as though to live only in intense obedience, never only with land, as though simply to possess and manage;[13] always *with land* and *with Yahweh*, always receiving gifts from land, always being addressed by Yahweh, always being assured and summoned, always being both nourished and claimed, always being of the family of earth, but always and at the same time Yahweh's peculiar listening partner in historical covenant. The crisis of Israel at the boundary and the power of Deuteronomy at the boundary are in precisely insisting upon both Yahweh and land. It is likely that conventional Christianity has wanted always to talk about Yahweh and neglect land. And conversely, secular humanism wants always to talk only of land and never of Yahweh. And most of us live in both worlds and settle for an uneasy schizophrenia, schizophrenia because we don't know what else to do, uneasy because we know better. Deuteronomy knew better also and insisted that Israel is now situated to receive land gifts and to be addressed words by Yahweh, and it must both receive and listen.

In that dialectic land is something different. It is not only giver of nourishing gifts. It is bearer of historical words. Israel had a peculiar notion that land is not natural setting but historical arena, place not just

11. Compare Walter Harrelson, *From Fertility Cult to Worship* (New York: Doubleday, 1969) 12–13. Harrelson intends to correct the one-sided emphasis upon history to the neglect of "nature."

12. George E. Mendenhall refers to the United Monarchy as a process of "paganization" of Israel, "The Monarchy," *Int* 29 (1975) 160.

13. This dialectic points to the central dynamic of Israel's tradition. The Mosaic tradition stressed obedience to Yahweh in ways that minimized the land. The Davidic tradition conversely stressed the land and neglected the Torah. The holding together of Torah and land is the central problem for Israel and protects against the twin dangers of works righteousness and cheap grace. Compare Peter Diepold, *Israels Land*, BWANT 95 (Stuttgart: Kohlhammer, 1972) 100.

for satiation but also for listening, for words being spoken with their rich implications of doing and caring and deciding, and their strange affirmation of newness.

The gifted land is covenanted land. It is not only nourishing space. It is also covenanted place. The Jordan is entry not into safe space but into a context of covenant. The gift is for celebration. It is based on the risk that satiated people can stay in history and keep listening. It is a bold question, as yet unresolved, whether only the hungry will listen, or whether placed people can stay in history with the Lord of history. No wonder they paused at Jordan!

The Land as Temptation

The gift of the land provides secured people with dangerous alternatives. One alternative is to keep the gift as gift, to maintain the dialectic with land/with Yahweh, knowing one is gifted by land/addressed by Yahweh. This alternative is to maintain the rich vitality of the covenant.

But already at the boundary Israel reflected on alternative handlings of the gift. Israel knows very early that the need to rework identity in the land can lead to a new identity that perverts the land, distorts Yahweh, and destroys Israel. The land, source of life, has within it seductive power. It invites Israel to enter life apart from covenant, to reduce covenant place with all its demand and possibilities to serene space apart from history, without contingency, without demand, without mystery.

Israel does not have many resources with which to resist the temptation.[14] The chief one is memory. At the boundary Israel is urged to remember.[15] In the first instance remembering is important completely apart from the substance of memory. Remembering is a historical activity. To practice it is to affirm one's historicity. It is to acknowledge that there is movement and change, that there is contingency and discontinuity. It is to reflect upon the dissonance between how it was and how it is. Thus is posed the peculiarly historical problem of continuity and discontinuity, of how we shall take seriously things that abide along with the things that are given and denied, that are yearned for and lost.

---

14. Bächli, *Israel*, 70–113, names four "weapons" for Israel's resistance: preacher, law, cult, and power.

15. Compare Edward Blair, "An Appeal to Remembrance," *Int* 15 (1961) 41–47, and the articles accompanying that of Blair. It is instructive that the entire German hermeneutical discussion of "representation" focused on Deuteronomy. More recently Robert Coles has studied displacement and land temptation in American culture and has stressed the impor-

Land can be a place for historical remembering, for action that affirms the abrasive historicity of our existence. But land can also be, as Deuteronomy saw so clearly, the enemy of memory, the destroyer of historical precariousness. The central temptation of the land for Israel is that Israel will cease to remember and settle for how it is and imagine not only that it was always so but that it will always be so. Guaranteed security dulls the memory. Guaranteed satiation erodes the capacity to maintain the distance and linkage between how it was and how it is and deadens the capacity to be open to how it might yet be. Where that distance and linkage are gone, one can no longer recall a time before the gift and then we can scarcely remember that it is gift. One can hardly reexperience one's pre-satiation days. The temptation of satiation is to transform a historical gift given in a moment of covenant that separates no-gift and gift existence. And it becomes an eternally guaranteed situation without change or demand, evoking neither risk nor gratitude.[16]

Israel's central temptation is to forget and so cease to be a historical people, open either to the Lord of history or to his blessings yet to be given. Settled into an eternally guaranteed situation, one scarcely knows that one is indeed addressed by the voice in history who gives gifts and makes claims. And if one is not addressed, then one does not need to answer. And if one does not answer, then one is free not to care, not to decide, not to hope, and not to celebrate.[17]

Of course the border reflections of Deuteronomy are not interested in memory as an empty formal construct. The substance of Israel's memory is clear. It concerns Yahweh, his actions toward Israel, the incredible willingness and capacity he has shown in transforming Israel's history from slavery to wilderness to security in land. Remembering Yahweh is not simply an act of religious devotion. It is confessing a relation that keeps life historical, that assures that newness comes from outside us, that life is not at our disposal,[18] that gifts can be given, that amazement and gratitude are

tance of representation, "The Cold Tough World of the Affluent Family," *PsychT* (November, 1975) 67ff.

16. Jürgen Moltmann, *Theology of Hope: On the Ground and the Implications of a Christian Eschatology,* trans. J. W. Leitch (New York: Harper & Row, 1965), has contrasted promissory faith and religion of epiphany. In the latter there is no newness, but only a disclosure of what always is. In such a context nothing is hoped for and there can be no serious covenanting.

17. Compare Moltmann, *The Experiment Hope,* trans. M. D. Meeks (Philadelphia: Fortress Press, 1975) 70–84, on apathy.

18. Compare Abraham Heschel, "To accept the sacred is an acknowledgment that certain things are not available to us, are not at our disposal," *Who Is Man?* (Stanford: Stanford Univ. Press, 1965) 48.

possible.[19] Remembering Yahweh is for Israel the source of the qualities of humanness and humanness that are its distinctive heritage.[20] Nothing less is at issue in this warning to Israel than whether Israel will live a life rooted in words freely spoken and gifts freely given, or whether Israel will live a life of apathy under coercion, devoid both of passion and victory.[21]

And so the preachers at the Jordan, each time they speak of the land, move to warning:

> ... Then take heed lest you forget Yahweh, who brought you out of the land of Egypt, out of the house of bondage. (Deut 6:12)

> Take heed lest you forget Yahweh your God, by not keeping his commandments and his ordinances and his statues ... lest, when you have eaten and are full ... then your heart be lifted up, and you forget Yahweh your God, who brought you out of the land of Egypt, out of the house of bondage, who led you through the great and terrible wilderness, ... who fed you in the wilderness with manna. ... Beware lest you say in your heart, "My power and the might of my hand have gotten me this wealth." (Deut 8:11-17)

> Take heed lest your heart be deceived, and you turn aside. . . . (Deut 11:16).

The first of these is reference to Exodus. Remember that the satiated ones were the enslaved ones and only Yahweh could and did change that. In the bodies of the Israelites is the memory of slavery and only the other One could change that. Note in Exod 16:3 they yearn for enslavement.

The second more fully developed statement describes the alternative to remembering, namely, the seduction of imagining it was always so and Israel made it so. In such a consciousness, Israel is no longer recipient of

19. We may note the intersection of a cluster of pertinent motifs in this connection in the work of Heschel. On the one hand, Heschel, before anyone else, wrote on the pathos of God, *The Prophets* (New York: Harper & Row, 1962) 252–78. On the other hand, he has written most eloquently of embarrassment and celebration as the quintessence of mature humanness, *Who Is Man?* And he also eloquently understood Sabbath as a faith statement about God's healing, restful world, *The Sabbath: Its Meaning for Modern Man* (New York: Farrar, Straus and Young, 1951).

20. On our understanding and reading of the text and our passion for humanness, which may be screened out by our tendentious reading, compare José Porfirio Miranda, *Marx and the Bible: A Critique of the Philosophy of Oppression*, trans. J. Eagleson (Maryknoll, N.Y.: Orbis, 1974).

21. See Peter L. Berger et al., *The Homeless Mind: Modernization and Consciousness* (New York: Random, 1973), on both the causes and consequences of coerced, fragmented life.

land but controller, no longer creature of grace but manager of achievement. There is no more radical word than that in Deut 8:18: "Yahweh, your God, . . . it is he who gives you power to get wealth." Israel is offered a covenantal understanding of power, power that is not vested in Israel but in the other One who meets Israel at the point of need. Secure consumers can scarcely reexperience crunch-points like slavery and sojourn and so Israel forgot. In the land the people ceased to be Israel.

In all three warnings two common elements appear. First, Israel can be seduced by other gods:

> You shall not go after other gods, of the gods of the peoples who are round about you. (6:14)

> And if you forget Yahweh your God and go after other gods and serve them and worship them, I solemnly warn you this day. . . . (8:19)

> Take heed lest your heart be deceived and you turn aside and serve other gods and worship them. . . . (11:16)

The temptation of other gods is almost a cliché in Deuteronomy. It is surely a formula that is not dealt with in any open or discursive way. It is rather the bottom-line, nonnegotiable premise of land entry, and therefore does not need to be explicated at the boundary.

As a formal assertion, it is enough to affirm that Yahweh will not tolerate rival loyalties because he is a jealous God, insisting on singular and exclusive loyalty.[22] Therefore any attention to other gods evokes his anger, which is intolerant and destructive. Of course the temptation to idolatry and consequent anger of Yahweh can be left as a positive principle of abstract theology. It is a warning that, if never questioned, never needs to be explained.

But as a positive principle it does not recognize the subtle insight of the tradition. The depth of the warning is not due to pettiness on Yahweh's part. It has to do with the character of Yahweh and the character of the other gods. Yahweh is the one who by his liberating speech and wilderness presence has created a people in history with a peculiar consciousness. They are people who know they are addressed by life-giving words that

---

22. Compare George Ernest Wright, *The Old Testament against Its Environment*, SBT 1/2 (London: SCM, 1950) 30–41, and Norman K. Gottwald, "Biblical Theology or Biblical Sociology?" *Radical Religion* 2 (1975) 46–57.

bestow the free gift of historical existence on the radically undeserving.[23]
Thus Deuteronomy makes much of free election as the root of gifted existence (7:6-11; 9:4-5; 14:1-2). Israel finds itself in history as one who had no
right to exist. Slaves become a historical community. Sojourners become
secured in land. Slaves have no reason to expect to be addressed or called
by name, surely not to be liberated. Wilderness wanderers have no reason
to expect to be secured in land. But it happens—all hoped for but
unplanned. None of it achieved, all of it given. Indeed the attempt to
achieve it ended in disaster (Num 14:39-45). Yahweh is the Lord of *gifted
existence,* taken freely and without merit. And the way to sustain gifted
existence is to stay singularly with the gift-giver.

In the land Israel encounters alternative possibilities. It experiences
guaranteed satiation, and with such a way of life, it needs an appropriate
theology. Living with guaranteed satiation, it needs gods—surely other
than Yahweh—who are committed to their own guaranteed satiation,
who can function as symbolic legitimation for Israel's pursuit of satiation.
And sure enough, there are such gods who make themselves available.
They present themselves as practical choices, usable loyalties put at the
disposal of Israel as means of securing its own existence. That is the central temptation of the land, that it seems to contain in its own gifts adequate means to secure existence. The sources of fertility are in the land
itself.[24] The possibility of strength is in the mineral-laden hills. The
promise of rain is in clouds managed by technique. And the gods who
claim these gifts are subject to manipulation, ready to serve human ends,
the ends of satiation. As everything else in this consciousness, so these
gods; everything is put at disposal, usable for self-security.[25]

The land tempts Israel to escape from history with Yahweh, to substitute for the vitality and precariousness of history the sureness, sameness,
and closedness of dull existence in secure land without decision, without
promise, without word, without mystery. Land folk want to pretend that
life is not precarious and history is not contingent. In the land of sureness

23. Gottwald, "Biblical Theology," is surely correct in seeing that Israel's notion of
monotheism is sociologically shaped. But as a theological statement, the claim cannot be
reduced to an echo of sociological reality. Theologically we must insist that it is the jealous
God who evoked Israel as a people with a peculiar sociological character, and not the other
way around.

24. On the sexuality of Yahweh and the matter of generativity, see Gottwald, "Biblical
Theology," 53–55. The refusal to attribute sexuality to Yahweh is centered in resistance to the
notion that creation itself contains its own resources for generativity.

25. The argument pursued here rejects the notion that *technē* is a neutral tool for good or
ill. Israel discovered *technē* to be an ideological reality affirming that life can be self-secured.

there are no risks to be taken, but only modest taxes to be paid. In the land of sameness there are no newnesses to be faced or hoped for but only institutions to honor. In the land of closedness there are no unexplained dimensions that may yet reach us, but only rituals to perform. There is only complacent self-indulgence or there is uneasy despair, or perhaps there are both.

Either way or both ways, Yahweh will not permit that to happen to Israel. That is not Israel's destiny and it cannot regard itself as so fated. And so Deuteronomy announces Israel's ultimate contingency. It can lose the good land.

Land is in history with Yahweh. It is never contextless space. It is always a place where memories of slavery and manna are recalled and where hopes of fidelity and well-being are articulated. Land is always where Israel must come to terms with the Lord of memories and hopes. It is always the place for promises and demands, for words spoken and heard. And those who would have it otherwise, those who wish turf without being addressed, perish. Deuteronomy's most mature reflection is that gift land may become coerced space. The heirs of promise may become participants in the history of banishment (Deut 8:20).

The central temptation of the land is coveting. There is no clearer picture than the disaster in the valley of Achor, Joshua 7. The narrative is programmatic for Israel's land entry. Israel is a community under gift (see 8:1). That is how land is obtained and held, according to this tradition. The introduction of self-seeking in a world of gifts is an attempt to shift the grounds for security. It is an attempt to replace precarious trust with control, to substitute self-possession for covenantal assurance. Israel's memory is that land held in this way disturbs the well-being of all Israel. The temptation to private well-being is a way to death.[26]

---

26. See the sharp critique by Miranda, *Marx*, chap. 1. One cannot always determine whether the critique concerns actual economic realities or simply an uncaring attitude toward community. It is likely that such a distinction is in itself ideological. The Old Testament offers two paradigms for coveting and its death-bringing force, i.e., the David–Bathsheba–Uriah episode and the Adam–Eve narrative. It is likely that in the history of tradition the two are related. Certainly they provide a central symbol for the destructive power of coveting for self-security. Compare Mic 2:1-2. See the connections I have suggested between the David and Adam stories, "David and His Theologian," *CBQ* 30 (1968) 100–164. There can be little doubt that the two narratives reflect the same cultural world, that of urbanized monarchy. For a characterization of that cultural world, see the polemical statements of George E. Mendenhall, "The Monarchy," 155–70, and "Samuel's 'Broken Rib': Deuteronomy 32," in *No Famine in the Land: Studies in Honor of John L. McKenzie*, ed. J. W. Flanagan and A. W. Robinson (Missoula, Mont.: Scholars, 1975) 63–73.

The central question at the boundary is this: Can Israel live in the land without being seduced by the gods, without the temptation of coveting having its way? Can Israel live in the land with all the precarious trust of landlessness? All the experience of Israel would answer negatively. But Deuteronomy clings to a better vision of Israel, believing that in the land, faithful people can resist the temptation to be too secure, and can maintain the buoyancy of covenant, by saying "yes" to Yahweh, "no" to the gods. And on such a premise Israel need not perish but dwell in the land, even to sons' sons.

The Land as Task

Land with Yahweh brings responsibility. The same land that is gift freely given is task sharply put. Landed Israel is under mandate. "Everyone to whom much is given, of him will much be required" (Luke 12:48). Interestingly in Luke 12:41-48, Jesus' saying is precisely in the context of possessions, owners, and stewards. It is a radical idea challenging our usual notions of possessions, for we think much possession makes one immune from caring.

Deuteronomy at the boundary knew otherwise. And so the boundary is the place of Torah. Torah, according to tradition, is from Sinai. But it is freshly presented, interpreted, and urged at the boundary. Surely a case can be made that Torah becomes relevant in decisive ways for Israel only when it is landed, not in the yearnings of the fathers, not in the weariness of slavery, not in the precariousness of sojourn, but singularly in the land. Only in land is Israel primarily people of Torah.

Torah consists in guidelines for land management[27] (thus correlating with the concern for stewards in the parable of Luke 12:41-48). Torah of course has to do with obedience to Yahweh, with honoring covenant. But Israel's Torah is markedly uninterested in a religion of obedience as such. It is rather interested in care for land, so that it is never forgotten from whence came the land and to whom it is entrusted and by whom. Thus in Joshua 1 at the moment of land entry, Joshua makes a characteristic appeal:

> Only be strong and very courageous, being careful to do according to
> all the law which Moses my servant commanded you; turn not from
> it to the right hand or to the left, that you may have good success

---

27. James A. Sanders, "Torah and Christ," *Int* 29 (1975) 372–90, has characterized Torah as including *ethos,* ethics, and life-style, all of which apply to our concern.

wherever you go. This book of the law shall not depart out of your
mouth, but you shall meditate on it day and night, that you may be
careful to do according to all that is written in it; for then you shall
make your way prosperous, and then you shall have good success.
(Josh 1:7-8)

The rhetoric is peculiar because it is an imperative to martial bravery
and courage. But what is asked is not courage to destroy enemies, but
courage to keep Torah. Perhaps the opportunity to forget Torah, that is, to
disregard the historical character of the land, is Israel's central enemy to
be resisted. The only courage Israel needs is that for honoring Torah.
What takes most courage for Israel is the affirmation about land as
covenanted place and the denial that it is contextless space to be filled as
Israel chooses.

Torah is Israel's way of living gifted life. It is not necessary here to
review all the wrongheaded notions of Torah under the general notions of
works righteousness.[28] It is enough to affirm that Torah is for Israel the
way to enjoy gifts. Torah-honoring leads to "success" and "prosperity." But
in this and similar contexts, prosperity and success are not carefully
planned achievements or manufactured blessings rooted in human ingenuity. Rather they are blessings freely bestowed. They come not because
Israel is diligent or clever but because Israel has understood the character
of gift and the ways in which gift comes.

The link between Torah and land is central. It seems so obvious, but so
radical. In a coercive society, exactly the opposite is true. The ones who
have made it, the ones who control the land and the machinery of governance are the ones who need not so vigorously obey. They are the ones
who can fix tickets or prices as needed, the ones before whom the judge
blinks and the revenue officer winks (see Mic 3:11). It is the landless poor
and disadvantaged who are subject to exacting legal claims of careful
money management, precise work performance, careful devotion to all
social jots and tittles, not only last hired and first fired, but first suspected,
last acquitted.

At the boundary Israel declares that in the land of gift the opposite is
the case. The landed are the ones called to Torah, to honor it without tam-
pering or modifying or compromising. Torah exists so that Israel will not
forget whose land it is and how it was given to us. Only the landed are

28. Sanders, *Torah*, 381, makes the point well: "It is gospel and then law—both completely
intertwined, inextricable one from the other. There is no such thing in the concept of Torah
as law without story. . . ."

tempted to forget. Only the well-off and seemingly satiated are tempted to forget the history of barrenness and slavery, of hunger and manner, of gifts and promises kept beyond all human expectation. Torah is precisely to preserve memory for those most tempted to forget. Torah is not to cramp behavior, not to coerce or control, but to keep Israel in its historicality with Yahweh and with land. At the boundary the tradition knows that Israel's temptation in its new security will be to flee to a nonhistorical consciousness. Torah is precisely to sustain memory in Israel of its long history with Yahweh, a history of gift and land entry as a protest to the history of banishment.

Of course the Torah is rich and varied, and all manner of emphases can be noted. But in the context of land-remembering and land management, let us note especially three tasks set by Torah. We have already commented on exclusion of (a) other gods and (b) coveting. Perhaps they are the two points of reference in the Decalogue for land management. They provide the frame in which the Decalogue is set. The first is concerned with resisting the seduction of coercion. The second, placed last in the Decalogue, is concerned with keeping land as gift and refusing possession of it. In that context these items may be noted:

1. The first is prohibition of images. Images are something other than "other gods," which we have already discussed. Images refer to making controllable representations of our best loyalties and visions.[29] They are efforts to reduce to manageable and predictable form the sources of value and power in our lives.

    Surely images are a peculiar temptation to the landed. Characteristically when one is able to plan and manage everything else, one yearns to make a comfortable place in life even for ultimate values that can be managed. Thus mystery is reduced to manageable size. God is put at the disposal of his people. Transcendence is domesticated. When the land is fully controlled, it is easy to imagine that the land has been generated by the community and can be used for its own objectives (Deut 8:17).

    Images are a way of removing our land from history, a way of forgetting the terror that surrounds the land and the blood let even in and for our land. Images have a way of leveling memories and hopes into the deception that it is all present and given now, that there were no pre-image times nor will there be times yet to come without

---

29. Compare Gerhard von Rad, *Old Testament Theology,* vol. 1: *The Theology of Israel's Historical Traditions,* trans. D. M. G. Stalker (New York: Harper, 1962) 212–19. See Gabriel Vahanian, *Wait without Idols* (New York: Braziller, 1964), for a more broadly based presentation of an iconoclastic approach to biblical faith.

images.[30] And if time is made timeless[31] by images that endure and never change, no newness can come; there will be no new healings but also no disruptive vision and no land-loss. The world of images is a world without terror, without rage, without the compelling announcement ever to leave the land for a better one. Images are for seeing, probably seeing too clearly and knowing too much.[32]

2. The second task of landed Israel is to keep Sabbath. Sabbath in the earliest teaching is for freeing slaves (Exod 21:1-11; Deut 15:12-18), later for resting land (Leviticus 25)[33] and for canceling debts (Deut 15:1-11). We have yet to learn of the radical meaning of Sabbath for landed people.[34]

While the history of the festival is ambiguous its radical affirmation to Israel cannot be missed. It is a central affirmation to Israel about the character of life and land as gift. It is the institutional reminder to Israel that cessation from frantic activity will not cause the world to disintegrate or society to collapse. Sabbath sets a boundary to our best, most intense efforts to manage life and organize land for our security and well-being.

Sabbath is a voice of gift in a frantic coercive self-securing world. Land Sabbath is a reminder that (a) land is not *from* us but is a gift *to* us, and (b) land is not fully given over to our satiation. Land has its own rights over against us and even its own existence. It is in covenant with us but not totally at our disposal. Sabbath is for honoring land. In some traditions of course (Gen 2:1-4a), the rest is in context of creation,

---

30. Perhaps only landless ones can have historical hope because they yearn for a decisive transformation. Those in the land are so fixed on what is already given that they do not hope and where hope is gone, history is not possible. There can then be no distance between what is and what is promised. Moltmann, *Theology of Hope,* speaks of the "utopia of the status quo" (23). See his comments on the religion of epiphany (95–102).

31. Walter H. Capps, *Time Invades the Cathedral: Tensions in the School of Hope* (Philadelphia: Fortress Press, 1972) 33–36 and *passim,* insists on an understanding of reality that allows for a dawning *Novum.* He discerns how the reduction of history to timelessness serves a sociological interest, i.e., images that result in a static god serving socioeconomic interests (34).

32. See the remarkable distinctions made by Erwin W. Strauss, "Aesthesiology and Hallucinations," in *Existence: A New Dimension in Psychiatry and Psychology,* ed. R. May et al. (New York: Basic, 1958) 157–62 on seeing and hearing. Rolf P. Knierim addresses the problem of knowing and seeing in "Revelation in the Old Testament," in *The Task of Old Testament Theology: Method and Cases* (Grand Rapids: Eerdmans, 1995) 139–70.

33. John H. Yoder, *The Politics of Jesus: Vicit Agnus Noster* (Grand Rapids: Eerdmans, 1972) 64–77, has made jubilee of the land a primary motif in his radical interpretation of the gospel.

34. See Heschel, *The Sabbath,* and Hans Walter Wolff, *Anthropology of the Old Testament,* trans. M. Kohl (Philadelphia: Fortress, 1975) 135–42.

whereby it is announced that rest is characteristic of the history of the land from the beginning, and indeed rest is essential to the history of God himself.[35]

But at the boundary, the tradition of Deuteronomy appeals for Sabbath on more historical grounds. Sabbath is rooted in the history of Exodus, which led to the land of fulfillment. And keeping Sabbath is a way of affirming the power and authority of the history that brought Israel to the land. Sabbath is a way of remembering to which history Israel belongs and the way in which it is related both to Yahweh and to land.

Debt Sabbath is a dramatic affirmation that human society does not rest finally on buying and selling, owing and collecting. Landed people are accustomed to managing things. And as we manage things we would manage people. We manage them by taxation and interest rates, by debts and mortgages and soon everyone is either owner of others or part of the owned. When we forget our history we think that is the way it has always been and is supposed to be. Sabbath in Israel is the affirmation that people, like land, cannot be finally owned or managed. They are in covenant with us, and therefore lines of dignity and respect and freedom are drawn around them that must be honored by people who will have the land as a covenanted place.

Slave release is only an extreme form of debt cancellation. Sabbath for slaves is the recognition that Sabbath is an occasion of public amnesty; the world is restored to its rightful posture, and society is reorganized according to covenantal relations. Sabbath does not make sense in contextless space. But it is indispensable in a society and land whose people intend to be historical. History has to do with the acknowledgment that our much frantic effort cannot secure our existence, that our planning can't eliminate contingency from our common life. We are secured only in the give and take of memory and hope among members of the covenanting community who have agreed to discern their common contingency in a certain way.

Landed people are tempted to create a *sabbathless* society in which land is never rested, debts are never canceled, slaves are never released, nothing is changed from the way it now is and has always been. The give and take of historicality can be eliminated, and all of life can be reduced to a smoothly functioning machine. That is the meaning of

35. Sabbath is a dramatic protest against our characteristic homelessness and the fatigue in which it results. Links may be made between Berger's essay on "homelessness" and Paul Tournier's understanding of fatigue, *Fatigue in Modern Society*, trans. J. H. Farley (Richmond: John Knox, 1965).

the producer-consumer consciousness that tempts Israel to betray the meaning of the land.

Sabbathless existence is for coveting without limit because there are no more covenanted brothers and sisters. Amos knew that and saw it happening:

> Hear this, you who trample upon the needy,
>   and bring the poor of the land to an end,
> saying, "When will the new moon be over,
>   that we may sell grain?
> And the sabbath,
>   that we may offer wheat for sale,
> that we may make the ephah small and the shekel great,
>   and deal deceitfully with the false balances,
> that we may buy the poor for silver
>   and the needy for a pair of sandals,
>   and sell the refuse of the wheat?" (Amos 8:4-6)

Sabbaths are the only events that protect the poor from being bought and sold. If Sabbaths can be eliminated, life will be emptied of history. Land will be void of covenant. Everything can be bought and sold. Brothers and sisters, like land, become commodities. No wonder Israel at the boundary regarded Sabbath as a peculiar task.

3. A third task for landed Israel, announced at the boundary, is care for the brother and sister. They are variously characterized: the poor (Exod 23:6; Deut 15:7-11), the stranger (Exod 21:21-24; 23:9), the sojourner (Deut 10:19), the widow and orphan (Deut 24:19-22), and the Levite (Deut 14:27). This diverse list has one feature of commonality. They are those who have no standing ground in the community. They are without land and so without power and consequently without dignity. They have "no portion or inheritance with you" (Deut 14:27). The landed are given as a task at the boundary the care of these when they come to the land. It is one of the tasks that goes with covenanted land and keeps the land as covenanted reality; these who seem to have no claim must be honored and cared for.

At the boundary all these landless poor are redefined as brother and sister, that is, as full participants in the promises of covenant (Lev 25:25-55; Deut 15:1-11, 12-18; 22:1-4). "Brother and sister" is a covenantal phrase.[36]

---

36. See John Priest, "The Covenant of Brothers," *JBL* 84 (1965) 400–406, and Michael Fishbane, "The Treaty of Background of Amos 1:11 and Related Matters," *JBL* 89 (1970) 313–18.

It is a term like "neighbor," used to describe those for whom special care must be taken, for whom the memories are also operative and for whom the hopes are still applicable:

> And if your brother becomes poor, and cannot maintain himself with you, you shall maintain him; as a stranger and sojourner he shall live with you. Take no interest from him or increase, but fear your God; that your brother may live beside you. . . . I am Yahweh your God, who brought you forth out of the land of Egypt to give you the land of Canaan, and to be your God. (Lev 25:35-38)

Land is for sharing with all the heirs of the covenant, even those who have no power to claim it. Something about land makes one forget them, makes one insensitive to them. Israel at the boundary believed the new land is precisely for caring for brothers and sisters. Israel had the hope and vision at the boundary that covenantal relations can still operate in the land. Israel refused to think that being landed and covenanting were inimical to each other.

Land is an opportunity to pervert justice (Deut 24:17-18; see Amos 5:10-12). Land tends to diminish the value and even the presence of the brother or sister. Israel knew the only defense against such self-deception is a sense of brothers and sisters being in history with us. They are the limits set on coveting.

The tasks of Israel in the land are subtle but so obvious. They are not so easy to circumvent as tax laws, inheritance laws, property laws, because they touch the elemental dimensions of covenant:

1. Have no images that will take us from history.
2. Keep Sabbath so that life is not coercive.
3. Honor covenant brothers and sisters, who may not have power but do have dignity.

Land is given in covenant. Israel's central task is to keep it so, never to perceive its land in a social or historical vacuum. In a vacuum all kinds of coercive deeds are possible and even legitimate. But they speak no words, give no gifts, keep no promises. Coercive deeds can never yield life, which after all is Israel's deepest yearning.

The Land as Threat

It takes courage to enter the new land. In Joshua 1, leader and people are admonished three times to act with boldness and confidence against enormous odds:

> Be strong and of good courage.... (v. 6)
> Only be strong and very courageous.... (v. 7)
> Have I not commanded you? Be strong and of good courage; be not
> frightened, neither be dismayed.... (v. 9).

And the chapter concludes with the same assertion: "Only be strong and of good courage" (v. 18).[37] This "formula of encouragement" is utilized at the boundary because Israel is called to a new task against hopeless odds. The Bible is not romantic about the prospect of the land being organized in an alternative way.[38]

That is how the land situation appeared to Israel at the boundary. Already in the sojourn tradition where it is affirmed that the land is good, already there Israel knows fearful reluctance to enter the land:

> The land, through which we have gone, to spy it out, is a land that devours its inhabitants; and all the people we saw in it are men of great stature. And there we saw the Nephilim (the sons of Anak, who come from the Nephilim); and we seemed to ourselves like grasshoppers, and so we seemed to them. (Num 13:32-33)

Nobody doubted that the land is bounteous and attractive. But the land of promise is never an eagerly waiting vacuum anticipating Israel. Nor is it an unambiguous arena for faith. It is always filled with Canaanites. That is how the promise comes. And Israel knew that Canaanites are always more impressive than Israelites.[39] It is the nature of the Canaanites[40] to control the hardware and all the other means of leverage. They are cruel and unaccommodating, and they do not do anything for the morale of Israel. In the historical vacuum of wilderness, Israel could manage with some self-respect. But in the new land the contrast is too great and daily visible. It becomes a meeting between giants and grasshoppers, between powerful agents of force and hopeless victims incapable of resistance or assertion. It is the new land that creates the contrast and creates in Israel a sense of fear and hopelessness. It is the very land of promise, the purpose of the whole journey of faith, which causes the failure of nerve. If only Israel

---

37. On the formula see Dennis J. McCarthy, "An Installation Genre?" *JBL* 90 (1971) 31–41.

38. The formula of encouragement is appropriate as well to Mendenhall's proposal that the land is reoriented away from royal, bureaucratic models. Thus the covenantal vision of Israel is a challenge to a powerful status quo.

39. On the contrast see G. Ernest Wright, *Biblical Archaeology* (Philadelphia: Westminster, 1957) 8, and the sociological interpretation of Mendenhall, *The Tenth Generation,* 12–13.

40. "Canaanites" here is used not as an ethnic term but as a sociopolitical term. On such an understanding, see Van Seters, *Abraham,* chap. 3.

could avoid the land and could know that Yahweh would settle for a people short of promise fulfilled, then giants would not be visible and grasshopper self-images would not surface.

Israel always wants to play it safe short of the land. God's people always want to settle for something short of promises, because promises being fulfilled remind Israel how vulnerable it is, how exposed it is, and how precarious it all is. Promiseless existence is safer. The Bible knows from the beginning that promises are always kept in the midst of threats. Tables are always prepared in "the presence of my enemies" (Ps. 23:5), and if one would eat at the table, one must eat in the presence of enemies. The land is precisely for those and only for those who sense their precariousness and act in their vulnerability.

The entire memory of this moment for Israel is one of Israel's cowardice, ineptness, and incompetence in the face of the land. Israel was ill-prepared and ill-qualified, and clearly the land-entry, whatever its historical character, had little chance of success. What an enormous promise of success and prosperity is Josh 1:8 in the face of such possibilities. The memory affirms that Israel characteristically acted in fear, tried to avoid receiving the promise, or tried by clever strategy to minimize the risk. Israel is always Abraham lying to save his skin (Gen 12:10-20). And always the cowardly generation resisting the call to entry:

> Yet you would not go up, but rebelled against the command of Yahweh your God; and you murmured in your tents, and said, "Because Yahweh hated us he has brought us forth out of the land of Egypt, to give us into the hand of the Amorites to destroy us.... Our brethren have made our hearts melt, saying, 'The people are greater and taller than we; the cities are great and fortified up to heaven; and moreover we have seen the sons of the Anakim there.'" (Deut 1:26-28)

After more assurances, this generation was rejected because it was fearful:

> Yet in spite of this word you did not believe Yahweh your God....
> And Yahweh heard your words, and was angered, and he swore, "Not one of these men of this evil generation shall see the good land which I swore to give to your fathers." (Deut 1:32-35)

Israel's destiny is fearful, and Israel would rather not face it. In the land entry tradition Israel is driven by promise and summoned by fulfillment to ambiguous places of newness when old places seem more assured, simple, and manageable. It concerns Israel being called into new unmanageable situations of blessing and her resistance to them.

The land-giving memories are about how promises are kept among God's people. They are not kept in splendid purity but always in ragged fearfulness. They are never unmixed triumphs but always processions of grasshoppers in the face of the giants. The land of promise, whenever Israel comes there, is filled with enemies of the promise. They are the agents of management, the spokesmen for prosperity and property, for competence and coercion. They possess the land and have organized it. The land is willy-nilly ordered by people who control the tools of production and consumption and are ready to accommodate all others into the system.

But Israel's mandate is not to join the Canaanites. It is to engage the Canaanites so that the management objectives for the land can be radically transformed. Israel is to enter the land in trust, confident that the word of promise that has brought it this far will not fail now. Israel is to reject both easy accommodation and self-assured belligerence. It is to enter in bold confidence with nothing more than the word of promise spoken originally and consistently in its history (see Josh 1:3, 6). Israel is to have the buoyant, blind conviction that creatures of the word can in any circumstance trust the word that will destroy all its enemies. The radicalness of the motif cannot be overstated.

Such a view may seem problematic to us, if not absurd. It is at least romantic to think land will be given in such a way. But surely the problem is not in Israel's memory but in our consciousness. We are so consumed (see Num 13:32, "devoured") by notions of winning or conquering land that we cannot entertain such a gift notion. It is important for us to acknowledge that this notion (from our perspective an absurdity) is not marginal or incidental. It forms the focus for Israel's faith. To trust is to believe land is faithfully given (see 1 Cor 1:22-31).

5.

"ONE FROM AMONG YOUR BRETHREN"

L AND MUST BE MANAGED. EVEN LAND GIVEN MUST BE TAKEN CARE OF. Those who possess it must take responsibility for it. When Israel crossed the Jordan and secured itself in the new land of promise and ful-fillment, it discovered that the concerns, burdens, and ambiguities of management were inescapable. For Israel they were new because it had not known such matters in the wilderness. They came with the land. It must be managed, ordered, and administered. It must be used well, first in order not to lose it, second in order to enhance it.

The Jordan is for Israel the juncture between two histories. The first history is one of *landlessness on the way to the land:*

PROMISE	FULFILLMENT
Go from your country and your kindred and your father's house to the land that I will show you. (Gen 12:1)	Thus Yahweh gave to Israel all the land which he swore to give to their fathers. . . . Not one of all the good promises which Yahweh had made to the house of Israel had failed; all came to pass. (Josh 21:43-45)[1]

That history began in trustful departure and ended in glorious possession. Sojourners became heirs. The major demand of that history is to trust a promise. The major temptation is to doubt the promise and to quit.

1. This way of structuring the material is of course taken over from Gerhard von Rad, "The Problem of the Hexateuch," in *The Problem of the Hexateuch and Other Essays,* trans. E. W. T. Dicken (New York: McGraw-Hill, 1966), especially 67–74.

The second history of Israel is the history on the other side of the Jordan. It is the history of *landed Israel in the process of losing the land:*

PROMISE	FULFILLMENT
Go from your country and your· kindred and your father's house to the land that I will show you. (Gen 12:1)	Thus Yahweh gave to Israel all the land which he swore to give to their fathers. . . . Not one of all the good promises which Yahweh had made to the house of Israel had failed; all came to pass. (Josh 21:43-45)[1]

This history began in secure settling and possession. It ended in shattering exile in which King Jehoiachin is treated as the chief exile in Babylon:

> Evil-merodach king of Babylon, in the year that he began to reign, graciously freed Jehoiachin king of Judah from prison; and he spoke kindly to him, and gave him a seat above the seats of the kings who were with him in Babylon. So Jehoiachin put off his prison garments. And every day of his life he dined regularly at the king's table; and for his allowance, a regular allowance was given him by the king, every day a portion, as long as he lived. (2 Kgs 25:27-30)

But he was still an exile! Heirs became exiles. The major demand of that history is caring management of the turf. The major temptation is to use up the land in wasteful, careless, self-indulgent ways and so to lose it. In the first history Israel kept the trust and refused to quit. In the second history Israel resisted the demand, yielded to the temptation, and so the narrative ends in exile. The literature of Judges, 1 and 2 Samuel, and 1 and 2

2. This way of shaping the material is not based on a literary judgment, for while the "first history" clearly follows the Yahwist, the "second history" deals only with a portion of the Deuteronomic history. The inability to deal with the relation of von Rad's hypothesis on J and Noth's hypothesis on Dtr at the same time is problematic in any case. See Douglas A. Knight, *Rediscovering the Traditions of Israel: The Development of the Traditio-Historical Research of the Old Testament, with Special Consideration of Scandinavian Contributions,* SBLDS 9 (Missoula, Mont.: Society of Biblical Literature, 1973) 158–63.

In what follows I have tried to discern the structure of the material itself which cuts through the various traditions. I believe such a method is faithful to the intention of the material, for it is beyond dispute that the crossing of the Jordan into land changed the character of Israel. On the decisive speech at the boundary, see George E. Mendenhall, "Samuel's 'Broken Rib': Deuteronomy 32," in *No Famine in the Land: Studies in Honor of John L. McKenzie,* ed. J. W. Flanagan and A. W. Robinson (Missoula, Mont.: Scholars Press, 1975) 63–74 and Walter Beyerlin, "Gattung und Herkunft des Rahmens im Richterbuch," in *Tradition und Situation: Studien zur alttestamentlichen Prophetie. Artur Weiser zum 70. Geburtstag,* ed. E. Wurthwein and O. Kaiser (Göttingen: Vandenhoeck and Ruprecht, 1963) 1–29.

Kings is the account of the tortuous route by which heirs became exiles, the same ones who in Genesis doubted ever becoming heirs and were surprised by grace. When exile came, they were surprised again.

On Managing the Land

Israel had to make decisions about how to manage the land. It had to devise institutions of governance it never needed before.[3] That is so of every newly landed person or community. The new situation requires new organization. In this history, there are essentially two models of land management we may note.[4] The first was the appearing of judges who engaged primarily in crisis intervention, avowedly at the behest of Yahweh. While that form of management proposed to be responsive and faithful to Yahweh, it proved to be ineffective. It lacked the resilience and durability to give the land or the people the sustained, disciplined attention they required. Quite clearly turf needs intense and sustained attention if it is both to be kept and enhanced. For those purposes, the judges were insufficient.[5]

The second and alternative form of land management that Israel attempted was kingship. In the Bible, "king" refers to those who presided over the organized life of Israel and so had responsibility for the land. In our discussion, the term will be used in a second sense as well, to refer in an impressionistic way to all people entrusted with the power and authority to choose social ends and deploy resources for those ends. This second history of Israel from Judg 2:7 to 2 Kgs 25:27-30 concerns the anxious pursuit of a form of governance and management that will keep and enhance the land and so give to Israel the joy, freedom, and security that were contained in the old promises. In the Philistine crisis of the eleventh century B.C.E., judges were no adequate apparatus for those ends, and so Israel tried kingship.[6]

3. See the programmatic statement of George E. Mendenhall, "The Monarchy," *Int* 29 (1975) 155–70.

4. The narrative of Gideon is an early and obvious example of the tension about the two ways of governance. More generally see Joseph Blenkinsopp, "The Quest of the Historical Saul," in *No Famine in the Land*, 75–99.

5. It is not the particular office of judge that is inadequate, but the entire "tribalism" that yielded to organization and bureaucratization. Tribalism, which need not be associated with nomadism, clearly had a very different notion of land.

6. The location of Judg 1:1—2:5 in terms of literary and tradition history is problematic. But in terms of the two histories suggested here, we may observe that the unit is appropriately placed between the histories as a transitional statement in which they are in the land, but not in fact in control. For a statement locating the material in the traditions, see Sigmund Mowinckel, *Tetrateuch—Pentateuch—Hexateuch*, BZAW 90 (Berlin: Töpelmann, 1964) 9–32.

Israel reflected on the nature of kingship that was appropriate to the land, recognizing early that a legitimate form of management must be consistent with the character of the land as gift. The traditions on kingship in Israel are diverse and complicated because of the lack of consensus in Israel about the meaning and legitimacy as well as the character of the institution. Clearly Israel's memories from the landless side of the Jordan provided no models[7] for kingship because such sustained institutions of management were neither needed nor possible there. Thus when it looked to find models for the land side of the Jordan, it looked to how other people managed land in the same context of security:

> ". . . now appoint for us a king to govern us like all the nations." . . .
> "No! but we will have a king over us, that we also may be like all the nations, and that our king may govern us and go out before us and fight our battles." (1 Sam 8:5, 19-20)

But that was precisely the issue, and Israel tried to solve it too easily. It proposed to manage land like all the others around it.

But the speeches at the boundary in Deuteronomy make exactly the opposite insistence. Israel is to be in the land differently. And if it is to be in the land differently, it will have to manage it differently, which calls for a different, distinctive notion of kingship. Thus the *form* of land management in Israel may be "like the others,"[8] even with a king and the apparatus commonly associated with that institution, but the *intent* is to be peculiar, as peculiar as Israel and its relationship to the land are peculiar. Other kings incline to control the land as a possession. This king is to manage the land as a gift entrusted to him but never possessed by him.

When Israel craved for kingship like the others, it was attracted precisely to those examples that presumed to manage their own existence and seize initiative for their own well-being in history.[9] Whereas life on

7. Mendenhall, "The Monarchy," 160, among others speaks of "models." The use of the term itself is important for an understanding of sociological interpretation now being urged especially by Mendenhall and Gottwald. It makes clear that these persons in the tradition are to be understood as embodiments of broad and deep movements in the community, and not simply as individual actors.

8. "Being like the nations" is discerned by the Dtr as crucial in land-loss. See the warning of Josh 23:7 and the concluding verdict of 2 Kgs 17:24-40. On the way of the nations see Isa 47:7-10; Ezek 27:3; 28:2; 29:3; and the fine discussion of Donald E. Gowan, *When Man Becomes God: Humanism and Hybris in the Old Testament*, PTMS 6 (Pittsburgh: Pickwick, 1975).

9. Mendenhall, "The Monarchy," speaks of the monarchy in the model of the "typical Syro-Hittite state." Compare T. N. D. Mettinger, *Solomonic State Officials: A Study of the Civil Government Officials of the Israelite Monarchy*, CBOT 5 (Lund: Gleerup, 1971), who traces the influence of Canaanite and Egyptian influences on the structures of the United Monarchy.

the other side had been utterly derived from Yahweh, now the yearning was to eliminate all of that uncertainty and derive life from policies and institutions totally under human mastery. Thus the request for kingship was a proposal to shift decisively the foundations of communal life in Israel.[10]

Israel believed the *form* could be imitated and a special *intent* and character could be devised for Israel. Such an odd notion of land management is presented to Israel in Deut 17:14-20, the only formal statement on the institution in the tradition from the boundary.[11] The model for land management offered there consists of three parts. First, permission is given to have a king, but demanding limits are set on his character:

> When you come to the land which Yahweh your God gives you, and you possess it and dwell in it, and then say, "I will set a king over me, like all the nations that are round about me"; you may indeed set as king over you him whom Yahweh your God will choose. One from among your brethren you shall set as king over you; you may not put a foreigner over you, who is not your brother. (Deut 17:14-15)

The contrast is clear and sharp: a brother, not a foreigner.[12] The issue is not pure blood or tribal connection but that the land must be managed by someone nurtured in the understandings and memories of Israel. If the land is not to be wrongly handled, the king must remember barrenness and birth, slavery and freedom, hunger and manna, and above all the speeches at the boundary. "One from the brethren" means one in the context of covenant, one whose discernment of power concerns gifts and tasks, one who will not reduce society to coercion and people to slaves. This teaching thus calls for a radical redefinition of what kingship is all about.[13] It is not to control the land, but to enhance the land for the sake

10. I am following the judgment of Mendenhall and Gottwald on the sharp contrast between premonarchic and monarchic presentations of Israel. A more benign reading is possible, which understands the monarchy as faithfully derived from the old traditions. It is of course characteristically in the interest of the "new regime" to shape the memory so that continuity is stressed.

11. There is of course an extensive literature on this passage and its assessment of the monarchy. See the discussion and documentation of Werner H. Schmidt, "Kritik am Königtum," in *Probleme biblischer Theologie: Gerhard von Rad zum 70. Geburtstag,* ed. H. W. Wolff (Munich: Kaiser, 1971) 440–61.

12. It is clear that "brother" refers to a covenant partner. Compare John Priest, "A Covenant of Brothers," *JBL* 84 (1965) 400–406; Michael Fishbane, "The Treaty Background of Amos 1:11 and Related Matters," *JBL* 89 (1970) 313–18; and Dennis J. McCarthy, *Old Testament Covenant* (Richmond: John Knox, 1972) 33.

13. See Paul Lehmann, *The Transfiguration of Politics* (New York: Harper & Row, 1975), especially his exposition of John 18:33-40; 19:1-16.

of the covenant partners to whom the king is bound by common loyalties and memories.

The second element concerns the prohibitions that this peculiar king must honor: "Only he must not multiply horses for himself, or cause the people to return to Egypt in order to multiply horses. And he must not multiply wives for himself, lest his heart turn away: nor shall he greatly multiply for himself silver and gold" (vv. 16-17). Horses are for armaments; thus amassing horses constitutes an effort to become self-reliant, to eliminate the very precariousness at the center of covenantal existence in or out of the land. Kingship shall not try to overcome the precariousness that belongs to covenantal history. But surely that is the point of being a king or having a land, to eradicate contingency! So much for horses. Clearly Israel has a very different notion of kingship and land management than any of its neighboring peoples. Wives are a temptation to landed folk. In part they symbolize self-indulgence when acquired in multiple fashion, but more importantly multiple marriages have to do with political marriages, with commitments that will create a reliable network of alliances, again a way of being secure on one's own terms. The third prohibition, silver and gold, is more of the same, to enhance one's own existence. That surely is a normal way of being a king. But it is not for Israel.

It takes little imagination to see what the absence of these prohibitions would do to covenant brothers and sisters. In a regime oriented to self-security, it is highly probable that citizens become resources to be used or spent or traded or manipulated for the sake of the regime.[14] What is rejected in this warning is land management organized around commodities and securities in which king and people value no initiative or security other than those they devise.

The third element is the positive alternative to those self-securing efforts:

> And when he sits on the throne of his kingdom, he shall write for himself in a book a copy of this law, from that which is in charge of the Levitical priests; and it shall be with him, and he shall read in it all the days of his life, that he may learn to fear Yahweh his God, by keeping all the words of this law and these statues, and doing them; that his heart may not be lifted up above his brethren, and that he

14. Lewis Mumford, *The Myth of the Machine*, vol. 1: *Technics and Human Development* (New York: Harcourt, Brace and World, 1966), has most effectively shown that the emergence of imperial kingship in the ancient world is not a matter of the emergence simply of new leaders but of a radically changed consciousness.

> may not turn aside from the commandment, either to the right hand
> or to the left; so that he may continue long in his kingdom, he and
> his children, in Israel. (Deut 17:18-20)

The central activity of the king is to read the Torah, that is, the primary
function of the king is to keep management focused on the central memory and vision of Israel. The king is, in this passage, not charged with
technical decisions or details of administration. His role is to preside over
a government in a way that constantly affirms the peculiar destiny of
Israel. It is hard to imagine a more radical statement about the relation
between institution and commitment, between power and faith. Clearly
the issue is settled in an unexpected way. Unlike all neighbors, the king is
subjected to the Torah. The institution is to serve the fundamental commitments that have priority and authority over the institution of king.
Power is put in the service of a special faith and a peculiar vision. Such a
view of kingship asserts a dominant conviction of the Bible that is against
the wisdom of the world. Note the promise of the last sentence of the unit.
Torah reading will preserve Israel in the land. The way to keep the land
and power over it is to turn attention from land to Torah. By implication
the way to lose land is to be anxious about it to the neglect of Torah.
(Compare the enigmatic statements of Jesus in Matt 6:25-33; 23:23-24; and
Luke 9:23-25, which are wholly consistent with this view. Obviously it
sounded strange when he asserted it, even as it must have when articulated in Deuteronomy.)

The Torah tells the king he is a brother of the other brothers and sisters. The Torah is not simply the Decalogue or a collection of laws, but it
means the fundamental affirmation that Israel's sources are in Yahweh's
graciousness, and Israel's character is to be holy to Yahweh.[15] Land management in Israel is to be at ease about the land, but very much involved
for the covenant partners. This is not simply humanitarianism but it is
Israel's insight into the riddle of the land and how it is kept and how it is
lost.[16] Land is not, if viewed as gift, for self-security but for the brother
and sister. Land is not given to the calculating, but to the "meek," that is,
to the ones who do not presume.

15. See James A. Sanders, "Torah and Christ," *Int* 29 (1975) 372–90, for a peculiarly sensitive statement of this matter.

16. Moshe Weinfeld has suggested that wisdom teaching lies behind the humanitarianism of Deuteronomy, "The Origin of the Humanism in Deuteronomy," *JBL* 80 (1961) 241–47.
See more fully, Weinfeld, *Deuteronomy and the Deuteronomic School* (Oxford: Clarendon,
1972).

The view of the land in the text is land as history, that is, land as an element in the give and take of covenanted community. Both land and people are alive to precariousness. Both live and have their vitality because of the links to Yahweh, which are always dynamic and under change. It is the temptations of kings ("like the other nations") with horses, wives, and silver and gold to want to flee history and withdraw into a closed, managed space where nothing is ever given or asked or lost. If land can be taken out of the context of covenant in which speaking and answering happen and can be regarded simply as a turf possessed, then it is safe, unambiguous, and purely an object to be handled. Neither the king nor anyone else in Israel is permitted to take the land of covenant and turn it into absolute, royal space.

Alternatives to Royal Management

This theory of governance provided a critique of tempting alternatives. The alternative is described in 1 Sam 8:11-17, and Israel is warned that such a model will undo Israel.[17] In the alternative to be rejected (a) the king is primarily a confiscator, (b) Israel is reduced to slavery (see Deut 17:16; Hos 8:13; 9:3, 6), back in Egypt as though Exodus history had not begun, (c) Israel is cut off from Yahweh, and there is no more covenantal history (1 Sam 8:18), and (d) land is lost (1 Sam 12:25). The royal apparatus designed to keep and enhance the land will cause Israel to lose it (see Prov 13:23). Thus the alternatives are clear. Governance by a king will be either (a) "like all the nations that are round about," or (b) "one from among your covenant partners." It cannot be both ways. One leads to slavery, alienation, and finally expulsion. The other way leads to solidarity and well-being. And Israel must choose.[18]

A major presentation of David as land-manager is the narrative of 2 Samuel 11–12, the account of Bathsheba and Uriah.[19] In this story the

17. See I. Mendelsohn, "Samuel's Denunciation of Kingship," *BASOR* 143 (1956) 17–22. See Gottwald's shrewd discernment of that issue sociologically, "Biblical Theology or Biblical Sociology?" *Radical Religion* 2 (1975) 46–57.

18. Psalm 72 provides a major statement of how the two themes are held together. The language moves among the themes of (a) fertility, (b) political triumphalism, and (c) care for the powerless. But it is clear that care for the powerless is the major preoccupation of the king and the source of fertility and well-being. Israel had discerned that care for the "least" (Torah) is not an optional decision of the king but is more fundamental to well-being in land than is the office of the king. King and not Torah is an optional, historical choice. On the discernment of what land does to people, see John Steinbeck, *The Grapes of Wrath* (New York: Viking, 1939) especially 42–51.

19. See Walter Brueggemann, "The Trusted Creature," *CBQ* 31 (1969) 484–98; "Life and Death in Tenth Century Israel," *JAAR* 40 (1972) 96–109; and David M. Gunn, "David and the

king is secure. He does not accompany his troops into battle, but remains at home with too much leisure time. The story puts the issue rapidly (11:2-5). He sees her. He wants her. He takes her. And then she is pregnant. David had presumed himself immune from Torah, as kings always are tempted to presume.[20] The story in subtle fashion raises the question of the relation of king, Torah, and land. Is the king free to do what he will with his extensive turf? Is he still "one from the brothers," or is he not part of but over them? And if apart from them, why should his heart not "be lifted up above his brethren"?

The subsequent narrative forms a remarkable contrast. David writes a letter (11:14). Nathan says, "Thus says Yahweh" (12:7). Too much should not be made of writing, but we may usefully reflect on the dynamics of writing and speaking.[21] Israel is characteristically inclined to speak, not to write. To speak is to address and evoke response. It is the medium of direct address that allows for alternative responses and maintains space for free interaction between parties. Speech is the appropriate medium for covenantal promises and demands. But writing tends to be, by contrast, one-way communication. It is exact and precisely delivered, carefully measured. Above all it is communication that neither invites nor permits response. There is no give and take but only a directive. It is not a letter that engages another and invites a free response, but it is a decree presuming not exchange but obedience. It is the form of communication that sends Uriah to his death and covers for the king in a detached managerial way.

Gift of the Kingdom," *Semeia* 3 (1975) 14–45. The polarity he discerns of gift and grasp is an especially helpful one.

20. See R. A. Carlson, *David, the Chosen King: A Traditio-Historical Approach to the Second Book of Samuel,* trans. E. J. Sharpe and S. Rudman (Stockholm: Almqvist & Wiksell, 1964) 181 and *passim.*

21. John Steinbeck, *Grapes,* 317, has shrewdly presented the power of writing as a means of confiscation when it is controlled by the bureaucracy in the service of established interests: "Owners no longer worked their farms. *They farmed on paper;* and they forgot the land." The Okies learned to avoid anyone with writing equipment for writing meant land-loss.

I have been able to locate only three other biblical narratives in which kings write in the sense that David did here. One is in 1 Kgs 21:8-14, in which Jezebel writes documents to frame Naboth and secure land for the king by illegal confiscation. The second is in 2 Kgs 5:5-7, in which the king of Syria sends a letter commanding the king of Israel to heal, i.e., healing on demand, by royal memo.

The third incident of writing is in 2 Kgs 10:1-11 when Jehu executes a coup by writing directives. These three uses of royal directives in writing stand as a sign for the way in which royal management tries to secure turf at the expense of the others. Interestingly, in each of the three, the royal letter is confronted by prophetic word; by Elijah (1 Kgs 21:17), by Elisha (2 Kgs 5:14), and again by Elijah (2 Kgs 10:10). The land-giving, land-taking word will not be circumscribed by a royal form of controlling communication.

David had become a practitioner of one-way bureaucratic communication intended to cover the open, unresolved space between king and Torah. Surely something happened to this man who had gone so willingly into extremities with his fellows. What had happened to him was land! Land required and made possible a new form of communication that no longer communicated but only dispatched and commanded. The ones receiving the directives were not covenant members but functionaries in the ordering and retention of land.[22] The directive has no interest in either Joab or Uriah but only in David and preservation of his turf. The situation of land transforms modes of communication and with it the modes of all relations.[23]

The counter-theme to the managing memo of the king that controls is the word of God, borne by Nathan, that cuts through the closed situation of royal control and calls to accountability. The word is expressed subtly in the parable but unmistakably in the words following the parable.[24] In the very world the landed king thought he controlled, this other One has his sovereign say: "I delivered you. . . . I gave you. . . . I gave you. . . . I would add to you . . ." (2 Sam 12:7-8). The language echoes and parallels the same emphasis in the legitimating oracle of 2 Sam 7:8-11: "I took you. . . . I have been with you. . . . I will make for you. . . . I will appoint. . . . I will give you. . . ." There is no doubt who is subject and who is object, who is giver and who is receiver of all he is and has. The structure of the two speeches calls into harsh question the worldview of the king who thought he could order his own world and therefore constructed a mode of communication in which king is always subject of every active verb and acts on every object. The word of Yahweh, twice pronounced by Nathan, suggests an alternative grammar in which Yahweh as land-giver, and not king as land-holder, retains initiative.

The primary issue is announced in this same sequence. "Why have you despised the word of Yahweh . . . ?" (2 Sam 12:9), and the echo: "You have

22. This is central to what Mumford means by the "Machine" in his title cited in note 14. Citizens lose their identity and have only utilitarian value, but in the service of a royal myth of order. Compare pp. 168–202.

23. This is behind Marshall McLuhan's enigmatic statements in *The Gutenberg Galaxy: The Making of Typographic Man* (Toronto: Toronto Univ. Press, 1962); and idem, *Understanding Media: The Extensions of Man* (New York: McGraw-Hill, 1964) on modes of communication and modes of relationship in society. The emergence of coercive language serves to alienate and to define relations in terms of production and consumption.

24. See Rolf Rendtorff, "Reflections on the Early History of Prophecy in Israel," *History and Hermeneutic*, ed. R. W. Funk (New York: Harper & Row, 1967) 27, and more generally, James M. Robinson, "The Internal Word in History," in *No Famine in the Land*, 293–98. Compare John Dominic Crossan, "Jesus and Pacifism," in ibid., 201–7.

utterly scorned Yahweh . . ." (v. 14).[25] That is, why have you attempted to live in a closed world over which you presided, forgetting that you are established by his gift, forgetting that he has yet more to give and forgetting that you are accountable to him? The word is the affirmation that there are sources of life and initiative that lie outside the power of the king. The cool, reasoned grammar of David is to be contrasted with the vigorous initiative of Yahweh in the song of Hannah:

> Yahweh kills and brings to life;
>   he brings down to Sheol and raises up.
> Yahweh makes poor and makes rich;
>   he brings low, he also exalts.
> He raises up the poor from the dust;
>   he lifts the needy from the ash heap. . . . (1 Sam 2:6-8)

Land between Word and Memo

The contrasting mood and grammar of *Hannah's song* and *David's memo* represent two perceptions of life: the one from desperate but hopeful people without land, the other from secure, anxious people with land. One relies completely on the initiative of the promise-maker and promise-keeper and takes the form of doxology. The other relies completely on royal management and takes the form of directive. And Nathan holds to the odd notion that a royal land-manager can turn from directives to doxologies in his communication.[26]

The assertion of Nathan in 2 Sam 12:9 should not simply be labelled "prophetic." In another tradition close to this narrative the wisdom teacher observes what happens to those who despise the word and fashion their own life: "He who despises the word brings destruction on himself, but he who respects the commandment will be rewarded" (Prov 13:13).[27] William McKane refers to the despising as "intellectual arrogance" that presumes too much.[28] The issue is sharply joined: king versus prophet, memo versus word, management versus intrusion, control versus disruption, planning versus inscrutable mystery. The king tries to have life on his

---

25. The term is not the same as in v. 9. But it clearly receives major stress as it is stated as an infinite absolute.

26. The movement from directive to doxology is a decisive example of the shifted language world to which Robinson and Crossan are referring. Subsequent interpretation likely will need to pay more attention to the battle for a faithful language world.

27. On the links between wisdom and the Succession Narrative, see Hans-Jürgen Hermisson, "Weisheit und Geschichte," in *Probleme biblischer Theologie*, 137–48.

28. So William McKane, *Proverbs*, OTL (Philadelphia: Westminster, 1970) 454.

own terms and nearly destroys himself, or as v. 10 asserts, ultimately does destroy not only himself but the future of his dynasty. The offense is adultery and murder. And the result of despising: *a sword.* Land is held in relation to word. Land is lost without word. Even the king must learn that man (king) lives by word, not just by bread: by what is given and not by what is controlled.[29] This has been announced at the boundary (Deut 8:3). But Israel does not remember.

It is the complexity and majesty of David that he has not fully drawn the flag around himself. He is still reachable by the word and so he repents, that is, responds to the irresistible word (v. 13). Repentance to which he is called is for a total reorientation, a recognition that we are object and not subject, a reorientation most improbable for the landed.[30] (Jeremiah thought it not only improbable but impossible for the landed; Jer 13:23.) We need not speculate about David's motives or his prudence. It is enough to see that, even here, he who would keep his land will lose it, but he who would risk his land may keep it. But being landed makes the word seem remote and improbable, not to say irrelevant. The issue is posed clearly by a *memo-writing king* and a *word-hearing prophet.* And the story leaves David with his throne, but in an altered mood. Interestingly, Psalm 51, said to be the situation in this crisis, ends with the same word: "The sacrifice acceptable to God is a broken spirit; a broken and contrite heart, O God, thou wilt not *despise*" (Ps 51:17).[31] The landed king may despise the word. Strangely the same God does not despise those who retain land as gift. The rule of the king is not the last word and he had best remember it.

Of course David's relation to his throne is complex and dialectical. Twice the narrative has David risk the kingdom in an act of radical trust:

29. See especially Gunn, "David and the Gift," 22–29, on gift and grasp. Bread can be grasped, word must be given.

30. Repentance may mean abandonment of a universe of discourse. Obviously such a shift in language will involve the dismantling of much of the monarchy that depends on that language. In contemporary discussion, this is a theme especially important to Rubem A. Alves, *Tomorrow's Child: Imagination, Creativity, and the Rebirth of Culture* (New York: Harper & Row, 1972), in which he urges an alternative language of imagination.

31. Paul D. Hanson, *The Dawn of Apocalyptic: The Historical and Sociological Roots of Jewish Apocalyptic Eschatology,* rev. ed. (Philadelphia: Fortress, 1979), has made a major case for understanding the brokenhearted in historical and political terms as those who have been oppressed, disenfranchised, and deprived of their land. See p. 111 and *passim* on the theme of the "ethos of the humble and broken of spirit." Compare Isa. 57:15; 61:1. Hanson has made unmistakable the connection between the piety of humbleness and the sociology of being deprived of land.

> If I find favor in the eyes of Yahweh, he will bring me back and let me see both it and his habitation; but if he says, "I have no pleasure in you," behold, here I am, let him do to me what seems good to him. (2 Sam 15:25-26)

> Behold, my own son seeks my life; how much more now may this Benjaminite! Let him alone, and let him curse; for Yahweh has bidden him. It may be that Yahweh will look upon my affliction, and that Yahweh will repay me with good for this cursing of me today. (2 Sam 16:11-12)[32]

In both cases he risks himself completely and places himself at the disposal of Yahweh. In both cases by running risk he found himself secure in the providence of Yahweh. In one other incident (2 Sam 23:13-17), David shows himself a man who lived by risk and not by memo or by sword.[33] Though yearning for water from Bethlehem, he refused to drink what his men got for him at risk to their own lives. He did not seize and gulp like a secure landowner but he poured it out in a sacramental act of solidarity with his covenant brothers (a king "from among the brothers" as he here remembers). Perhaps worth noting is the judgment of most scholars that this is in fact a narrative reporting an episode from his early period, before he was so secured in the land, and therefore yet free to act differently. If that is true, as seems likely, we may discern in David a process by which he became increasingly landed, increasingly secure, increasingly cynical, and increasingly less open to risk, to his fellows, and to the word of Yahweh—less likely to recall the assertions at the boundary!

The ambivalence is gone in David's son Solomon. There is no hint of the openness to contingency that so compellingly characterized David at times. Solomon is a king totally secure in his land, which he got for himself, totally committed to keeping his land on his own terms and insensitive to either the cry of his fellows or the gifts and claims of Yahweh.[34] The evidence seems unmistakable. First Kings 4 is a picture of a settled bureaucracy preoccupied with itself.[35]

32. See Walter Brueggemann, "On Trust and Freedom: A Study of Faith in the Succession Narrative," *Int* 26 (1972) 3–19.

33. See Walter Brueggemann, *In Man We Trust: The Neglected Side of Biblical Faith* (Richmond: John Knox, 1972) 36–37.

34. See ibid., 67–77, in which I have drawn a sharp contrast between David and Solomon, a contrast that is clearly reflected in the form of the narrative.

35. Solomon embodies the bureaucracy, discerned by Mumford, which produced the homelessness for Israel about which Peter Berger has written.

4:1-6 presents the bureaucracy, culminating in the minister of labor affairs.[36] The program is not only labor, but forced labor (see 5:13; 9:15-22).[37]

4:7-19 presents a remarkable bureaucratic decision that reorganizes Israel into effective taxation districts, completely and no doubt deliberately disregarding the human bonds of normal tribal groupings. Effectiveness is what it is all about, and the significance of human bonds must yield to effectiveness. Israel for the first time is totally organized and administered. The business of this kind of management is to reduce various human components into administrative packages. Israel had not been so reduced since Pharaoh had organized and administered Israel. Solomon creates a situation not unlike that of Pharaoh.[38]

4:22-28 reports the well-being and consumptive values that govern Israel, a picture of uninterrupted bliss. Land seems not really losable.

To ensure against losing the land, Solomon further secures himself by (a) fortification, arms, and the strengthening of the garrisons at every crucial place on the border (1 Kgs 9:15) and (b) a network of strategic marriages that surely enhances his standing in neighboring courts (1 Kgs 9:16; 11:1-5). The picture is unmistakably an utterly secure regime, all achieved by strategy and manipulation, as though land is supremely property to be kept and not gift to be received.

All this is capped by the building of the temple, the ultimate achievement of his reign. The temple serves to give theological legitimacy and visible religiosity to the entire program of the regime. The evidence is beyond dispute that he so manipulates Israel's public worship that it becomes a cult for a static God, lacking in the power, vigor, and freedom of the God of the old traditions.[39] This God, in contrast to the exodus

---

36. On the historical data behind forced labor see Mendelsohn, "Samuel's Denunciation," and Mumford, *Myth*, 194–202. Reference should be made to Emile Durkheim's thesis on the division of labor and its role in the emergence of anomie.

37. The evidence of 1 Kgs 5:13 and 9:15-22 is mixed as to whether the program was confined to non-Israelites. It seems unlikely, in terms of the sociological understandings suggested here, that such a distinction would have been important to or honored by the regime.

38. On the significance of Solomonic tax districts (1 Kgs 4:7-19) see R. de Vaux, *Ancient Israel* (New York: McGraw-Hill, 1961) 133–38. The disregard of tribal lines for the sake of economic interest fits well with Berger's theory of componentiality. See Baruch Halpern, "Sectionalism and Schism," *JBL* 93 (1974) 519–32, with reference to Wright's work.

39. Solomon's temple, congenial as it is to the myths powering his regime, is an embodiment of "religion of epiphany," in which God does not act but only abides. See Jürgen Moltmann, *Theology of Hope: On the Ground and the Implications of a Christian Eschatology*, trans. J. W. Leitch (New York: Harper & Row, 1967) 43, 50–69.

deliverer, is a domesticated preserver of the regime. He dwells in silent, obedient, uninterrupted, and uninterrupting security:

> Yahweh has set the sun in the heavens,
>> but has said that he would dwell in thick darkness.
> I have built thee an exalted house,
>> a place for thee to dwell in for ever. (1 Kgs 8:12-13)[40]

Yahweh is now cornered in the temple. His business is support of the regime, to grant legitimacy to it and to effect forgiveness for it as is necessary.

The God who had given land and intended it to be handled as gift is now made patron of the king who now has the land. In the Solomonic period even God now apparently has no claim on the land. He is guest and not host. Religion becomes a decoration rather than a foundation. The God of the temple is subordinated to the royal regime. It is no longer remembered in public Israel that he maintains his freedom and that the land is indeed and always his. Solomon, not Yahweh, is clearly in charge with only a few charitable nods in the direction of Yahweh.

Presumably this king, unlike his father David, has managed a land arrangement without disruptive word. The point of it all is to secure himself against that word that calls all landholding into question. And this king, like all such land-managers, learns only late and unhappily that it is never finally that way. The word from Yahweh makes three decisive disruptions in Solomon's serene tea party. First at the beginning, in the very charter for Solomon, clearly it is from the free word that Solomon has his legitimacy. The word gives a gift: "Behold, *I give you* a wise and discerning mind, so that none like you has been before you and none like you shall arise after you. *I give you* also what you have not asked, both riches and honor, so that no other king shall compare with you, all your days" (1 Kgs 3:12-13). The word makes a claim: "And if you will walk in my ways, keeping my statutes and my commandments, as your father David walked, then *I will lengthen* your days" (v. 14).[41] That is how it is from the beginning. The monarchy is rooted in the word.

The second and most remarkable appearance of Yahweh's word is in 9:1-9. It occurs just when the temple is completed and an era of good

---

40. While the textual problems are difficult and parts must appeal to LXX, the intention of the text is clear. It is commonly regarded as an authentic and programmatic statement for the new temple, albeit with a Canaanite theology.

41. Characteristically, this statement from Dtr subordinates the king to the Torah. It is likely that in king and Torah are embodied the two principles by which community tries to secure and hold land.

feeling is inaugurated. The very house designed to silence the word of Yahweh is completed. And just then it comes again:

> . . . *if* you will walk before me, as David your father walked, with integrity of heart and uprightness, doing according to all that I have commanded you, and keeping my statutes and my ordinances, *then* I will establish your royal throne over Israel for ever, as I promised David your father. . . . But *if* you turn aside from following me, you or your children, and do not keep my commandments and my statutes which I have set before you, but go and serve other gods and worship them, *then I will cut off Israel from the land* which I have given them; and the house which I have consecrated for my name I will cast out of my sight. . . . (1 Kgs 9:4-7)[42]

The land is still conditional, and the announcement of it is made at the center of unconditional possession, in the midst of the Solomonic deception. The term used, *karat*, is in other contexts the antithesis of *yara'*, to possess. Thus the loss is clearly intended as the negation of the possession. The land still requires obedience, and without that, no other guarantee—temple or garrison, wives or wisdom—can keep the land.

There must be high irony in the way the narrative reports Solomon's response. The word of the condition is greeted with cold disregard, ignored as the king goes his merry, managing way: "At the end of twenty years, in which Solomon had built the two houses, the house of Yahweh and the king's house, and Hiram king of Tyre had supplied Solomon the cedar and cypress timber and gold, as much as he desired, King Solomon gave to Hiram twenty cities in the land of Galilee" (1 Kgs 9:10). It is as though the word of vv. 1-9 had not been spoken. Kings secure in land can proceed as though the word had not been spoken. As the narrative suggests, it is this very manipulative act in disregard of the word of Yahweh that finally leads to the loss of the land. David had indeed scorned the word of Yahweh in the Uriah episode. But the scorning of the word by Solomon is much more massive and institutional. And in either case, it leads to land loss.

Curiously the demands of Yahweh for integrity and righteousness (1 Kgs 9:4) and the conditions for holding land (see Ps 89:14; Prov 8:30;

---

42. This statement is symmetrical to the promise of 1 Kgs 3:3-14 and is decisive for Dtr. It is the first clear statement about land-loss being under way and therefore is structurally crucial for Dtr. The divide in the history comes between 1 Kings 8 and temple dedication and 1 Kings 9 with this harsh word. I am not convinced by the conclusion of Frank Moore Cross that this text must be from another edition (*Canaanite Myth and Hebrew Epic: Essays in the History of the Religion of Israel* [Cambridge: Harvard Univ. Press, 1973] 287).

Isa 11:4-5) are articulated in the mouth of the foreigner, queen of Sheba. Everybody knows it except the king. Everybody understands what the land is about except Solomon who thinks land can be had and held for quite other reasons.

The third and ultimate coming of the word is in 1 Kgs 11:29-39 by the prophet Ahijah: "Behold, I am about to tear the kingdom from the hand of Solomon, and will give you ten tribes . . . because he has forsaken me, and worshiped Ashtoreth . . . and has not walked in my ways, doing what is right in my sight and keeping my statutes and my ordinances, as David his father did" (vv. 31-33). The land will be lost. The kingdom will be revoked. The glory of Jerusalem will be diminished. To be sure the dynasty does survive for a time, but only in reduced form. The empire of Solomon is left in shambles for Israel to ponder. It is Israel's primary attempt to have life on her own terms. Nothing here of Torah, but only horses, wives, silver and gold (Deut 17:14-20). Israel has known since the boundary that it could not be done. But in the land, boundary talk seems remote and not pertinent.

But land is not what it seems, because it is always gift. History is not what it seems because there is always the word. Nathan was right. The sword does linger in such contexts (2 Sam 12:10)! Solomon has done his best to eliminate the "if" from history. He has tried by religion, by organization, and by arsenal to silence the word. He has forgotten to be "one from the covenant partners." So comes death.

6.

"BECAUSE YOU FORGOT ME"

K INGS ARE NOT FREE TO MANAGE THE LAND AS THEY WISH IN ISRAEL. The land is not to be perceived in Israel as it is among the nations. That is a perennial lesson Israel had to learn and to perceive otherwise is a perennial temptation. Israel kept thinking it could be like the other nations (1 Sam 8:5, 20) and only discovered painfully that it was not possible. The land of Israel must be understood peculiarly because Israel itself was a peculiar people.

The visible peculiarity of Israel includes an additional component in the apparatus of her governance, namely, the prophet. It is the prophet who stood vis-à-vis the king to assert continually dimensions of governance and land management that kings prefer to disregard. It is an urgent question, then and now, (a) whether royal land management will acknowledge the prophetic dimensions of land perception and (b) whether land will be lost by kings who silence or disregard prophets. The presence of prophets in Israel characteristically causes problems for kings who want to be like other nations and other kings, because the prophets always announce to kings the peculiarity of Israel and the peculiar means by which land is kept. For all their trouble, one should not be insensitive to the extraordinary fact of their existence. That they even existed is radically peculiar, even if they are not heeded or honored. That fact alone makes a difference in how the Bible thinks about land.[1]

---

1. On the historical relation of prophet and king, see Rolf Rendtorff, "Reflections on the Early History of Prophecy in Israel," in *History and Hermeneutic* ed. R. W. Funk (New York: Harper & Row, 1967) 14–34. Paul D. Hanson, "Old Testament Apocalyptic Reexamined," *Int* 25 (1971) 454–79, concludes, "Prophecy arose with kingship. The prophet established himself alongside the king as spokesman of a point of view which often opposed the royal theology, a view drawing heavily upon the traditions of the League. . . . Yet if one aspect of his prophetic office stands out, it is his activity as a statesman, one fully involved in the politics

The Land, the Prophet, and the King

Remarkably the prophetic component of land entry is articulated in Deuteronomy at the boundary. In the same cluster of traditions in which the king is authorized, the prophet is presented to Israel, authorized by Moses, and described according to his authority and function (Deut 18:9-22).[2] Three elements make it important to announce the prophet as constitutive for Israel's understanding of her new situation in the land.

1. The prophet is precisely for the time in the land: "When you come into the land . . . Yahweh your God will raise up for you a prophet" (Deut 18:9-15). At that time a prophet is needed, and one is given. The land creates a situation in which the new decisive word of Yahweh must be made visible to Israel. It is the condition of being in the land that creates a prophetic situation.

2. The unit on the prophet follows soon after that on the king. To be sure, the section concerns a variety of officials so that the grouping is natural.[3] But beyond that general cluster, it is probably the potential power and danger of the king that evoke the guarantee of a prophet. Indeed Rolf Rendtorff has made a compelling case for the complementarity of the two. Prophets are intended precisely to address kings. It is because of kings that prophets appear.

3. The structure of Deut 18:9-22 contrasts the gifts of the prophet in Israel with the temptation of the land, namely, magical practices of self-securing and manipulation:[4] "There shall not be found among

of his nation, one constantly confronting the king with Yahweh's will." See Jacques Ellul, *The Politics of God and the Politics of Man*, trans. G. W. Bromiley (Grand Rapids: Eerdmans, 1972), for a powerful presentation of the tension between prophets and kings. Also important for this discussion is Frank Crüsemann, *Der Widerstand gegen das Königtum: die antiköniglichen Texte des Alten Testamentes und der Kampf um den frühen israelitischen Staat*, WMANT 49 (Neukirchen-Vluyn: Neukirchener, 1978).

2. Norbert Lohfink, "The Deuteronomists and the Idea of Division of Power" (paper delivered at SBL, Los Angeles, 1972) argued that Deut 16:18—18:22 is a type of constitution to delineate various offices, to provide a balance of power and "to guarantee anew the rule of God in Israel."

3. Calum M. Carmichael, *The Laws of Deuteronomy* (Ithaca: Cornell Univ. Press, 1974) 96–117, has proposed a very different reason for the grouping, based on repetition of concerns from chapters 12 and 13. While the proposal is rich and ingenious, it seems doubtful that the clustering of materials of leadership roles can be understood without reference to that commonality of content.

4. On the contrast between magic and reliance upon historical word see Klaus Koch, "Wort und Einheit des Schöpfergottes in Memphis und Jerusalem," *ZTK* 62 (1965) 292. On the same issue in the contemporary context see Theodor W. Adorno, "Theses Against Occultism," *Telos* 19 (1974) 7. He comments, "The attraction of the occult is a symptom of

you any one who burns his son or his daughter as an offering, any one who practices divination, a soothsayer, or an augur, or a sorcerer, or a charmer, or a medium, or a wizard, or a necromancer" (vv. 10-11). The land and the illusion of self-sufficiency seduce and lull people into managing their lives and their land in ways that seem beyond the terrors of history. The prophet, by contrast, is Israel's single source of insight and guidance. He exists to affirm continually to Israel its precariousness and contingency in the face of more attractive but illegitimate alternatives. The prophet is intended precisely for speech (a) in the *land,* (b) in the face of the *king,* (c) against idolatrous forms of *self-securing.*

The prophet is neither rooted in the model of "other nations" nor selected by Israel like the king. He is, by contrast, *raised up by Yahweh.* The language of resurrection is used to announce this one who strangely and peculiarly derives authority from Yahweh as does none other. But he has one important point of commonality with the king. He also is "from among you, from your brethren," that is, he is steeped in covenant and prepared to speak out of it. The king might conceivably be a foreigner, although that also is prohibited by the teaching; but a prophet is unthinkable from any such source. He can come only out of the life and faith and history of Israel with Yahweh. He is designated to articulate that consciousness against all other seductions of power and security. He is to assure that the land be discerned in covenantal ways. Thus the meeting of king and prophet provides a paradigm for one with "lifted heart" and one "raised of Yahweh," one a self-securing manager, the other committed to land as gift.

1 Kings 21: The Land, the Torah, and Coveting

One such model of king/prophet confrontation over land management is that of Ahab and Elijah in 1 Kings 21. The narrative begins with an encounter of Ahab and Naboth (vv. 1-2), each expressing a view of the land. Ahab regards the land as a tradable commodity: "Give me your vineyard, that I may have it for a vegetable garden, because it is near my house; I will give you a better vineyard for it; or, if it seems good to you, I will give you its value in money" (v. 2). In contrast, for Naboth land is not a *tradable*

---

retrogression of consciousness . . ." (7). Robert E. Neale, *In Praise of Play: Toward a Psychology of Religion* (New York: Harper & Row, 1969) 115, asserts, "Magic is the attempt to control the sacred." Both "retrogression of consciousness" and "attempt to control the sacred" reflect what happened to Israel when she attempted to live in the land.

commodity, but an *inalienable inheritance:* "Yahweh forbid that I should give you the inheritance of my fathers . . . I will not give you the inheritance of my fathers" (vv. 3-4). The exchange sharply expressed two views of land. That of Naboth represents traditional covenantal language in which the land is not owned in a way that permits its disposal. It is "inheritance," which means it is held in trust from generation to generation, beginning in gift and continuing so, and land management is concerned with preservation and enhancement of the gift for the coming generations. Naboth is responsible for the land, but is not in control over it. It is the case not that the land belongs to him but that he belongs to the land. Naboth perceives himself and the land in a covenantal relation, with the relation between the two having a history of fidelity that did not begin with him and will not end with him. Thus the term "inheritance" insists that the land be understood as a dimension of family history. Of course Ahab and surely Jezebel had no notion of that, because kings characteristically think everything is to be bought and sold and traded and conquered. The statements imply two views of royal management. Ahab intends to deal equitably but believes royal prerogatives have weight. By contrast Naboth gives no credibility to royal claims. He regards the king as also subject to more historical, covenantal views of land management. The exchange embodies the alternatives expressed in Deut 18:9-22, the one providing means of self-security, the other the risks and openness of covenantal history.

The response of Jezebel (vv. 5-7) introduces a new element presenting (a) Canaanite kingship as an institution that can rule and manipulate, (b) a mercantile view of land in which land is a commodity to be secured by whatever means, and (c) an alien view of Torah that makes the king immune from its demands. Thus in the speech and action of Jezebel covenantal views of kingship, land, and Torah are all called into question. The narrative hints that Ahab, in contrast to his wife, is at least cognizant of peculiarly Israelite perceptions, for he is prepared to honor the resistance of Naboth even if he does not like it. The distortion comes from Jezebel, clearly not "one from among the covenant partners." Her presence embodies an alien view of kingship, land, and Torah. She has no appreciation at all for the inalienable quality of a family inheritance. "Inheritance" as a land notion directly contradicts royal notions of land management that know no limitation and that sanction confiscation and royal prerogatives generally. The idea of inheritance affirms that there are enduring and resilient networks of meaning and relationship into which one is placed, and these are fundamental to the shape of society. The queen believes, as Peter Berger has observed, that persons and property are replaceable parts, each a component in a grand royal design that can be shuffled and rearranged at the whim of the managers. The queen believes societal arrangements are a human artifact,[5] and therefore they can be handled with freedom and inventiveness, thus denying the shape of societal relations ordained in covenant and not subject to such administration.

Jezebel's complete misunderstanding of Israelite notions of king, land, and Torah is evident in her rebuke and assurance to Ahab: "Do you now govern Israel? . . . I will give you the vineyard" (v. 7). The first comment shows that *govern* (literally, "do kingship") means total control with capacity to dispose of land as one prefers. The second comment misunderstands *inheritance* because she proposes to give what cannot be given and in any case is not in her power to give. Inheritances are not given in Israel, surely not by a royal officer. In the queen's view, quite in contrast to that of Naboth, land is negotiable, that is, it is a piece of property handled objectively and with detachment and rationality. How modern she is!

The conspiracy of vv. 8-14 presents a view of monarch not inconsistent with that of 1 Sam 8:10-18. The main function of the king is to *take,* and there are no higher norms or principles that govern the king or protect his subjects according to that notion. The will of the monarch, as capricious as it may be, is all that matters. The narrative contains two noteworthy features. First, the queen *writes,* that is, issues a directive, not unlike David's action against Uriah. Monarchy represents in Israel the emergence of written communication that is bureaucratic and impersonal.[6] It is consistent with a notion of kingship outside the context of covenant.

Second, the queen *uses* the Torah for her own ends. Thus in her false charge she appeals to the norm of Torah: "You shall not revile God, nor curse a ruler of your people" (Exod 22:28). But for her the teaching is not a norm. It is a tool like everything else to serve royal interests. It is not a principle for the queen but only an instrument for manipulation. Here is a ruler who no longer submits herself to Torah, but now controls Torah, just as she intends to control land and to control citizens.

But the issue is not yet joined. The action really only begins in v. 17 with the appearance of Elijah, spokesman for Yahweh, champion of Naboth, enemy of this kind of royalty.[7] Until now the narrative is preliminary to the

---

5. Notice the opening sentence of Max L. Stackhouse, *Ethics and the Urban Ethos: An Essay in Social Theory and Theological Reconstruction* (Boston: Beacon, 1972) 1, "The modern setting of man is an artifact." When that is true, royal-urban power is without restraint. So it was in Ahab's Israel.

6. Lewis Mumford, *The Myth of the Machine* (New York: Harcourt, Brace and World, 1966) 192, correctly makes the connection.

7. I am aware of arguments that the narrative is not originally a unity. Compare H. Seebass, "Der Fall Naboth in 1 Reg. XXI" *VT* 24 (1974) 474–88; Peter Welten, "Naboths Weinberg,"

essential confrontation. The narrative discloses in its movement a factor about land that Jezebel completely missed. She presumed that in securing land she had only to cope with public opinion and conventional legal practice. And she managed to circumvent both of these. By v. 16 the narrative appears to reach a conclusion as the land issue is resolved. "And as soon as Ahab heard that Naboth was dead, Ahab arose to go down to the vineyard of Naboth the Jezreelite, to take possession of it."[8]

But now it is clear that the hedge against royal confiscation is not only a social usage that might be overcome, but the intentionality of Yahweh himself. And that changes everything in ways that this Phoenician princess could not comprehend. It is Yahweh who has assigned land. When Yahweh gives it, it is gift-land. One is not free to pervert that peculiar character of land. The relation of Naboth and land is not owner/property but heir/gift, and that is true even in the face of the king, not to say the queen.

The speech of Elijah is crisp and unmistakable. There is first a question of indictment: "Thus says Yahweh: 'Have you killed, and also taken possession?'" (v. 19).[9] Two offenses, guilty of both—killing and taking, both in the repertoire of Canaan but not of Israel. And then an answer of verdict: "Thus says Yahweh: 'In the place where dogs licked up the blood of Naboth shall dogs lick your own blood.'" The land will be avenged precisely because land is not give over to any human agent, but is a sign and function in covenant. Thus arrayed against the monarchy are both the traditionalism of Naboth and the purpose of Yahweh.[10]

EvT 33 (1973) 18–32; John Gray, I and II Kings, OTL (Philadelphia: Westminster, 1963) 385–87; Odil Hannes Steck, Überlieferung und Zeitsgeschichte in den Elia-Erzählungen, WMANT 26 (Neukirchen-Vluyn: Neukirchener, 1968) 32–77; and Georg Fohrer, Elias, ATANT 53 (Zurich: Zwingli, 1968). In any case, we are here dealing with the narrative in its completed form. For sociological and literary analyses, see the important essays in Robert B. Coote, ed., Elijah and Elisha in Socioliterary Perspective, Semeia Studies (Atlanta: Scholars, 1992).

8. It is worth noting the very different texture of nahalah and yara', corollary to a very different sense of land. See Seebass, "Der Fall Naboth," 476, and the careful note by E. Hammershaimb, "On the Ethics of the Old Testament Prophets," in Congress Volume: Oxford, 1959, VTSup 7 (Leiden: Brill, 1960) 95 n.1.

9. The double meaning of yara' as both "possess" and "dispossess" is important here! Such possessing of course happens only when another is dispossessed. While that is obviously true whenever land is seized, it is especially stressed in the context of royal land.

10. See the data on land confiscation summarized by Moshe Weinfeld, Deuteronomy and the Deuteronomic School (Oxford: Clarendon, 1972) 264–66. See F. C. Fensham, "Common Trends in Curses of the Near Eastern Treaties and Kudurru—Inscriptions Compared with Maledictions of Amos and Isaiah," ZAW 75 (1963) 155–75. His evidence suggests the urgency of protection against land confiscation.

This plus factor of Yahweh's purpose for land had been affirmed both in the legal and sapiential traditions of Israel:

> In the inheritance which you will hold in the land that Yahweh your God gives you to possess, you shall not remove your neighbor's landmark, which the men of old have set. (Deut 19:14)

> Remove not the ancient landmark which your fathers have set. (Prov 22:28)

> Do not remove an ancient landmark or enter the fields of the fatherless; for their Redeemer is strong; he will plead their cause against you. (Prov 23:10-11)

More vigorously Yahweh is presented as an active intervener:

> Yahweh tears down the house of the proud, but maintains the widow's boundaries. (Prov 15:25)

Yahweh is the Lord of tearing down and building up.[11] In our narrative he tears down the proud, that is, those of elevated heart (see Deut 17:20) and builds up the "widow," that is, those who have lost power and standing in the community.

Most remarkable and most radical is the alliance of Yahweh with the poor against those who would seek to take the land from them. Prophets characteristically condemn avarice in land seizure:

> Woe to those who join house to house,
>   who add field to field,
> until there is no more room,
>   and you are made to dwell alone
>   in the midst of the land. (Isa 5:8)
> Woe to those who devise wickedness

> and work evil upon their beds!
> When the morning dawns, they perform it,
>   because it is in the power of their hand.
> They covet fields, and seize them;
>   and houses, and take them away;
> they oppress a man and his house,
>   a man and his inheritance. (Mic 2:1-2)

---

11. On tearing down and building up, see 1 Sam 2:7-8 and the tradition history study of Robert Bach, "Bauen und Pflanzen," in *Studien zur Theologie der alttestamentlichen Überlieferungen*, ed. R. Rendtorff and K. Koch (Neukirchen-Vluyn: Neukirchener, 1961) 7–32.

This last could well be a commentary on the Naboth episode. The ones who take the land are characterized by a sequence of harsh verbs: they covet, they seize, they take, they oppress. And the offense is against the man, but also against the inheritance, and if so, then against the God who arranged it so. Such a proprietary attitude toward land is oppression of the land as well. It takes the land out of covenant and reduces it to control. The character of the land itself as covenanted, gifted land is disregarded and can now bring only trouble. The prophet announces the end, the end of haughtiness in which one takes priority over another, the one who has forgotten about covenant partners. It is clear that this is not simply gentle concern for poor folks, but it has to do with Yahweh, with his character and his commitments. He is allied with the poor against the rapacious wealthy. That is who he is and no royal wishing will have it otherwise.[12]

The speech of Elijah announces a surprising thing, one not heard often by kings. When one in power forgets brothers and sisters, it is not only the brother and sister who suffer but the one who "lifted his heart over them." The king is subject to the Torah and may not manage the land in any other way. The verdict of Elijah contains a word from Yahweh that always surprised the self-serving landed:

> Behold,
> I will bring evil upon you;
> I will utterly sweep you away, and
> [I] will cut off from Ahab every male....
> I will make your house like the house of Jeroboam.... (1 Kgs 21:21-22)

The first formula is like that against David (2 Sam 12:11), which in itself is radical enough—God against the landed. The second formula is more radical and echoes the threat of Samuel against landed monarchy (1 Sam 12:15) although the language is different. The third and fourth statements, by appeal to historical example, announce the end of monarchy, the end of promise, the end of landedness, the end of royal history. Royal history is terminated by the Lord of the land who is the Lord of the Torah. The grammar of the narrative is instructive. Jezebel had asserted, "I will give." But when the resolution comes, it is Yahweh who says, "I, I": I will bring, I will sweep away, I will cut off, I will make. The initiative has passed from the royal family back to the land-giving God. He finally presides.

---

12. On the character of Yahweh as identified with the landless poor, see Norman K. Gottwald, "Biblical Theology or Biblical Sociology?" *Radical Religion* 2 (1975) 46–57. See the sharp contrast in Psalm 82 between Yahweh's character and that of the other gods who are declared to be no-gods because of their indifference to the poor.

The Royal Road to Exile

Of course such an understanding of land is against every Canaanite and every modern notion of land. It is an understanding of land in a history of gifts graciously given and of radical breaks in history that begin in Exodus and wilderness and that come to full expression in crucifixion and resurrection. The narrative notes that Ahab repented and that he was humbled and rent his clothes (v. 27).[13] At the last moment the king affirms openness to the purposes of Yahweh for land.

Is it too much to relate the theme to Jesus' observation about landless and landed? "Every one who exalts himself will be humbled, and he who humbles himself will be exalted" (Luke 14:11; see also 18:14; Matt 18:4; 23:12). The Bible discerns that the promised future is not in kings with high hearts but with covenant partners like Naboth on whose behalf Yahweh intervenes. That is the characteristic affirmation of Elijah's presence that the king could not tolerate. Elijah embodies not only a powerful word but a radically alternative history. Especially in 1 Kgs 17:8-16, by the authority of Yahweh Elijah puts himself at the disposal of a landless widow in an alien territory, and the presence of God's word gives security and joy to the landless one:

> And she went and did as Elijah said; and she, and he, and her household ate for many days. The jar of meal was not spent, neither did the cruse of oil fail, according to the word of Yahweh which he spoke by Elijah. (17:15-16)

The care of Yahweh for the landless in this episode of course is reasserted by Jesus in his Nazareth confrontation:

> But in truth, I tell you, there were many widows in Israel in the days of Elijah, when the heaven was shut up three years and six months, when there came a great famine over all the land; and Elijah was sent to none of them but only to Zarephath, in the land of Sidon, to a woman who was a widow. (Luke 4:25-26)

Jesus' statement asserts that God is not concerned with the landed, even in Israel. He acts especially for the landless as did Elijah and as did the prophet of the exile (Isa 61:1-14),[14] whom Jesus quotes in Luke

---

13. E. W. Nicholson, *Preaching to the Exiles: A Study of the Prose Tradition in the Book of Jeremiah* (Oxford: Blackwell, 1970) 43, makes a sharp distinction between kings who receive the word and rend their garments and kings who resist the word and refuse to rend their garments.

14. See Paul D. Hanson, *The Dawn of Apocalyptic: The Historical and Sociological Roots of Jewish Apocalyptic Eschatology,* rev. ed. (Philadelphia: Fortress Press, 1979) 46–77.

4:18-19. That proclamation of Yahweh for the landless sounds this
way:

> ... good news to the poor.
> He has sent me to proclaim release to the captives
> and recovering of sight to the blind,
> to set at liberty those who are oppressed. ...

Thus the Elijah/Naboth/Jezebel/Ahab sequence stands as a focus for traditions that are an embarrassing interruption in royal history. It is a pause
that asserts that kings do not finally rule as they seem to, because Yahweh's
care for the land is inalienable. No amount of royal finesse can change that.
It is still covenant word and not royal hardware that governs land.

And so the narrative concludes in 2 Kgs 9:30-37 with the total elimination of the royal presence from history. Even the will that it be buried is
voided. The word will permit it no safe place in history or in land. And
that word against monarchy includes not only action against king but
against the whole royal future as announced in 1 Kgs 21:21-22. "And when
he came to Samaria, he slew all that remained to Ahab in Samaria, till he
had wiped them out, according to the word of Yahweh which he spoke to
Elijah" (2 Kgs 10:17). Royal history cannot be sustained against the keeper
of promises to those who will receive gifts and trust them. The narrative
is abrasive, and it offends the sensitivity of those who would wish for a
sweeter gospel. But the narrative will not be misunderstood. Yahweh has
taken sides and he acts powerfully for the landless, powerfully enough to
overcome and defeat the enormous power of those who control land and
sit on thrones.[15]

The history of Israel in its classical period is presented as a tension
between *royally secured land* and *covenanted precarious land*. The narrative of 1 Kings 21 presents the clearest embodiment of that tension. But it
is also apparent in other contexts. The prophet Amos is consistent in his
announcement of land-loss, especially to those who are complacent in
their luxuriant self-indulgence:

> "Hear this word, you cows of Bashan,
>   who are in the mountain of Samaria,
>   who oppress the poor, who crush the needy,
>   who say to their husbands, 'Bring, that we may drink?'

---

15. This is the central theme of James H. Cone, *God of the Oppressed*, rev. ed. (Maryknoll,
N.Y.: Orbis, 1997).

Yahweh has sworn by his holiness
    that, behold, the days are coming upon you,
     when they shall take you away with hooks,
    even the last of you with fishhooks.
And you shall go out through the breaches,
    every one straight before her;
    and you shall be cast forth into Harmon," says Yahweh.
(Amos 4:1-3)

Exile follows self-indulgent consumerism:

Woe to those who are at ease in Zion,
    and to those who feel secure on the mountain of Samaria. . . .
Woe to those who lie upon beds of ivory,
    and stretch themselves upon their couches,
and eat lambs from the flock,
    and calves from the midst of the stall;
who sing idle songs to the sound of the harp,
    and like David invent for themselves instruments of music;
who drink wine in bowls,
    and anoint themselves with the finest oils,
    but are not grieved over the ruin of Joseph! (6:1-6)

The passage describes with rich imagery the self-seeking complacency to which Israel in the land is seduced. It is the very temptation about which Israel was warned at the boundary (see Deut 8:11-20). And the conclusion is that the land will be exiled, the revelry of the self-satisfied will be silenced: "Therefore they shall now be the first of those to go into exile, and the revelry of those who stretch themselves shall pass away" (Amos 6:7). That history will end. It is not the way to life or to the future.

The dramatic peak of Amos's preaching, as has often been recognized, is the encounter with Amaziah, priest of Bethel, in which two discernments of history are presented. Two understandings of land are articulated (7:10-17). Amaziah asserts the same royal theology of Solomon in his temple or of Jezebel in her manipulative acts: "And Amaziah said to Amos, 'O seer, go, flee away to the land of Judah, and eat bread there, and prophesy there; but never again prophesy at Bethel, for it is the king's sanctuary, and it is a temple of the kingdom'" (7:12-13). The text is a monument to royal continuity. The king is immune from holy demand. History is closed and land is manageable. And against that Amos presents this other view of land and of history, that they are always precarious:

Therefore thus says Yahweh:
"Your wife shall be a harlot in the city,
and your sons and your daughters shall fall by the sword,
and your land shall be parceled out by line;
you yourself shall die in an unclean land,
and Israel shall surely go into exile away from its land." (Amos 7:17)

Now the unspeakable has been spoken. It echoes the curses that land managed outside of covenant will be lost (Deut 28:63-68). History can be ended. The sentence of Amos builds from lesser to greater tragedy:

a. queen
b. princes and princesses
c. the land
d. the king himself
e. Israel

Each experience inverts a previous blessing. Thus it is a recital of tragic reversals[16] when the prosperous history of the king seemed irreversible. Thus:

The queen becomes harlot.

The princes and princesses, symbol of future, are dead.

The promised and possessed land is reassigned to others.

The king, focus of corporate life, is not only dead, but is dead apart from his land.

Israel, people of promise in land of promise, is off land in exile. And as though to stress the last, so that the point is not missed, the verb *exile* is expressed as infinitive absolute. This is the surest announcement of the prophet: people of promise now promised only landlessness.

In other contexts the theme of tragic reversal is assurance to Israel. Especially in the vivid image of humiliated Babylon:

Come down and sit in the dust,
    O virgin daughter of Babylon;
sit on the ground without a throne,
    O daughter of the Chaldeans!
For you shall no more be called
    tender and delicate.
Take the millstones and grind meal,
    put off your veil,
Strip off your robe, uncover your legs,
    pass through the rivers.

16. The term is that of Norman K. Gottwald, *Studies in the Book of Lamentations*, SBT 1/14 (Chicago: Allenson, 1954) chap. 3.

> Your nakedness shall be uncovered,
> and your shame shall be seen. (Isa 47:1-3)

The contrast is sharp and total. But that is Babylon, and for Amos the same sharp total inversion is for none other than Israel. The landed are recalled to the forsaken history of landlessness.[17]

Each of the statements of Amos makes a total reversal and a drastic undoing. The last two are the most telling. A king is scarcely a king in a land where he is not only not ruler, but where the norms of ritual cleanness do not prevail (compare later regarding Jehoiachin in 2 Kgs 25:27-30). And the juxtaposition of that last line is powerful to the point of being unbearable: *Israel/exile!*

Amaziah and the royal house surely had equated Israel and land, or even king and land. And the land they valued was no longer gift-land but controlled land.[18] The announcement of Amos is not unlike that of Elijah. In a dramatic encounter of the two histories, it is asserted that kings who violate Torah, who refuse to treat the land and the brothers and sisters in a covenantal way, will be dethroned, such land possessors will be dispossessed, and Israel must again affirm its identity and destiny without land. Kings, the very land-managers entrusted to care for the land, are the instruments of land-loss.

The same issue is stated in even more depth by Hosea. Elijah had been concerned only with a dynasty. Amos had spoken at a time of peak prosperity. Hosea by contrast speaks in the very face of land-loss and so has a remarkable tone of pathos in this poetry.

The pathos of Hosea is in his discernment of history as divorce.[19] The radical imagery shows boldness in two ways. Concerning form, he uses the idiom of marriage and fertility but turns the imagery to speak of fickleness, harlotry, and divorce. Concerning substance, the divorce theme negates all security, all possession of land, all control of the apparatus of well-being. Divorce is unthinkable in fertility religion because fertility religion characteristically celebrates growth and well-being. It contains

---

17. R. E. Clements, *Prophecy and Covenant,* SBT 1/43 (Naperville: Allenson, 1965) 40, argues that earlier prophets had announced judgment but Amos first announced the end of Israel.

18. The extent to which the land was for control and coercion is evident in their inability to tolerate Sabbath, a sign that coercion and control are not the way Yahweh orders land or society; compare Amos 8:4-6.

19. See Abraham Heschel, *The Prophets* (New York: Harper & Row, 1962) 47–60, and Walter Brueggemann, *Tradition for Crisis (A Study in Hosea)* (Richmond: John Knox, 1968) 110–23.

no categories of fidelity or betrayal and therefore cannot speak of divorce. But covenant has to do with fidelity and betrayal, with embrace and abandonment. And that is the radical turn Hosea has discerned in the midst of his people. He utilizes fertility images to speak of *covenantal* realities. And he announces by that odd and inventive combination of form and substance that the covenant is ended. It is voided, and with it the covenant gift, the land, is also forfeited. Covenant history, which had its fruition in the land, is now terminated. And the payoff is landlessness:

> . . . lest I strip her naked
> and make her as in the day she was born,
> and make her like a wilderness,
> and set her like a parched land,
> and slay her with thirst. (Hos 2:3)[20]

Israel assumes its land gifts come from other sources:

> For she said, "I will go after my lovers,
> who give me my bread and my water,
> my wool and my flax, my oil and my drink." (v. 5)

And if from other sources, they are not so radical or holy, not so total in demand, not so rich in promise. They are sources that can be accommodated, and that is how Israel prefers it. How convenient if undemanding sources give it all. All on demand and without demand.

Israel does not know the real sources (Hos 2:8). In land it becomes increasingly incapable of knowing.[21] It controls a lot of data as royal consciousness does, but this knowing consists in bowing before and trusting in, and this it cannot do. Israel's knowing is all of a monologic kind, of subject handling object, but knowing Yahweh as covenantal Lord escapes it, as it always does those bent on singularly self-sufficient management.

20. On the form, see Hans Walter Wolff, *Amos the Prophet: The Man and His Background*, trans. F. R. McCurley (Philadelphia: Fortress Press, 1973) 51–53, and the parallel use of Deut 8:11-17.

21. It is now beyond dispute that "know" means to acknowledge covenant loyalty and the accompanying demands. Herbert B. Huffmon, "The Treaty Background of Hebrew *Yada'*," *BASOR* 181 (1966) 31–37. Huffmon and Simon B. Parker, "A Further Note on the Treaty Background of Hebrew *Yada'*," *BASOR* 184 (1966) 36–38. See Hans Walter Wolff, "Wissen um Gott bei Hosea also Urform von Theologie," in *Gesammelte Studien zum Alten Testament*, ThB 22 (Munich: Kaiser, 1964) 182–205, and José Porfirio Miranda, *Marx and the Bible: A Critique of the Philosophy of Oppression*, trans. J. Eagleson (Maryknoll, N.Y.: Orbis, 1974) 44–53, for an application to current parallel problems of covenant and urban consciousness.

Yahweh announces what Israel is incapable of knowing: "It was I who gave her the grain, the wine, and the oil" (v. 8). And the sure consequence: the gifts are losable!

> Therefore I will take back
> my grain . . .
> . . . my wine . . .
> . . . my wool . . .
> . . . my flax. . . . (v. 9)

Yahweh is a fertility God.[22] As he announced at the boundary, he will give growth and produce, covenant blessings for covenant land. But when land is taken out of covenant, that is, detached from Torah, subject to coveting, cynical of brothers and sisters, exile must surely come. His fertility for land is always covenantal fertility. As covenantal land is freely given, it can be surely taken away:

> *And I will put an end* to all her mirth,
>   her feasts, her new moods, her sabbaths,
>   and all her appointed feasts.
> *And I will lay waste* her vines and her fig trees. . . .
> *I will make them a forest.* . . .
> *And I will punish her* for the feast days of the Baals
>   when she burned incense to them
>   and decked herself with her ring and jewelry,
>   and went after her lovers,
>   *and forgot me,* says Yahweh. (2:11-13)

The voice of the end is relentless and devastating. I will end, I will lay waste, I will make a forest, I will punish. And all because of forgetting. The certain result of harlotry and forsaking is exile.

The antithesis is sharp and consistent: Yahweh and land gods, trust and fickleness. Everything is perceived in binary opposites. Israel has memories to treasure, vows to honor, choices to make, loyalties to affirm. The tradition from the boundary believed such things were possible even in the land. But the land has done something to Israel. The ones warned about forgetting (Deut 8:11) remember nothing. Land has caused amnesia (Deut 32:15-18). Israel has forgotten everything about from whence it came, who gave the land, the demands that come with it.

22. Compare W. Harrelson, *From Fertility Cult to Worship* (Garden City, N.Y.: Doubleday, 1969) 12–18.

Prophets are to speak to kings. They are to speak about land linked to history, about turf in covenant. They say "yes" to kings, "yes" about God's faithful promises. They say "no" to kings, "no" to reducing land to property. "Yes" or "no" is the language of covenant, the voice of covenantal history. It speaks the amazement of "yes" and the terror of "no." It is always either/or.

Kings seek to silence "yes" and "no" and make it all timeless sameness. They do not remember being spoken to or having answered, being addressed or being given an identity. And when landed folk do not remember, it all ends. And so the land is losable. There is perishing (Hos 9:17; 10:15; 12:8-19). History with Yahweh and with land can end.

7.

THE PUSH TOWARD
LANDLESSNESS—AND BEYOND

ISRAEL'S ROYAL HISTORY IN THE LAND MOVED INEXORABLY TOWARD
exile. Kings tend to think about the next crisis rather than the general
drift and destiny of the community. Kings in Israel refused or were unable
to think that exile could be their ultimate end. But the prophets, the partners and challengers of kings, knew where Israel was headed—to exile. It
is the business of the prophets to discern what kings cannot see and to
articulate what kings cannot bear. Their spectrum of expectation and their
rigor in honesty are beyond royal possibilities. So they think unthinkable
thoughts and speak unspeakable words that kings can never tolerate or
dare to face. And none of that alternative discernment and articulation is
more radical than the notion of exile in the face of a landed king.

Jeremiah and the Terror of Land-Loss

None saw this alternative picture more clearly than Jeremiah. And none
expressed it more poignantly. In the Old Testament he is the poet of the
land par excellence.[1] None was more visibly rooted in the old traditions of
tribal Israel when land was held, after the manner of Naboth, with the
vitality of gratitude and newness.[2] None saw more clearly than he that

---

1. See Peter Diepold, *Israels Land,* BWANT 95 (Stuttgart: Kohlhammer, 1972), for an
excellent discussion of the land theme in Jeremiah; and Walter Brueggemann, "Israel's Sense
of Place in Jeremiah," in *Rhetorical Criticism: Essays in Honor of James Muilenburg,* ed. J. J.
Jackson and M. Kesller, PTMS 1 (Pittsburgh: Pickwick, 1974) 149–65.

2. These links are suggested in Jeremiah's derivation from Anathoth and in his links to
Hosea and Deuteronomy. See the early study of Karl Gross, "Hoseas Einfluss auf Jeremias

land cannot be held the way royal Israel tried to hold it. He knew unmistakably that land would be lost. None treasured the land more than he and none understood more clearly than he the flow of royal history toward exile. And all the others denied it in their royal self-deception.

Jeremiah more than anyone else is the embodiment of terror. It is the embodiment in his person of the whole history of Israel, the breaking of what had been promised forever, the collapse of what was eternally guaranteed. And in Jeremiah there is an extraordinary coming together of external upheaval, poetic articulation in power, and the irresistible coming of the Holy One in terror.[3] His message to Israel, who thought it was ultimately secure and at home, is the coming ultimate homelessness.[4] The mother of Israel—Israel in the land—should be celebrating but the child Israel is dead:

> A voice is heard in Ramah,
>> lamentation and bitter weeping.
> Rachel is weeping for her children;
>> she refuses to be comforted for her children,
>> because they are not. (31:15)

No comfort. They are not! Rachel grieves, and Jeremiah announces to those secure in the land that things that are, will not be (see 1 Cor 1:28).

The beginning of the lordly disruption of landed complacency is in the call of Jeremiah (1:4-10). The breaking in of Yahweh is in the peculiar clus-

---

Anschauungen," *NKZ* 42 (1931) 242–56, 327–43, and the thorough review of Foster R. McCurley Jr., "The Home of Deuteronomy Revisited: A Methodological Analysis of the Northern Theory," in *A Light unto My Path: Old Testament Studies in Honor of Jacob M. Myers,* ed. H. N. Bream, et al. (Philadelphia: Temple University Press, 1974) 295–317. If Deuteronomy 32 is as old and central as Mendenhall has argued, then the links to Jeremiah suggested by William L. Holladay, "Jeremiah and Moses: Further Observations," *JBL* (1965) 17–27 are most important.

3. Compare William L. Holladay, "The Covenant with the Patriarchs Overturned: Jeremiah's Intention in 'Terror on Every Side' (Jer. 20:1-6)," *JBL* 91 (1972) 305–20.

4. I am using "homelessness" here not simply as being away from Palestine but in the more radical sense of *anomie,* which is the meaning of Berger's "homelessness." This tradition of homelessness in Christian theology culminates in Jesus crucified. Not accidentally has H. Wheeler Robinson discerned the theme of the cross especially in Hosea, Jeremiah, Job, and Second Isaiah: *The Cross in Hosea* (Philadelphia: Westminster, 1949), and *The Cross in the Old Testament* (Philadelphia: Westminster, 1955). All four traditions are either from the old memories of landlessness or are reflections on exile. Jürgen Moltmann, *The Crucified God: The Cross of Christ as the Foundation and Criticism of Christian Theology,* trans. R. A. Wilson and J. Bowden (New York: Harper & Row, 1974) 39, 58, and *passim,* speaks of Jesus as the one radically "homeless" and "rootless."

ter of verbs: "I knew, I appointed, I consecrated." And he will have his way. He will have his way against the protesting young man as he will have his way against the resistant kings. He will have his way, and that is what Jeremiah embodies against his own will and against all the yearnings of his fellows. The call is in the service of the message. And the message is:

> . . . to pluck up and to break down,
> to destroy and to overthrow,
> to build and to plant. (Jer 1:10)

That is the point of the call. That is the point of Jeremiah's words. That is the only unbearable point for the landed, managing kings, for it affirms against all of them that initiative is retained by Yahweh. Finally he will preside over this history, in or out of the land. The land imagery is unmistakable. The message is for tearing down and plucking up, for destroying and overthrowing. To be sure, the words are answered by two others, but the imbalance is clear. The weight is on the ending, not the beginning. Jeremiah knew, long before the others could face it, that history in land moves to exile.

The subsequent word of 1:13-19 shows that both Jeremiah and Yahweh understood early that the word that must be spoken is against all conventional wisdom and will not receive a welcome hearing. No longer is the surprising word that the land is losable. But now it is that the land is being lost and will be lost. He announces not an unthinkable possibility but an unacceptable certainly. And the words are fighting words, in conflict with an alternative notion of reality: "They will fight against you" (v. 19). The central issue of the poetry is now set; it concerns well-being in the land, and he must say, "It is over." History is ended. It is a word that calls into question everything held dear. Jeremiah has gone beyond his predecessors in the prophetic tradition. He no longer imagines possible futures, but now concludes about the end: "They are not!"

This conflict between the perception of land being lost and being retained is deep and to the death. It is at the center of all of the poetry, but nowhere more so than in the complaints that begin in 11:18-20, 12:1-2 with disputes between Jeremiah and his fellows. The harsh reality of the word endangers the person of the messenger. But the resentment is displaced. The issue is not about a misguided poet but about the flow of history toward exile. And Yahweh's response to Jeremiah dealing with the displaced anger is relentless and unbending (11:21-23, 12:5-6). The dialogue moves with new intensity in 15:15-21 so that the dispute is no longer with the citizenry but between Yahweh and his poet. Jeremiah has postured himself as an alienated man, as precursor of exile. As the people cannot envision exile for themselves, so Jeremiah must ask about his treatment, which ends in abandonment, when he has been as faithful as he knew how (v. 17). And the lot of Jeremiah inevitably rejected and in exile is an embodiment of Israel's future about which nothing can be done.

Perhaps there is a fresh clue here about the complaints. While many scholars have treated them as internal struggles of a sensitive person, and some have tried to understand them institutionally, it may be that the land/exile theme illuminates them differently. The dispute is not about Yahweh's private dealing with Jeremiah but about the great public crisis that comes to light between Yahweh who is Lord and Jeremiah's contemporaries who will manage land their own way.[5] The central issue in the texts is how land is kept and how it is lost and who makes those decisions. Jeremiah has embodied in his own person the dispute about these questions, for he knows in his body (4:19, 6:24) how it really is. But he cannot bear it. It is enough to experience the rejection of his fellows. It is more than enough to be caught with a sovereign proclamation that evokes anger and anguish that such a time would come in Israel's history. As sensitive as he is, that word is surely harsh for Jeremiah too, because he knows in his own person that talk of exile is of ultimate seriousness, and it must not be taken lightly.

While Jeremiah carries in his poetry this deep anguish with Yahweh, the anguish of Israel for its precious land, he permits Israel a glimpse of history ending in exile. His words announce a startling future to his people. The end is coming and the land will be lost. This was anticipated in his call (vv. 1:13-16). But the more powerful statement of it is in the war poetry.[6] The war poetry is not so much a bulletin providing information about troop movement and imperial policy as it is an effort to bring Israel to an awareness of its true faith-situation. The prophet's attempt to bring Israel to this awareness required radical imagery for the sake of an intense aesthetic experience. Israel had become numbed and dull, stupid (4:22), having lost the capacity to be embarrassed (8:12).[7] In its alienated security

5. On the proposal of Henning Graf Reventlow concerning the laments of Jeremiah and their identity as public and not personal, see the comments of John Bright, "Jeremiah's Complaints—Liturgy or Expressions of Personal Distress?" in *Proclamation and Presence: Old Testament Essays in Honour of Gwynne Henton Davies*, ed. J. I. Durham and J. R. Porter (Richmond: John Knox, 1970) 189–214; and Sheldon H. Blank, "The Prophet as Paradigm," in *Essays on Old Testament Ethics (J. Philip Hyatt, In Memoriam)*, ed. J. L. Crenshaw and J. T. Willis (New York: Ktav, 1974) 113–30. Nevertheless, Blank sees Jeremiah as a paradigm for exiled Israel.

6. John Bright, *Jeremiah*, AB 21 (Garden City, N.Y.: Doubleday, 1965) 33–34.

7. Abraham Heschel, *Who Is Man?* (Stanford: Stanford University Press, 1965) 113, asserts: "The end of embarrassment would be the end of humanity." That is what Jeremiah had seen in his contemporaries, and he announced the end of their humanity and their history.

it had settled for nonreflective apathy, surely the last achievement of amnesia in the land.[8] Because covenantal realities had lost their power for Israel, it knew itself to be neither addressed nor accountable. It believed history could have neither endings nor beginnings (Zeph 1:12). It believed that it was on its own, with some security but without capacity to discern or respond. Jeremiah articulates to Israel his own pathos, the pathos of Yahweh, which is pathos over land-loss.[9] The interiority of Israel's faith is perhaps the central issue, not loss of land but loss of pathos. Must land make its holders apathetic? Have we that to learn from Marx, that being in land without caring for community ends history? Israel cannot even hurt over its loss. No wonder at the boundary Israel was warned to take heed (Deut 8:11-20).

So land-loss means the end of history. And it will surely come. It comes because a relentless army moves from the north (see 1:13-16). The "north" is of course a geographical reference and it is finally about Babylon. But the term also contains a numinous quality designed to bring terror to Israel because it is an unnamed enemy with awesome power:

> Blow the trumpet through the land;
>> cry aloud and say,
> "Assemble, and let us go
>> into the fortified cities!"
> Raise a standard toward Zion,
>> flee for safety, stay not. . . .
> A lion has gone up from his thicket,
>> a destroyer of nations has set out;
>> he has gone forth from his place
> to make your land a waste;
>> our cities will be ruins without inhabitant. (4:5-7)

He comes with relentless speed and power and one can only flee:

> Behold, he comes up like clouds,
>> his chariots like the whirlwind;
> his horses are swifter than eagles—
>> woe to us, for we are ruined! . . .
> Warn the nations that he is coming;
>> announce to Jerusalem,
> "Besiegers come from a distant land;
>> they shout against the cities of Judah. . . ."

8. On apathy as a theological agenda, see Moltmann, *The Crucified God*, 270–278, and *The Experiment Hope*, trans. M. D. Meeks (Philadelphia: Fortress Press, 1975) chap. 6.

9. See Abraham Heschel, *The Prophets* (New York: Harper & Row, 1965) 103–36.

Disaster follows hard on disaster,
    the whole land is laid waste. (4:13-20)

He is still a distance off, but one can hear. One can hear and knows it won't stop:

At the noise of horseman and archer
    every city takes to flight;
they enter thickets; they climb among rocks;
    all the cities are forsaken,
    and no man dwells in them. (4:29)

That coming nation is never named.[10] Such reticence adds to the power of it. The enemy is unnamed and, if unnamed, cannot be resisted or tamed, nor can safety even be negotiated. The "unnamed It" to come is nonnegotiable. Its identity is hidden. Its coming is inscrutable but it comes. And there will be an end to everything.

"Behold, a people is coming from the north country,
    a great nation is stirring from the farthest parts of the earth.
They lay hold on bow and spear,
    they are cruel and have no mercy,
    the sound of them is like the roaring sea;
they ride upon horses,
    set in array as a man for battle,
    against you, O daughter of Zion!" (6:22-23)

Not only does the enemy come. But it is an enemy called by Yahweh. The destroyer is indeed an identifiable historical force. But it is a historical agent commissioned and sent. The one who will take the land away from Israel is not some alien power, but it is the Holy One who gave the land. Yahweh himself wills the end of Israel's history in the land. Thus the end of Israel in land and the loss to Babylon is because "I am bringing":

Behold, I am bringing upon you
    a nation from afar, O house of Israel. . . . (5:15)

. . . for the fierce anger of Yahweh
    has not turned back from us. (4:8)

---

10. George Adam Smith, *The Book of the Twelve Prophets I,* rev. ed. (New York: Harper & Row, 1929) calls it "the unnamed *It*."

... before Yahweh, before his fierce anger. (4:26)

... for I bring evil from the north,
and great destruction. (4:6)

It is hard enough for landed people to believe land will be lost. It is
harder to imagine Yahweh will do it. But that is the center of this message: the announcement that Yahweh had made a decision for the end of
his people in his land. And surely this is nowhere more remarkably articulated than in two prose passages in which Yahweh's course of action is
presented:

> Because you have not obeyed my words, behold, I will send for all
> the tribes of the north, says Yahweh, and for Nebuchadrezzar the
> king of Babylon, *my servant,* and I will bring them against this land
> and its inhabitants, and against all these nations round about; I will
> utterly destroy them, and make them a horror, a hissing, and an
> everlasting reproach. (25:8-9)

> Now I have given all these lands into the hand of Nebuchadnezzar,
> the king of Babylon, *my servant,* and I have given him also the beasts
> of the field to serve him. (27:6)

Nebuchadnezzar, clearly the central enemy of landed Israel, is Yahweh's
servant and instrument, doing his work (see Isa 10:5, 47:6).[11] Nebuchadnezzar the land-grabber, the quintessence of imperial expansionism that
threatened Israel, is doing the work of Yahweh. No wonder Jeremiah is
called traitor. His argument is that land-loss is not only inevitable, but it
is the intention of Yahweh (see 21:7; 22:25; 28:14; 29:21). This history ends
not for lack of ingenuity or by accident but by the purpose of Yahweh.
Israel no longer fits his purpose. Such a conclusion might claim to be
more symmetrical and to presume to know too much for us. The prophet
testifies to the freedom and sovereignty of God against a people who has
presumed upon its land and has claimed for itself freedom and autonomy
against the rule of Yahweh. And thus land is lost and history is closed!

The geographical, political loss is great enough. But Jeremiah urgently
presents the shocking awareness of the enmity that is at the center of it.
Land is not lost, history is not denied, because of some political eventuality,

11. See George Telcs, "Jeremiah and Nebuchadnezzar: King of Justice," *CJT* 15 (1969)
122–30; and T. W. Overholt, "King Nebuchadnezzar in the Jeremiah Tradition" *CBQ* 30
(1968) 39–48. For a different explanation of the text, see Werner Lemke, "Nebuchadnezzar,
My Servant," *CBQ* (1966) 45–50.

but because of the enmity of holiness in the midst of history. We of course do not believe that in our time about turns in land and in history. But they did not then either. Thus Jeremiah, most powerful and most pathos-filled of all Israel's poets, announces to Israel that its time in the land is over. Because Yahweh rules!

Kings as a Way to Land-Loss

The end of the land of course means the collapse of all public institutions and all symbolic expressions of well-being and coherence. None is more telling than Jeremiah's extraordinary articulation of kingship that loses land and kingship that keeps land. For him Jehoiachin (Shallum) and Josiah are models of land-losing and land-keeping kings.[12] He describes the presumptuous royal power that takes it all for granted:

> "Woe to him who builds his house by unrighteousness,
>   and his upper rooms by injustice;
> who makes his neighbor serve him for nothing,
>   and does not give him his wages;
> who says, 'I will build myself a great house
>   with spacious upper rooms,'
> and cuts out windows for it,
>   paneling it with cedar,
>   and painting it with vermilion." (22:13-14)

The word pairs governing the image are clear: not righteous/not justice, cedar/vermilion. He has discerned that kings and such landed ones tend to choose between cedar and righteousness, between justice and vermilion (see Deut 16:18-20, and especially v. 20: "Justice, and only justice, you shall follow, that you may live and *inherit the land* which Yahweh your God gives you").

Then Jeremiah sets two rhetorical questions that concern the relation of land/Torah/kingship:

> Do you think you are a king
>   because you complete in cedar?
> Did not your father eat and drink
>   and do justice and righteousness? (Jer 22:15)

---

12. Telcs, "Jeremiah" develops a convincing ideological contrast between Josiah who cared for the poor and Jehoiachin who exploited the poor.

The first question asks about king and cedar, about power and self-seeking, about order and coveting, about whether cedar is definitive for royal power. The second presents an alternative model of kingship in his father, Josiah, a *Mosaic* effort at *Davidic* power. That of course is what the contrast of Josiah and Jehoiachin is all about. Jehoiachin embodies the worst pretensions of the dynasty after the manner of Solomon. Josiah embodies an effort to redefine the dynasty in terms of Torah.[13] As Jehoiachin preferred cedar to righteousness and vermilion to justice, so Josiah settled for justice and righteousness. He took his clue for keeping land from the voice at the boundary. Father and son, land-keeper and land-loser, Mosaic responsibility and Solomonic self-seeking, are set in sharp contrast:

> He judged the cause of the poor and needy;
> > then it was well.
> Is this not to know me?
> > says Yahweh.
> But you have eyes and heart
> > only for your dishonest gain,
> for shedding innocent blood,
> > and for practicing oppression and violence. (Jer 22:16-17)

The issue is an urgent one because the poet is asking about losing land and keeping it. Then comes the inevitable "therefore," a "therefore" not only concerning king, but concerning the whole people, a "therefore" very old in the tradition and earlier announced by Amos:

> Therefore thus says Yahweh:
> "Your *wife* shall be a harlot in the city,
> > and your *sons and your daughters* shall fall by the sword,
> > and your land shall be parceled out by line;
> you *yourself* shall die in an unclean land,
> > and *Israel* shall surely go into exile away from its land."
> (Amos 7:17)

The poet must place a "therefore" in the center of the land. And the end is the ignominious separation of land and king, the loss of place and the end of power. Yahweh brings to nought that which is, after the manner of Jezebel, the land-grabber who ended without a trace, and history was as though she had not been (2 Kgs. 9:36-37):

---

13. See E. W. Nicholson, *Preaching to the Exiles: A Study of the Prose Tradition in the Book of Jeremiah* (Oxford: Blackwell, 1970) 42–57.

Therefore . . .
"They shall not lament for him, saying,
   'Ah my brother!' or 'Ah sister!'
They shall not lament for him, saying,
   'Ah lord!' or 'Ah his majesty!'
With the burial of an ass he shall be buried,
   dragged and cast forth beyond the gates of Jerusalem." (Jer 22:18-19)

Beyond Jerusalem, outside the protected royal sanctuary, not like a king, but like a landless one. "He is cast forth" *('alak)*. He is spewed out, separated from his land, from every claim to presence and power. And he is Israel and what comes to the king surely comes to his people. He and they are abandoned, with none to comfort (compare the refrain in Lam 1:2, 9, 17, 21). That is Israel as well as its king. The symbolic world has disintegrated. Not only is the king dead, but the claims and pretensions of royalty are now without force. It is over. Land is gone. History is ended.

In the same cluster of tradition, the pathos intensifies for the helpless boy king Jehoiachin (Coniah), left to pay for the arrogance of the royal presumption that had gone before him:

Is this man Coniah a despised, broken pot,[14]
   a vessel no one cares for?
Why are he and his children hurled and cast
   into a land which they do not know? (Jer 22:28)

He, like his father, like his people, like the whole history of Israel, in this moment is hurled and cast into an alien land, which for Israel is no land at all. The king is again the bearer of the history of his people. The poet feels pathos about the exiled king quite in contrast to the abrasiveness of Amos in 7:17.

But just as the pathos for the vulnerable boy builds, the poet makes a curious turn. Just when he might grieve for the pitiful king he grieves for the land:

O land, land, land,
   hear the word of Yahweh!
Thus says Yahweh:

---

14. In Jer 18:1-11, 19:1-13, Israel is the pot. The prophet uses the image easily for both people and king, because he is concerned with *royal* Israel. It is royal Israel that goes into exile with Coniah.

"Write this man down as childless,
　　a man who shall not succeed in his days;
for none of his offspring shall succeed
　　in sitting on the throne of David,
　　and ruling again in Judah." (Jer 22:29-30)

The language recalls the state of Abraham and Sarah, without heir, without promise, and ultimately without land. Israel without land is no people. King without throne is no king. Land without Israel is no place. And now Israel, king and land, have come to parting and that is death.[15] It could have been otherwise with righteousness and justice. But in their stead there have been cedar and vermilion. Cedar and vermilion are the voices of exile claiming the people from the land. It could have been otherwise. But it is not. And it will not be. And in this moment the poet is numbed, and he is gripped in his innards by what could happen, even here. Micah had announced it with cool symmetry (see Mic 3:9-12; Jer 26:16-19), but now it comes and it can only be expressed, but scarcely embraced:

My anguish, my anguish! I writhe in pain!
　　Oh, the walls of my heart!
My heart is beating wildly;
　　I cannot keep silent;
for I hear the sound of the trumpet,
　　the alarm of war. (Jer 4:19)

My grief is beyond healing,
　　my heart is sick within me. (8:18)

He knew what those in the land were unable to discern. But it was happening nonetheless.

Jeremiah reflected long about the having of land and the losing of land. He apparently stands in the old tradition of those who understood what *inheritance* is all about.[16] He is impressed with the awesome reality of being entrusted with it, but he is equally urgent with the reality of its loss. He understands the covenantal dimension of landholding, the fact that being in land and possessing it depends on continual reference to

15. Robert Merton, *Social Theory and Social Structure: Toward the Codification of Theory and Research* (Glencoe, Ill.: Free Press, 1957) 131–94, has provided a helpful definition of *anomie*.

16. See Brueggemann, "Israel's Sense of Place," and the various essays of von Rad noted there.

Yahweh. He presents the grief of land-loss not from the perspective of Israel but from the view of Yahweh.

Thus he presents land-loss as pollution and as harlotry:

> "Would not that land be greatly polluted?
> You have played the harlot with many lovers;
>   and would you return to me?" says Yahweh. (Jer 3:1)

Land is polluted in that it has become impure by covenant breaking and violation of relation with Yahweh. It has been the scene of harlotry in that Israel has ceased to trust the land-giver and has engaged in alternative ways of securing its own existence. In these two terms Jeremiah employs (a) *priestly* language of a substantive violation of land that refers to material impurity and (b) *covenantal* language of infidelity to a solemn relation. In the first of these Jeremiah uses language that echoes priestly warning about purity and impurity:

> "Do you defile yourselves by any of these things, for by all these the nations I am casting out before you defiled themselves; and the land became defiled, so that I punished its iniquity, and the land vomited out its inhabitants. . . . lest the land vomit you out, when you defile it, as it vomited out the nation that was before you." (Lev 18:24-25, 28)

> "You shall not thus pollute the land in which you live; for blood pollutes the land, and no expiation can be made for the land, . . . except by the blood of him who shed it. You shall not defile the land in which you live, in the midst of which I dwell. . . ." (Num 35:33-34)

These statements appeal to a rather primitive idea of holiness in land, and Jeremiah has applied the warning to different understandings. But the result is the same: being vomited out. Israel is about to be rejected as were the most offensive of the heathen.

In the second language, concerning harlotry, the language is reminiscent of Hosea, but see also the older warnings: "Do not profane your daughter by making her a harlot, lest the land fall into harlotry and the land become full of wickedness" (Lev 19:29).

This harlotry not only is a violation of relation but implies a violation of land. Israel's disobedience and carelessness not only offends Yahweh who may respond in anger, but it also affects the land. The land has its own life and its own meaning, and the trouble disobedient Israel may bring goes beyond its own borders. It is the land that is finally abused.

Such action fouls the nest of Israel. And there is no alternative but to be rejected, because the land must be cared for.[17] It is valued by Yahweh, and he dwells there. Not only is Yahweh holy, but his land shall also be discerned as holy!

So Jeremiah announces his conclusion with the same word pair:

> You have *polluted* the land
>> with your vile *harlotry.* (Jer 3:2)[18]

And then he must announce the consequence of drought and finally of death. It cannot be otherwise for those who are against the land.

Harlotry is the way to lose land. Allegiance is the way to keep it. Israel in its fickleness came late to try relating to Yahweh:

> Have you not just now called to me,
>> "My father, thou art the friend of my youth—" (Jer 3:4)

But it is too late and too cheap. To be an heir, to have the inheritance, is to acknowledge the giver of land and call him "father." Israel tried that but only in desperation. The land comes from the father. But Israel had no sense of its own identity or place of belonging. Israel had been enjoying alternative identities with gods who could neither give nor keep the land:

> . . . say to a tree, "You are my father,"
>> and to a stone, "You gave me birth." (Jer 2:27)

So land and covenant, inheritance and fidelity, belong together. "Father" is a word spoken in covenant,[19] but it is also a word that may be spoken in fertility contexts, where it has to do not with *belonging to* but only with *producing.* Israel may appeal to father tree and mother stone, but that is not covenant. It is only an accommodating process, sure to lose the land (see Deut 4:28; 28:62).

---

17. See Alfred von Rohr Sauer, "Ecological Notes from the Old Testament," in *A Light unto My Path: Old Testament Studies in Honor of Jacob M. Myers,* ed. H. N. Bream, et al. (Philadelphia: Temple Univ. Press, 1974) 421–34.

18. Compare Diepold, *Israels Land,* 123.

19. See F. Charles Fensham, "Father and Son as Terminology for Treaty and Covenant," in *Near Eastern Studies in Honor of William Foxwell Albright,* ed. H. Goedicke (Baltimore: Johns Hopkins Univ. Press, 1971) 121–35; and Dennis J. McCarthy, "Notes on the Love of God in Deuteronomy and the Father-Son Relationship between Yahweh and Israel," *CBQ* 72 (1965) 144–47.

Israel rejected land from Yahweh. Jeremiah presents it from the perspective of Yahweh. He would be their father:

> I thought
> how I would set you among my sons,
> and give you a pleasant land,
>   a heritage most beauteous of all nations.
> And I thought you would call me, My Father,
>   and would not turn from following me. (Jer 3:19)

He would be father. To keep land, Israel must only say *'abi*, "my father," but it did not. And the land is lost. It is lost when it is taken from its covenant context.

The incapacity to say *'abi* is not just forgetting the right jargon or neglecting ritual formula. Jeremiah discerned that something enormous had happened to the mind and heart of Israel. It had been engaged for so long in a consumptive form of life, in self-seeking, that it became constitutionally impossible to address this other one in a committed way.[20] Israel had at least achieved autonomy (Jer 2:20, 5:5). It was alone in history with its land and thought it wanted it so. But that will not last, because land is covenantal. Israel was incapable of calling this other one by name, of addressing him. When that happens land is lost. Keeping land depends on saying *'abi*, on knowing that life is rooted in dialogue, of speaking and having to answer, of being surprised and precarious in the exchange that gives life. But that is over now. Land is lost, and history is ended.

So Jeremiah tells the whole story of Israel as the story of land. Israel had been committed to Yahweh, addressing the one who makes promises and keeps them. But after wilderness (see 2:2), after the boundary, there were attractive alternatives:

> They went far from me.... (Jer 2:5)

> and went after worthlessness, and became worthless?
> (Jer 2:5; see Hos 9:10)

They no longer recited their identity-giving credo. They forgot. They could not say:

> "Where is Yahweh
>   who brought us up from the *land* of Egypt,

20. On what is perhaps a frightening contemporary parallel, see Philip Rieff, *The Triumph of the Therapeutic: Uses of Faith after Freud* (New York: Harper & Row, 1966), who speaks of an absence of "binding address" in our "psychological" context.

who led us in the wilderness,
    in a *land* of deserts and pits,
in a *land* of drought and deep darkness,
    in a *land* that none passes through,
    where no man dwells?"
And I brought you into a plentiful *land,*
    to enjoy its fruits and its good things.
But when you came in you defiled my *land,*
    and made my heritage an abomination. (Jer 2:6-7)

The story of Israel is from the *land* of Egypt to the *land* of inheritance that now is the *land* of abomination. No stronger antithetical word pair can be imagined than heritage/abomination, most treasured gift/repulsive object of scorn. No wonder the poet says, "O land, land, land" (Jer 22:29). It all passed by so quickly—land of slavery, land of wilderness, land of fruitfulness, land, land, land. And it is gone! The secure heir has become the hunted prey (see Jer 2:14). Glory has been exchanged for shame (Jer 2:11; compare Hos 4:7). Well-being has been turned to anxiety and death. The land-giver has become the enemy (see Hos 5:14-15; 7:11-12).

Exile and the New History

The words of Jeremiah are subtle and dialectical. Of course he grieves about land-loss. He feels the pathos of God himself in the dissolution of people in land. He dreads its coming and he shrinks from it.

But his words are not a simple announcement of land-loss. They are the curious transformation of landlessness to announce that land-loss is the way of faith to the new land. That is, when Yahweh has willed land-loss, as he surely has, to cling to the land is an act of rebellion that can only fail. That is a fresh departure in Israel's faith: (a) Landholding is an act of disobedience (see Num 14:39-45). (b) Land-loss is an act of faith. Exile is the way to new life in new land. One can scarcely imagine a more radical, less likely understanding of history. In covenantal categories, embrace of curse is the root to blessing. In New Testament categories, embrace of death is the way to life (Luke 9:23-27; Rom 6:1-11). Thus in the movement among images, exile = death and restoration of land = life. Jeremiah announces the central scandal of the Bible, that radical loss and discontinuity do happen and are the source of real newness. So he holds what surely must have been a minority view, that the *exiles* are the real *heirs.* And conversely those who cling to the land are the ultimate exiles.

Thus Jeremiah transforms the evaluation of exile. Of the exiles he declares:

> Like these good figs, so I will regard as *good the exiles* from Judah,
> whom I have sent away from this place to the land of the Chaldeans.
> I will set my eyes upon them for good, and I will bring them back to
> this land. I will build them up, and not tear them down; I will plant
> them, and not uproot them. I will give them a heart to know that I
> am Yahweh; and they shall be my people and I will be their God, for
> they shall return to me with their whole heart. (Jer 24:4-7)

The restorative part of his commission in 1:10 is employed here. It concerns
return to land or resurrection to new life. The people outside the land now
have the attention of Yahweh as the land formerly had it (Deut 11:10). Now
his eyes are on exiles, not on land. The action of God is with the landless
ones.

Of the ones who cling to the land against his purposes, he says:

> "Like the bad figs which are so bad they cannot be eaten, so will I
> treat Zedekiah the king of Judah, his princes, the remnant of
> Jerusalem *who remain in this land,* and those who dwell in the land
> of Egypt. I will make them a horror. . . . And I will send sword,
> famine, and pestilence upon them, until they shall be utterly
> destroyed from the land which I gave to them and their fathers."
> (Jer 24:8-10)

The exiles whom the world does not value are the ones with the heart, for
whom the covenant formula is appropriate. The outsiders are the ones
who belong. The ones remaining in the land are the finally cursed ones
(Deut 28:37) and the ultimately destroyed ones. The cursed are blessed,
the blessed are cursed. That of course is nearly impossible for landed ones
ever to believe.

Jeremiah makes no snap judgment about this event, but has discerned
the central surprise of the tradition, that the sojourner gets the land, that
the barren one mothers the child of promise, the slave people triumphs
over Pharaoh, the desperate ones get fed (see Matt 5:6; Luke 6:21; and all
the Beatitudes on the theme of transformation).[21] Life is inverted. This
understanding of land is not the reading done by kings and empires, but
by this strange God who always provides his people an alternative reading
of land and landlessness. The dying ones will be the bearers of life.

So in a related text, there is a discounting of everything that landed history values—wisdom, might, riches, glory. This other One practices kind-

---

21. Dan O. Via Jr., *Kerygma and Comedy in the New Testament: A Structuralist Approach
to Hermeneutic* (Philadelphia: Fortress Press, 1975), has discerned this pattern in many New
Testament texts.

ness, mercy, righteousness in the land. That is the way of Josiah and the ones who always lose but are the wave of Yahweh's future (Jer 9:23-24; 1 Cor 1:26-30).

There is no more radical text than the parable of Jeremiah 24, for it is the Lord of land announcing landlessness as the way of the future.[22] Newness comes in discontinuity to those who have no claim. It is among exiles that he calls into existence things that do not exist (Rom 4:17). That is the power of resurrection, that the one without form or comeliness (Isa 53:2) is the heir to the future. It is among landholders that he brings to nought the things that are (1 Cor 1:28).

That is what is happening in Jeremiah 24: (a) He calls into existence that which is not (Rom 4:17). (b) He brings to nought the things that are (1 Cor 1:28). In this struggle over abandonment, displacement, and restoration are the seeds of crucifixion/resurrection faith. Landed or not, Israel is pressed to radical reliance on the One who works newness precisely where it can't seem to come. The scandal of Jeremiah 24 (and a model for much of the Bible under our theme) is that landed folks have no claims or significance. Landless exiles have the promise affirmed to them. It should not be. We in our having land do not believe it. Nor could Israel at the time her landed history came to a startling end.

It is a major theological and rhetorical achievement, never completely done, to turn the agenda of Israel to the exile and to see that just there is where the history of turf must find its next episode. Land is losable, and when lost, newness comes. Thus his word about good figs and bad figs is faithful to Hosea from whom he learned much. Hosea before him had seen that land is for forgetting and forfeiting (Hos 2:12-13). Conversely wilderness, that is, exile, is for remembering and seducing and covenant-making (2:14-20).

So history ended in landlessness. In fear Israel had come to seek a word from Yahweh, a word that would sustain its history as only a word could do. It asked for a word and got it: "There is." . . . "You shall be delivered into the hand of the king of Babylon" (Jer 37:17). And that was all. Israel ended where it had begun, landless. The landless have no history. It takes land to make history. Israel had no land and therefore no history. It was over.

History can end. It does end. And none knew it more surely or felt it more deeply than Jeremiah. But the One who tears down builds up. The One who plucks up plants (Jer 24:7), who brings what is to nought (1 Cor 1:28), is the One who can call into existence things that do not

22. See Nicholson, *Preaching,* 81–113.

exist (Rom 4:17). And that is the extraordinary thing in Israel's history. The Lord of history gives history to the landless who should have no history. He takes the barren as mother of promise. He takes the slaves as bearers of freedom. He takes the desperately hungry as heirs of the new land. And now he takes hopeless exiles as his new people.

There is another word from Yahweh. The word just considered had ended history. And now history begins anew, not continued but begun anew.[23] And the word is precisely to exiles. It is a word of scandal and assurance:

> Build houses and live in them; plant gardens and eat their produce. Take wives and have sons and daughters; take wives for your sons, and give your daughters in marriage, that they may bear sons and daughters; multiply there, and do not decrease [see Exod 1:7; Deut 10:22]. But seek the welfare of the city where I have sent you into exile, and pray to Yahweh on its behalf, for in its welfare you will find your welfare. (Jer 29:5-7)

The assurance is that what had seemed homelessness is for now a legitimate home. What has seemed barren exile is fruitful garden. What had seemed alienation is for now a place of binding interaction. His very word redefined a place for placeless Israel. The assurance is that the landless are not wordless. He speaks just when the silence of God seemed permanent. Exile is the place for a history-initiating word.

But the new word is also scandal. It is gospel in hard terms: "But seek the welfare of the city where I have sent you into exile, and pray to Yahweh on its behalf, for in its welfare you will find your welfare" (Jer 29:7). What a way to welfare, that hated Babylon is the place of well-being. Thus exile is not only place of unexpected word. It is also place of unexpected unacceptable vocation—exiles seeking welfare for others! Seek only justice and righteousness, even in anxiety, and get the kingdom (Matt 6:33). Seek *shalom*, and you'll get the land.

Exile is where Yahweh is with his people. But exile cannot contain him. He submits himself to the hopelessness of landlessness, but he is ruled by hope. He submits himself to the historylessness of exile, but he will make history. He enters the silence of exile but he will speak. And his speech, like his intention, is beyond the limits of exile. He is not defined by the possible or the expected: "For I know the plans I have for you, says Yah-

---

23. See Diepold, *Israels Land,* 149, 166; Walther Zimmerli speaks programmatically of a new beginning at the nadir, "Plans for Rebuilding after the Catastrophe of 587," in *I Am Yahweh,* trans. D. W. Stott, ed. W. Brueggemann (Atlanta: John Knox, 1982) 111.1.

weh, plans for welfare and not for evil, to give you a future and a hope. Then you will call upon me and come and pray to me, and I will hear you. You will seek me and find me; when you seek me with all your heart" (Jer 29:11-13). He has an alternative design (see Isa 55:8-9). He will be found (Deut 4:29-31; Isa 55:6-7). He will turn Israel's fortune.[24]

"I will be found by you, says Yahweh, and I will restore your fortunes and gather you from all the nations and all the places where I have driven you, says Yahweh, and I will bring you back to the place from which I sent you into exile" (Jer 29:14). That is the ultimate word of biblical faith. It is the word spoken to the first fathers in exile (Gen 12:1-3) and the affirmation of the last man at Calvary. It is the surprise of Easter that lies beyond all our landless and landed expectations. Exile ended history because the two are antithetical. But exile did not end Yahweh's will for history, and he will, as he has before, begin anew to make another history. The Bible never denies that there is landlessness or that it is deathly. But it rejects every suggestion that landlessness is finally the will of Yahweh. Exiles, like the old sojourners, live in this hope and for this plan that outdistances all reasonable hypotheses about history. The exiles know about endings and about waiting. They find it to be a beginning beyond expectation, nearly beyond celebration, but so his plan always is.

So Jeremiah anticipates the beginning of a new history that will begin where history is not supposed to begin, with the landless outcasts. Thus this same one who had his innards torn apart by the risk to death of his people who could discern nothing awaited a new coming of Yahweh who never finally wills landlessness.

His entry into the new history, and therefore the entry of Israel, is presented in the strange narrative of Jeremiah 32.[25] The narrative aspects are simple. Jeremiah goes to buy the land belonging to his family. He secures it by careful, legal means. He buys it precisely at the moment of total land-loss. There is no convincing human reason for such an act. Wisdom is violated, and he acts in the foolishness of God's power (1 Cor 1:18-31), the God who works newness precisely in such a time.

It is not a noticeable act, although it is publicly recorded. But it is an act quite parallel to that of father Abraham, who left everything for the sake of unlikely promise. In that case it was like this: "To your descendants I give this land" (Gen 15:18). And history had begun, and all the rest were

24. Elmer A. Martens, "Motivations for the Promise of Israel's Restoration to the Land in Jeremiah and Ezekiel" (Ann Arbor: University Microfilms, 1972) 172–96, has carefully considered the pertinent evidence for the formula.

25. Compare Diepold, *Israels Land*, 129–35.

waiting to see if he would. And this history begins in a like statement: "Houses and fields and vineyard shall again be bought in this land" (Jer 32:15). The rhetoric is not so clean as Gen 15:6 in which "Abraham believed Yahweh." But it is the same. Jeremiah believed Yahweh, and he acted. With this promise, an alternative history had begun, an alternative open only to trusting exiles who would receive land they could not seize. The promise is explicit and elaborated on in Jer 32:42-44:

> Just as I have brought all this great evil upon this people, so I will bring upon them all the good that I promise them. Fields shall be bought in this land of which you are saying, It is a desolation, without man or beast; it is given into the hands of the Chaldeans. Fields shall be bought for money, and deeds shall be signed and sealed and witnessed. . . .

It is waiting on his good word (see Josh 23:14-16), to see if that his how history is.

As usual, the act is simple and not hard to understand. It is the words that illuminate and draw our attention. Following the programmatic statement of Jer 32:15, vv. 16-35 offer two extended speeches characterizing the turn to the new history. The recital by Yahweh is in lawsuit speech, indictment and sentence. That is unexceptional, and it is intended that Israel should not miss the covenantal significance of land-loss. But remarkably, the statement is introduced in this way: "Behold, I am Yahweh, the God of all flesh; is anything too hard for me?" The question echoes that to Abraham in Gen 18:14. There it was the beginning of history by the One who brings into existence what is not. Here it is an end of history by the One who brings to nought what is. For Abraham and Sarah it seemed not possible for history to begin with a child of promise, for it violated their reason and conventional presupposition. For Jeremiah's time it seems not possible for history to end in exile, for that also violated the reason of conventional expectation. But Yahweh does begin history. He gives land. And he does end history. He takes away land. Israel does not deal with a safe, predictable, conventional God but with one free to work his purpose. And so this terrifying word *pela'*, "impossible," is used to assert his freedom against anything taken for granted. He does the thing that is too hard. He gives the land to Babylon that for so long seemed to belong to Israel. Impossible!

But the other speech, shrewdly set in juxtaposition to this history-ending assertion of Yahweh, is a prayer by Jeremiah who no longer reflects on land-loss, but is turned to the remarkable new word of v. 15 (vv. 16-25).

Jeremiah reflects on the potential of v. 15 and its future. He uses parallel words:

> "Ah Lord Yahweh ! It is thou who hast made the heavens and the earth by thy great power and by thy outstretched arm! *Nothing is too hard for thee,* who showest steadfast love . . . whose name is Yahweh of hosts . . . whose eyes are open to all the ways of men . . . who hast shown signs and wonders in the land of Egypt. . . . Thou didst bring thy people Israel out of the land of Egypt . . . thou gavest them this land. . . ." (Jer 32:17-22)

The prayer of Jeremiah (vv. 16-25) stands in heavy tension with the lawsuit speech of Yahweh (vv. 26-35) that follows. One looks back to the fracture. The other looks forward to amazement. And between the two, history has turned. One impossibility is as great as the other. The language has shifted. The lawsuit speech is about the disobedience of "they" (Israel) and that is how history ends. The prayer of Jeremiah is about the "Thou" of Yahweh and that is why history begins anew. Talk of "they" is about a hopeless past: speech about "Thou" is about hopeful future. The new history is radically different because it is rooted not in Israel but totally in Yahweh who does what is impossible. His most impossible deed is landed history for exiles. But that prayer is typological and makes the appeal for new impossibility by a recital of previous life-giving impossibilities.

The turn is assured and the promise is secured in the decisive announcement of Jer 32:37-41 (compare Gen 15:6):

> Behold,
> > I will gather them . . .
> > I will bring them back to this place, and
> > I will make them dwell in safety. . . .
> > I will give them one heart. . . .
> > I will make with them an everlasting covenant . . .
> > I will put the fear of me in their hearts. . . .
> > I will rejoice in doing them good, and
> > I will plant them in this land in faithfulness. . . .

And at the center of this extraordinary new initiative is the central formula of covenant: "And they shall be my people, and I will be their God." And history has begun again. It is like the old history in many ways, and appeal is richly made to old history. But it is radically different. Now the future of his history rests more totally with Yahweh. He takes new responsibility for history.

Jeremiah more than any other has led Israel into and through radical land-loss. He has penetrated the inscrutable will of Yahweh who wills exile and resolves to do his special new history precisely among exiles.

8.

"NONE TO COMFORT"

THE SECOND HISTORY OF ISRAEL, HISTORY IN THE LAND, CAME TO AN abrupt end when the landed ones thought it would not. The end of that history had begun very early, likely with the announcement to David that "the sword shall never depart from your house" (2 Sam 12:10).[1] But even if the end of that history were in process for a long time, few noticed it. And now in the words of Jeremiah and the invasion of Nebuchadnezzar, landed history was ended, unmistakably and irrevocably.

The kings could hardly entertain that radical notion. They engaged in self-deception and desperate hope. Zedekiah, for all landed Israel, put the question to Jeremiah, "Is there any word from Yahweh?" (Jer 37:17). And that now is the key question for Israel. That is characteristically the key question for landed ones losing land. When it is lost we wonder if that is all. Is the loss of land the end of covenant? Are the old traditions exhausted? Is the silence of God forever? Or is it an eclipse that will pass, and he will speak again? The question is not now a question about the nature of history, that is, does it persist and evolve in always new forms? It is a God question. It asks about the character of God, about his capacity to bring newness where all is ended, about his power to speak a word that will shatter the silence at the end of history. Can he speak a new word that will begin in a new shape what has so clearly ended? Nor can he squeeze some more history out of the old forms, but can he come from some other direction and give a new gift?

---

1. It is highly improbable that this verse belongs to Dtr, which constitutes the main material of this "history to exile." Nevertheless it is reasonable to conclude that Dtr has made use of this earlier material in a clearly programmatic way. Compare R. A. Carlson, *David the Chosen King: A Traditio-Historical Approach to the Second Book of Samuel*, E. J. Sharpe and S. Rudman (Stockholm: Almqvist & Wiksell, 1964) 76, 158–59, 213. This is supported by the shrewd observation of the parallel of 7:15.

The crunch at the end of the second history concerns continuity and discontinuity. Landed folks want to cling to continuities and believe that old forms surely continue. But the wrenching of 587 and the discernment of the prophets are about discontinuity. The land is really lost, and history is really ended. There is no king, no temple, no royal city, no Israel. It is ended. But at the same time those who dared to speak of a new history now beginning could do so only in terms of the old history, for they had no other images or models. But the use of such images inevitably suggested that the old history really continues in some way, when surely it does not.

But for all the continuity of images, this moment in biblical faith concerns clear, sharp discontinuity. We shall not understand the boldness and risk of announcing the new history rooted in exile, the life called forth from death (see Rom 4:17), unless we see that the old history is ended. Thus the beginnings of this third history, from exile to land, is as radical as the first history beginning in Gen 12:1-3; see Heb 11:12. This third history produced an enormous amount of literature, reflective material that considered in various ways the *brutality* of history ending and the *amazement* of history beginning again.[2] They are reflections by Israel who knew intuitively that if there is any new history for this people, it will be discerned only in this dead body of Israel. There is no other form it can take. And that is the enigma of hoping at all.

Lamentations and the "No" of God

Nowhere is the drastic discontinuity more clearly expressed than in the poetry of Lamentations. The tragic reversal of Israel concerns the end of what had seemed forever. So Israel is presented like a homeless, forsaken widow who has abruptly lost everything and has nowhere to turn for help (see Isa 47:1-7). This poetry most powerfully brings Israel into an articulation of landlessness, homelessness, abandonment. Israel in this poetry is between histories.

The governing word that seems to express this sense of ultimate homelessness is *'in,* the total, radical negation that Hans-Joachim Kraus calls the "no of God."[3] And now Israel receives his non-negotiable, unqualified "no" about every dimension of historical existence.

2. On the literature of the exile see Peter R. Ackroyd, *Exile and Restoration,* OTL (Philadelphia: Westminster, 1968), and Enno Janssen, *Juda in der Exilszeit: Ein Beitrag zur Frage der Entstehung des Judentums,* FRLANT 69 (Göttingen: Vandenhoeck & Ruprecht, 1956).

3. Hans-Joachim Kraus, *Klagelieder,* BKAT 20 (Neukirchen-Vluyn: Neukirchener, 1960) 34. See also Norman K. Gottwald, *Studies in the Book of Lamentations,* SBT 1/14 (Naperville, Ill.: Allenson, 1962).

Israel has "none to comfort" (1:2, 9, 17, 21). Israel has "none to help her" (1:7; see 1:3, 5:5, 5:8). It is the end of everything. "They are not" (see Jer 31:15; Lam. 5:7), and Israel must cope. Israel copes in this poetry in the staggering announcement of a new possibility rooted not in Israel but in the promise of Yahweh. In this most helpless circumstance, Israel can hope and can imagine a new history, one rooted in the character of God himself (3:22-24, 31-33).

Here is the vocabulary of the new history: *hesed, raham, 'emunah!* The language is that used in Hos 2:20 long before, in which a new beginning is announced by Yahweh after another debacle, that of the Northern Kingdom. It is a beginning not rooted in Israel but in the fidelity of Yahweh who keeps his promises. Israel must trust the land-giver and the land-promiser precisely when there is no land.

In the poetry of Lamentations Israel learns that this destroyed city is its home.[4] That is where it must be rooted. But it also learns that the language of promise is the only way to be there.[5] The language of Yahweh's faithful promise is the language for the exile. Only that language stands against rootlessness.

"I Will Restore Your Fortunes"

From hope comes a new history, from exile toward the land. That kind of newness is hard to talk about. And so in the years just after the expulsion from the land, there is a flood of new literature trying to talk about new history. Writers, speakers, poets try in a variety of ways to utter the unexpected and unutterable newness, that Yahweh begins a new history with exiles. And that new history is toward the land. Here we will consider four efforts to express the beginning of the new history, a new history begun in the same barrenness in which Abraham and Sarah began Israel's first trusting venture to land.

The first of these attempts to speak about another history when history in land is ended is Jeremiah. The very one who has spoken the most harsh, unwelcome words to Israel did not forget his entire commission. And now after the end of history, he addressed himself to the call "to build and to plant" (1:10).

4. Compare Heinrich Böll describes the pathos with which, as a postwar German, he discovered that "this destroyed city was his homeland," and that Germans cannot finally be *bodenlos* because their roots are in their language. It was so for Israel.

5. Jürgen Moltmann, *The Crucified God: The Cross of Christ as the Foundation and Criticism of Christian Theology,* trans. R. A. Wilson and J. Bowden (New York: Harper & Row, 1974) 173, contrasts the "language of promise" and the "language of facts."

The central phrase of Jeremiah's new initiative is in the formula *shuv shevot.* While there are several ways in which the phrase could be translated[6] we may retain the conventional reading, "restore fortunes." There are scattered earlier uses as in Zeph 2:7, in which the poet, surely before 587, announces the radical action of God in working a beginning just when the end had most surely come. (Compare also Amos 9:14, which may or may not be early, but surely reflects the same radical faith.) Norman K. Gottwald has seen that 587 B.C.E., the end of history in the land, is reported under the theme of tragic reversal, not only tragic, but total and radical. Now in this literature of Jeremiah, we have anticipation that this reversal will also be reversed. And it is the healing reversal of tragic reversal that is the meaning of Jeremiah's much used phrase.

It is also the case that this phrase says most decisively what the Bible wishes to say about exile and land. Indeed, here is the heart of the good news of the gospel: things that seem hopeless need not stay as they are. Things that seem hopelessly lost, closed, and dead are the very region of God's new action. The reversal of destiny is not some clever trick of human ingenuity, but it is the action of God himself when all human ingenuity has failed. Nor is the reversal of destiny some psychological or spiritual change, but it is the radical transformation of a historical, political situation.

That is the good news, that God transforms those who are displaced and makes them a home, gives to them secure turf. And the good news is precisely to exile and precisely when no prospect for land is anywhere visible. Those are the only terms on which the new history could be initiated and that is the central thrust of a biblical understanding of land, that it is freely given gift to undeserving exiles in a context without expectation by a God who is able radically to reorientate the character of historical existence. He is the one who inverts destinies and restores fortunes that are not only lost, but given up as hopeless:

> The bows of the mighty are broken,
>   but the feeble gird on strength.
> Those who were full have hired themselves out for bread,
>   but those who were hungry have ceased to hunger.
> The barren has borne seven,
>   but she who has many children is forlorn.
> Yahweh kills and brings to life;
>   he brings down to Sheol and raises up.

---

6. Compare Elmer A. Martens, "Motivations for the Promises of Israel's Restoration to the Land in Jeremiah and Ezekiel" (Ann Arbor: University Microfilms, 1972) 172–96.

> Yahweh makes poor and makes rich;
> > he brings low, he also exalts.
> He raises up the poor from the dust;
> > he lifts the needy from the ash heap,
> to make them sit with princes
> > and inherit a seat of honor. (1 Sam 2:4-8)

Clearly the issue of land and landlessness is in the picture here. This is the peculiar understanding of Yahweh-Israel-land held in the Bible. It is incredible to landed folks, unbelievable to exiles, but believed by the poets who articulated the new history when all history seemed ended.

So Jeremiah announces this remarkable transformation of historical existence. His announcement is about the reliable *hesed* of Yahweh when all seemed voided:

> The people who survived the sword
> > found grace in the wilderness;
> when Israel sought for rest,
> > Yahweh appeared to him from afar.
> I have loved you with an everlasting love;
> > therefore I have continued my faithfulness to you.
> Again I will build you, and you shall be built,
> > O virgin Israel! ...
> Again you shall plant vineyards
> > upon the mountains of Samaria,
> the planters shall plant,
> > and shall enjoy the fruit. (Jer 31:2-5)

The unexpected announcement is that love is everlasting (see the litany of Psalm 136), and it abides when temple, city, and king all are gone. Yahweh entrusted these institutions to Israel, and they have perished. The covenant loyalty he retained by his own initiative, and now it functions to do what no other can do. The word of this everlasting commitment is to build: The exhausted whore is renewed as a virgin (Isa 40:30-31; see Amos 5:2). Where there had been grief (31:15) now there is joy and dancing, for the new age has come (see 31:10-14). The prophet employs the formula of new history, again with the themes of rebuilding and rejoicing:

> Behold, I will restore the fortunes of the tents of Jacob,
> > and have compassion on his dwellings;
> the city shall be rebuilt upon its mound,
> > and the palace shall stand where it used to be.
> Out of them shall come songs of thanksgiving,
> > and the voices of those who make merry. (Jer 30:18-19)

The new history begins in his attentive compassion and ends with the covenant formula:

> Their prince shall be one of themselves [as prescribed in Deut 17:14-20],
>   their ruler shall come forth from their midst;
> I will make him draw near, and he shall approach me,
>   for who would dare of himself to approach me? says Yahweh.
> And you shall be my people,
>   and I will be your God. (Jer 30:21-22)[7]

The tradition of Jeremiah sees that any new history must finally be history that leads to Zion. W. D. Davies has shown that valuing the land is centrally expressed in the Jerusalem temple.[8] In this poetic vision, destroyed Jerusalem is not only restored, but it is established as center of a coherent, well-ordered communal life, the very antithesis of exile, in which there is satisfaction, rest, and renewal.

The prose passages of promise are probably derived from the poet. But the point is nonetheless sharp and clear. Newness comes where it is not expected because of the One who does surprises. He speaks and acts in the first person. He is cause and Lord of the new history:

> Behold, I will bring to it health and healing,
>   and I will heal them and reveal to them abundance of prosperity
>   and security.
> I will restore the fortunes of Judah and the fortunes of Israel,
>   and rebuild them as they were at first.
> I will cleanse them from all the guilt of their sin against me,
>   and I will forgive all the guilt of their sin and rebellion against
>   me.
> And this city shall be to me a name of joy, a praise and a glory before
> all the nations of the earth . . . they shall fear and tremble because of
> all the good and all the prosperity I provide for it. (33:6-9)

And the center of it all is transformed:

> In this place of which you say, "It is a waste without man or beast,"
> in the cities of Judah and the streets of Jerusalem that are desolate,

---

7. Hans Walter Wolff, *The Old Testament: A Guide to Its Writings*, trans. K. R. Crim (Philadelphia: Fortress Press, 1973) 32–35, 51–56, has shown how this formula expresses the intent of two exilic works P and Dtr, which have very different nuances, but together form the complement expressed in the formula.

8. W. D. Davies, *The Gospel and the Land: Early Christianity and Jewish Territorial Doctrine* (Los Angeles: Univ. of California Press, 1974) 130–54.

without man or inhabitant or beast, there shall be heard again the
voice of mirth and the voice of gladness, the voice of the bridegroom
and the voice of the bride, the voices of those who sing. . . . (vv. 10-11)

This poetry asks of its hearers incredible trust in a word against all the
data. Jeremiah is very clear. Israel does not belong to Babylon nor does it
belong to exile. It belongs to Yahweh in this alternative history, possessed
by these words that have no authority other than the compulsion of the
fidelity of their speaker. Finally the visionary must return to Israel's most
elemental promises:

If I have not established my covenant with day and night and the
ordinances of heaven and earth, then I will reject the descendants of
Jacob and David my servant and will not choose one of his descendants to rule over the seed of Abraham, Isaac, and Jacob. For I will
restore their fortunes, and will have mercy upon them. (33:25-26)

Israel must choose between the data at hand and the word so utterly free
of the data. That is always Israel's ultimate choice. And when it believes
the data at hand, it becomes either oppressed slave or cynical master. But
when it trusts the word of an alternative history, it is freed for peace and
joy, even in Babylon.

"This Land Shall Fall as Your Inheritance"

The second remarkable attempt to articulate the new history toward the
land is Ezekiel. The tradition of Ezekiel is as enigmatic and problematic as
any in the prophetic tradition. It is also the most radical, for it announces
both the end of land history and the beginning of new history in most
decisive terms. In the earlier chapters (4–5) he dramatizes the end. And
then in unmistakable terms he declares:

An end! The end has come upon the four corners of the land. Now
the end is upon you, and I will let loose my anger upon you, and will
judge you according to your ways; and I will punish you for all your
abominations. And my eye will not spare you, nor will I have pity;
but I will punish you for your ways, while your abominations are in
your midst. (Ezek 7:2-4)

Interestingly the harsh words are addressed not to Israel but to the land.
The end first articulated by Amos is now actualized.

In vv. 5-9 many of the same formulas are utilized in his heavily stylized
way, but now the address is to the inhabitants of the land:

> Disaster after disaster! Behold, it comes. An end has come, the end
> has come; it has awakened against you. Behold, it comes. Your doom
> has come to you, O inhabitant of the land; the time has come, the
> day is near, a day of tumult, and not of joyful shouting upon the
> mountains. (vv. 5-7)

The announcement of the crisis for the land, both from without and from
within, is total. The people are to be dislodged. The land itself is to be
rejected.

And then the prophet adds this other strange image: Yahweh himself
departs from the land and from the city. The damage being done because
of the abomination is not only to land and to people but to Yahweh himself. He does not simply choose to leave, but he is forced out by conditions
he cannot tolerate: "The guilt of the house of Israel and Judah is exceedingly great; the land is full of blood, and the city full of injustice; for they
say, 'Yahweh has forsaken the land, and Yahweh does not see'" (9:9; see
7:23). In 9:9, he apparently forsakes. But in 8:6, he is forced out: "Son of
man, do you see what they are doing, the great abominations that the
house of Israel are committing here, to drive me far from my sanctuary?"
The imagery is much more extreme than that of Jeremiah. In Jeremiah the
prophet and perhaps Yahweh grieve over Israel's exile. But now Yahweh
himself is an exile. He is situated, along with other exiles, in Babylon. In
making the image powerful, Ezekiel has radicalized the history of Yahweh.
Not only is history over for Israel. History has ended for Yahweh as well.
We have earlier seen Yahweh to be a God whose glory is seen in wilderness
(Exod 16:10). And in the New Testament Jesus on the cross is the presentation of the homeless God.[9] He is at the disposal of his people and is
forced out of his land by the work of his people.

In our consideration of land in the Bible, exile is not only a decisive
turn for the people of Israel, it is also a decisive turn in the history of God.
Ezekiel has a high vision of holiness of God, but he is equally aware of the
peculiarness of this God who is not serene in his place, not immune to the
tribulations of his people but is decisively affected by their destiny.

First, God himself is exiled. This surely is the only God in history who
is exiled. The text puts it both ways, that he is forced to leave and that he
chooses to leave. It is not enough that we see Israel as a people destined for
land but now it is clear that Yahweh is also intended for land. And the radical issue is now raised about land and its meaning for Yahweh's character.

Second, we have previously seen that Israel's occupation of land is
covenantal, and when covenant is violated, land is lost. But now it is clear

---

9. Moltmann, *The Crucified God*, chaps. 5 and 6.

that Yahweh's being in the land is also covenantal. His removal from the land is derived from covenant commitments. Surely there is no other God so at the disposal of his partner's actions. He suffers with and because of them. The end of history is a fresh staggering statement about Yahweh.

Third, Ezekiel's language consistently makes a double focus upon departure from land and departure from city. As we move into this third history, the city with its temple takes on increasing importance. Israel, according to the imagery of Ezekiel, is now with an emptiness at its center.[10] The central symbols of state religion are now void of meaning. History with its decisive and demanding movement robs every historical and institutional pretension, and Israel's watch becomes a reflection on absence.

Fourth, Yahweh's exile is with Israel. Biblical faith consistently refuses to choose between land and people. Nonetheless, if being in land is a covenantal commitment for both Israel and Yahweh, then it is also possible that exile is covenantal. As the glory was in the wilderness, so the glory is along with Israel in exile. This is the boldness and radicalness of Ezekiel's land thinking, that glory lives in exile, with this humiliated, abandoned people. It is in exile that Yahweh in his glory feeds Israel. It is in his exile that Yahweh begins history anew. The themes are unthinkable in such combination, but this new history begins precisely in such an unthinkable situation, where history to exiles for land must inevitably begin.

Yahweh's sovereignty is in his peculiar capacity to end history:

> And I will make the land a desolation and a waste; and her proud might shall come to an end; and the mountains of Israel shall be so desolate that none shall pass through. Then they will know that I am Yahweh, when I have made the land a desolation and a waste because of all their abominations which they have committed. (Ezek 33:28-29)

But his sovereignty is equally apparent to Ezekiel in his capacity to initiate history. Yahweh will not forever be exiled from his place. Nor will he forever permit his people to be landless. The prophet announces the new initiative of Yahweh when it all seemed over:

> It is not for your sake, O house of Israel, that I am about to act, but for my holy name, which you have profaned among the nations to which you came. And I will vindicate the holiness of my great name,

---

10. Ezekiel 9:3 and 10:4 affirm that "the glory has departed."

which has been profaned among the nations, and which you have
profaned among them. . . .
For I will take you from the nations, and
    gather you from all the countries, and
    bring you into your own land.
    I will sprinkle clean water upon you, and you shall be clean from
        all your uncleannesses, and from all your idols
    I will cleanse you. A new heart
    I will give you, and a new spirit
    I will put within you; and
    I will take out of your flesh the heart of stone and give you a heart
        of flesh. And
    I will put my spirit within you. . . .
You shall dwell in the land . . . and
you shall be my people, and I will be your God. (Ezek 36:22-28)

This extraordinary declaration contains a variety of important themes.
Yahweh's new act is on a different basis. It is no longer to value a people or
even to keep a promise, but it is for his own sake and reputation. If a new
history is now to begin, the ground for it must be rooted in Yahweh himself and not in Israel. That source for land history is as radical as the motif
of the exiled God. It is remarkably assured and, as W. Zimmerli has
asserted, is indeed *sola gratia*.[11] Nothing is required or expected of Israel—
which, of course, means Israel cannot damage land history as in the past.
The will for land for Israel is rooted in Yahweh's very character as a
covenant-maker and -keeper.

The old call for repentance (see 33:11-12) is no longer issued or
expected. It is no longer thought by Yahweh that obedience will yield a
new existence in the land.[12] Thus the motif of repentance is transformed
to the gift of new heart and new spirit. Now the possibility of land is
exclusively Yahweh's initiative. He works, as it were, from both sides of the
relationship, not only to address Israel but also to assure Israel's response.

In the midst of this enormous assertion, Ezekiel declares the
covenant formula of the Old Testament (see v. 28b). What of course has

11. Walther Zimmerli, "The Word of God in the Book of Ezekiel," in *History and
Hermeneutic*, ed. R. W. Funk (New York: Harper and Row, 1967) 13 concludes: "But what is
the purpose of all this emotional activity on the part of Yahweh? 'For the sake of my name':
thus runs the divine answer in the mouth of Ezekiel. In Ezekiel we hear a curious and strange
formulation of *sola gratia*."

12. Contrast the radical grace with the stress of Dtr. On the latter, see Hans Walter Wolff,
"The Kerygma of the Deuteronomic Historical Work," in *The Vitality of Old Testament Traditions*, ed. W. Brueggemann and H. W. Wolff (Atlanta: John Knox, 1975) 83–100.

often been noticed but less frequently remarked is that this formula is accompanied by a land formula: "You shall dwell in the land. . . . you shall be my people, and I will be your God." Surely the combination of *land formula* and *covenant formula* is not accidental. The two ideas, in land and in covenant, belong together. Ezekiel cannot imagine covenant apart from the land. Therefore what follows is not about covenant but about land as a covenant gift: "And I will summon the grain and make it abundant and lay no famine upon you. I will make the fruit of the tree and the increase of the field abundant" (vv. 29-30). (Compare the covenant renewal formula applied to land in Hos 2:21-22.) The description of land echoes the imagery of creation as well as the speeches of the boundary (Gen 1:22; 8:17). The speech also recalls the build/plant theme of Jeremiah:

> . . . I will cause the cities to be inhabited, and the waste places shall be rebuilt. . . . Then the nations that are left round about you shall know that I, Yahweh, have rebuilt the ruined places, and replanted that which was desolate. I, Yahweh, have spoken, and I will do it. (36:33-36)

And the assertion ends with a formula of recognition. "Then they will know that I am Yahweh" (v. 38b).

That is how he is known in his sovereignty. He is known as Yahweh when he ends history (33:29). Now he is known as Yahweh when he begins history. Israel and the nations are to discern this strange one unlike any other god who can create and destroy, who can bring light and darkness, who can deny land and bestow land.

In his bold imagery of resurrection in 37:1-14, the prophet again speaks about the end of exile and return to the land. Again it is being in land that is both the destiny of Israel and the mark of Yahweh's lordship:

> Behold, I will open your graves, and raise you from your graves, O my people; and I will bring you home into the land of Israel. . . . And I will put my Spirit within you, and you shall live, and I will place you in your own land; then you shall know that I, Yahweh, have spoken, and I have done it, says Yahweh. (37:12, 14)

Land is governed by word. Word is embodied in land arrangements. And the land-giving word does two things. First it brings Israel home, never meant to be homeless. Second, it establishes Yahweh's sovereignty. It is land that fully permits Israel to be Israel. It is land that fully permits Yahweh to be known as Yahweh. It is land that permits Yahweh and Israel to have history together.

Thus Ezekiel's speech envisions history beyond exile. That is the purpose of prophetic poetry, to permit exiles to live in the assurance of landedness that they need not merit, which Yahweh will not deny and which the nations, even Babylon, cannot prevent. In this history beyond exile, Ezekiel presents three images that bear upon our theme, although others might be noted.

First, Yahweh's exile is ended. He returns to the temple in the same manner in which he left it (see 43:1-5; 44:4). The glory that had departed to Babylon, or had been driven out, has now returned. Obviously the return is not to the same condition, for the temple has been radically restored. In this dramatic imagery, we may note its decisive implication for the temple, that it is symbolic center of the new history. But we must also note that Yahweh is no longer an exiled God. His new history has begun, and as it begins for him, so it begins for Israel.

The second image of land restoration is in 47:13—48:29.[13] Ezekiel engages in a powerful typology, so that the return to land and the reappropriation of the promise are presented after the manner of the land distribution of Joshua. The land has been conquered again by Yahweh. The land distribution proceeds as the original one, and as the first begins Israel's new history in the land, so this begins a new history in the land. The most characteristic word *nahalah*, used repeatedly in this text, affirms that the generation coming out of exile is recipient of all the old covenant promises. Thus the turn from exile to land is presented as God's decisive act of keeping his promise and enfranchising his people when apparently it could not happen. The use of *nahalah* obviously serves to link the generation of exile to the most formative and fundamental images of Israel's memory.

In addition to the details of distribution, we may note one remarkable departure from the old formulation in 47:21-23. Now the alien is treated like the native born. The promise is expansive and inclusive. The new history toward the land has a dimension of graciousness in it. The gift of land is now more decisively a free gift without qualification. It is a stunning statement (contrast 44:9) that aliens shall be included. As we shall see, subsequently the course of this third history is ambiguous and marked by conflict precisely because the aliens are given the inheritance. The very generosity of the gift poses deep problems for the new land and its possessors.

The third dimension of new land that we note is the restoration of the city of Jerusalem as the abode of God. Characteristically Ezekiel presents

---

13. See Georg Christian Macholz, "Noch Einmal: Planungen für der Wiederaufbau noch der Katastrophe von 587," *VT* 19 (1969) 322–52.

the new possibility with exhaustive detail. The new city will be the perfectly designed city. But the point of it all is that it is now to be named, "Yahweh is there" (Ezek 48:35). That is the name for the temple, for the city, for the land, for the history. The new history from exile is not just about free space but about a historical place in which the God of Israel's covenant (see 36:28) is present in the place formerly rejected. Thus rejected place is now inhabited space. Space abandoned by the land-giving God is claimed for the place-occupying God. Finally it is the abiding of the holy one that makes the land credible for Israel.

In this vision of rehabilitated space, Ezekiel has combined the old tribal tradition of *nahalah* and the ultimate royal-Priestly tradition of divine presence in the city. The theme presented in this double focus shows that both Yahweh and Israel together in covenant are in history again on the way to the land.

"Subdue and Fill the Land"

The voices that begin the new history are many and varied. One unlikely expression of the new history for exiles is stated in the Priestly tradition of the Tetrateuch.[14]

While the Priestly tradition is a meditation on cultic presence and a concern for God's glory when God's glory had departed[15] and may be an effort to legitimate certain religious practices and institutions, its major intent is to provide rootage for exiles without roots, to give assurance for those who surely must have doubted the power and/or legitimacy of their faith and practice.

The central theme of P is announced in Gen 1:1—2:4a, the creation story commonly assigned to this sixth-century effort. The land that God now creates for his people is contrasted with chaos (*tohu wabohu*, v. 2; compare Isa 45:18 also referring to exile as chaos). While chaos is a term that may refer in an ontological sense to formlessness, here it describes the historical formlessness of exile. The text contrasts Israel's land of future, characterized by all of Yahweh's blessings, with the land of the present, described as formless and void, dark, surely the experience of the faithful in Babylon.

14. See Walter Brueggemann, "The Kerygma of the Priestly Writers," in *The Vitality of Old Testament Traditions*, 101–13, and the comment of Frank Moore Cross, *Canaanite Myth and Hebrew Epic: Essays in the History of the Religion of Israel* (Cambridge: Harvard Univ. Press, 1973) 296, on P's concern for the land.

15. Claus Westermann, "Die Herrlichkeit Gottes in der Priesterschrift," in *Wort–Gebot–Glaube: Beiträge zur Theologie des Alten Testaments*, ed. H. J. Stoebe, ATANT 59 (Zurich: Zwingli, 1970) 227–49, has demonstrated that "glory" is a primary concern of P.

The promise at the center of this text (Gen 1:28) is a direct and intentional refutation of exilic hopelessness. These promise-blessing mandates are not contextless assertions but careful refutations of exile perceptions to open to Israel the prospect of an alternative history in an alternative land. The text is a denial of every Babylonian claim, every exilic pretension, and every Israelite doubt.[16]

It is in the context of exile that Israel told its best stories. Surely exile is not the only time Israel told stories. But it is important that the exile is the time when all the old stories were placed into a fixed form.[17] Israel went back into its memories, to the time when the history-making, history-summoning words were spoken that gave Israel enduring identity. A central theme of these stories for exiles is that to the *barren* is born the *child of promise*, to the one without future or hope (Jer 29:14) is given the impossible blessing (Gen 11:30; 18:9-15; 25:21; 29:31). Israel's stories now shaped into final form are not about barrenness. Nor are they about children of promise. The stories are about *children of promise to the barren.*[18] That motif is easily transposed: the land is always to the exiles. The old stories invited exiles to look again at their destiny. Their mothers and fathers were not for barrenness, so they are not for homelessness. The stories become protests against exile, denials that the exile of the present is the destiny of the future. Stories of the impossible births are the way these displaced hopers keep alive an alternative history. The stories prevent Israel from accepting the identity Babylon would bestow, for the empire wants to seduce the faithful into accepting a landless way outside history.[19]

16. Cross has noted the same formula in Lev 26:9 (*Canaanite Myth*, 296); see more fully the blessing of vv. 5-6. The refrain is unmistakable: "In the land securely," "in the land," "from the land," and "through your land." The formula both in Lev 26:9 and in Gen 1:28 is directed precisely to exiles who have ceased to yearn for the homeland. Like the secure land, P enjoins Israel also to rest Sabbath rest (Exod 31:12-17; Lev 25:2, 26). This is rest no Babylonian could deny Israel, because she is headed home to rest.

17. Special note should be taken of the important book of John Van Seters, *Abraham in History and Tradition* (New Haven: Yale Univ. Press, 1975). Van Seters has argued that the patriarchal stories are peculiarly appropriate to this period and that there is for many of them no evidence of any older form of them. While his argument is surely overstated and yet to be carefully assessed, it is beyond doubt that the stories have a peculiar appropriateness to this period, even though one may not follow Van Seters in his extreme critical views.

18. On the radical implications of this motif, see Mary C. Callaway, "The Mistress and the Maid," *Radical Religion* 2 (1975) 94–101. Callaway discerns in Paul's use of the motif (Gal 4:21-23) a "class reading" pertinent to our discussion.

19. For example, the narrative of Genesis 23, widely ascribed to P, provides Israel with a certain rootage in exile. Although Israel is a displaced people this narrative preserves assurance of a place in which Israel holds secure title to land; compare John Van Seters, *Abraham*, 293–95.

In the exile Israel told stories of rootage and belonging. It recited genealogies. To outsiders these genealogies seem a tedious bore, but to insiders, they are an index for locating rootage. The genealogies are a guarantee that Israel is not adrift in a vacuum of this present generation but has security and credentials. And as long as Israel can name names, utter their precious sounds, it has a belonging place that no hostile empire can deny.[20]

But the Priestly presentation is not just the action of desperate people collecting historical data. It is an artistic statement designed to give a sense of serenity, order, and coherence. It is constructed with remarkable intentionality. Nowhere is that intentionality clearer than in the formula announced at the beginning in the royal decree of Gen 1:28. It is an imperative but also an affirmation. It is demand but also guarantee. Israel's life is about one thing, secure well-being in control over land. It may well be a nonsensical wish uttered by exiles, but it is uttered by believing exiles, who never doubt that God's new history would end exile and yield rootage in land. God's will for Israel is against current circumstance. He will bring the new blessing to exiles. The same blessing is announced to Noah (Gen 9:1, 7), faithful Israel who trusted in chaos, and then to Abraham (Gen 16:2), to Jacob (28:3-4; 35:11), to Joseph (47:27; 48:3-4), and finally to the liberated ones in Egypt. Yahweh's will for land will finally triumph, and Israel can count on it.

Not Comforted—Comforted

Already in the eighth century, Hosea had announced that Israel is "not pitied" (1:6). And he had envisioned a time when it would again be "pitied" (2:23). In the sixth-century exile, Lamentations, as we have seen, had described Israel as "not comforted."

Hosea had envisioned a reversal and transfiguration of Israel's situation. In the exile, Second Isaiah envisions the same reversal of Israel's

---

20. The function and importance of genealogy have been stressed by Alex Haley, *Roots* (New York: Doubleday, 1976), in which he has shown the importance of genealogy to blacks who have had no remembered past and therefore no historical identity and no power for the historical present. Genealogy provides a "traceable history." Compare "Tracing Roots of the Black Family Tree," *St. Louis Post-Dispatch* (March 14, 1972) 4A. On the function of genealogy in the Old Testament, see Marshall D. Johnson, *The Purpose of Biblical Genealogies*, SNTSMS 8 (Cambridge: Cambridge Univ. Press, 1969); and K. C. Hanson, "The Herodians and Mediterranean Kinship. Part I: Genealogy and Descent," *BTB* 19 (1989) 75–84. Likely the genealogies are much more "interested" sociologically and historically than our usual historical approach would recognize (see Ezra 2:62-63).

exile. He announces that Israel is "comforted."[21] It is this radical transformation of Israel's situation that is at the center of Second Isaiah's
poetry and that requires such powerful lyrical style to say what must be
said.

The largeness of Second Isaiah's vision permits a convergence of many
traditions and the portrayal of many images. In the context of the present
discussion, it is the theme of *return to the land* that is central. It is Second
Isaiah more than any of his exilic antecedents who announces a turn in
history that will bring homeless Israel home again. Whatever else the
poetry means in terms of mission to Gentiles and vicarious, redemptive
suffering, the base line is the return of Israel home again. History is
inverted. Babylonian gods fall before Yahweh's power (46:1-4). Babylonian
tyranny yields to Persian liberation (45:1-7) at the behest of Yahweh. Dry
places in the wilderness are transformed into nourishment (41:17-19).
Forlorn Jerusalem will be restored and rebuilt (44:26). The temple will be
reactivated (44:28). All of that is the new thing (43:18-19) that explodes in
history just when it had seemed closed, managed, and controlled by hopeless, imperial policy.

The new thing is the beginning of a new history for Israel who had
given up on the old history and had concluded that no new history was
possible. It is unexpected history, newness incredible and unexplained,
generated not by kings and rulers, but by the action of the One who forms
light and creates darkness (45:7). The newness comes neither from Israel's
faith nor from Persian generosity. It comes when Yahweh reasserts his rule
over all turf and his restoration of his people in his land. Thus at the center of the poetry of the new history toward land is the enthronement formula of Yahweh's sovereignty:

> . . . say to the cities of Judah,
>   "Behold your God!"
> Behold Yahweh comes with might,
>   and his arm rules for him;
> behold, his reward is with him,
>   and his recompense before him. (Isa 40:9-10)

That is the gospel: "Behold your God!" He comes. He rules. He gathers.
He carries. He leads. That is the new history.

---

21. It is possible that "comfort" represents an important theme in Second Isaiah that con-
sciously responds to the "not comforted" theme of Lamentations. See the uses in Isa 49:13;
51:3, 12, 19; 52:9; and 54:11.

This assertion is matched by the second formula: "who says to Zion, 'Your God reigns'" (52:7).[22] There the cluster of terms presses to speak of newness: peace/good/good tidings/salvation. Second Isaiah makes a connection that will be important to the New Testament and for every homeless group, *Kingship of Yahweh leads to homecoming.* Rule by Yahweh means the end of homelessness because he is a God who wills land for his people. He wills neither chaos nor exile, neither alienation nor homelessness (Isa 45:18-19). He wills homecoming. He acts to have it so. That is the new thing, that in a history of homelessness his powerful purpose for home has intervened, and it is never the same again. To say this radical thing Second Isaiah must utilize the old royal traditions of establishment and rule in the land.

The old land tradition of Abraham and Sarah is used twice. The old promise is still the source of transformation:

> Look to Abraham your father
> and to Sarah who bore you;
> for when he was but one I called him,
> and I blessed him and made him many.
> For Yahweh will comfort Zion;
> he will comfort all her waste places,
> and will make her wilderness like Eden,
> her desert like the garden of Yahweh. (Isa 51:2-3)

Note the double use of "comfort" with the terms Zion and Eden. Transformation concerns well-being in historical placement.

In Isa 54:1-3, the tradition of Sarah's barrenness is again utilized to talk about placement of many heirs in a land filled with prosperity:

> For the children of the desolate one will be more
> than the children of her that is married, says Yahweh.
> Enlarge the place of your tent,
> and let the curtains of your habitations be stretched out;
> hold not back, lengthen your cords
> and strengthen your stakes.
> For you will spread abroad to the right and to the left,
> and your descendants will possess the nations
> and will people the desolate cities.

That tradition announces that Israel is for land and not for exile.

22. See Hans-Joachim Kraus, *Die Königsherrschaft Gottes im Alten Testament: Untersuchungen zu den Liedern von Jahwes Thronbesteigung,* BHT 13 (Tübingen: Mohr/Siebeck, 1951) 102–12, although his judgment about the relationship of Second Isaiah to the Psalmic tradition is doubtful.

The tradition of Noah, surely about the end of chaos and the coming of ordered space (see Gen 9:1, 7), is used for the new landed expectation:

> For this is like the days of Noah to me;
>   as I swore that the waters of Noah
>   should no more go over the earth,
> so I have sworn that I will not be angry with you
>   and will not rebuke you.
> For the mountains may depart
>   and the hills be removed,
> but my steadfast love shall not depart from you,
>   and my covenant of peace shall not be removed. ... (Isa 54:9-10)[23]

The eloquent vision of well-being is concluded with the use of *nahalah*: "This is the *heritage* of the servants of Yahweh and their vindication from me, says Yahweh" (54:17). The flood-tossed, chaos-exposed exiles are now secured. The flood story, reused in the sixth century, now celebrates the supreme, serene rule of God who can push back waters, push back empires, and who will give safe dry place to his people.

In a less emphatic way the tradition of David, land-gainer par excellence, is utilized to announce well-being in the new land (55:3).[24] That imagery slides easily into creation imagery (vv. 12-13; see 51:3), which in any case belongs in the stream of royal tradition. The Davidic appeal, derived from 2 Samuel 7, announces that the exiles are heirs to Yahweh's most fundamental promise of placed well-being.

All of these traditions, of Abraham, Noah, and David as well as that of creation, are about the free gift of land to Yahweh's covenant partner Israel. In all of these, the poet has promised prosperity (see 54:13) that displaces chaos and exile. Lament is turned to joy. Death is turned to life. Exile is turned to land. History is turned and Israel again lives by promises. The scorned captive is the honored ruler (49:7) while the arrogant ruler is a humiliated slave (47:1-5). The total turn of unexpected newness is the kind of which Hannah (1 Sam 2:4-8) and Mary (Luke 2:51-53) sang.

The motif of the new inheritance of land is pointedly articulated in Isa 49:8-9:

---

23. On the relation of chaos and exile, see Walter Brueggemann, "Kingship and Chaos (A Study in Tenth Century Theology)," *CBQ* 33 (1971) 317–32; and idem, "Weariness, Exile, and Chaos (A Motif in Royal Theology)," *CBQ* 34 (1972) 19–38.

24. Compare Otto Eissfeldt, "The Promises of Grace to David in Isaiah 55:1-5," in *Israel's Prophetic Heritage: Essays in Honor of James Muilenburg*, ed. B. W. Anderson and W. Harrelson (New York: Harper & Row, 1962) 196–207. The relation of this text to Lam 3:22-24 is worth noting.

In a time of favor I have answered you,
  in a day of salvation I have helped you;
I have kept you and given you
  as a covenant to the people,
to establish the land,
  to apportion the desolate heritages. . . .
They shall feed along the ways,
  on all bare heights shall be their pasture. . . .
for he who has pity on them will lead them,
  and by springs of water will guide them.
And I will make all my mountains a way,
  and my highways shall be raised up. . . .
For Yahweh has comforted his people,
  and will have compassion on his afflicted. (vv. 8-13)

The time of answering is for reestablishment of fertile, productive, nourishing earth (see Hos 2:21-22; 10:12). It is the restoration of livable turf. The land is redivided to prisoners and other outcasts. The land is gift given by the One who has pity (Hos 2:23), who leads and guides (compare Ps 23:1-3). The outcasts are given places and comforted. Indeed to be comforted is to be given place.

9.

JEALOUS FOR JERUSALEM

Exile history did move to land. History was again on its way. The history-initiating word has been spoken and a new thing was done.

Israel came once again to the land, and again it had to be managed. Israel was determined not to make deathly compromises as in the first entry. Joshua had found the land filled with Canaanites, and his management had to be in that context. Haggai, Zechariah, and Zerubbabel had found it surrounded by Samaritans, and later there were problems with the Edomites and "Arabs." From the landlessness of the exile, Israel came once again to Jerusalem.

Separatism as a Way to Save the Land

Israel had learned about the problem of syncretism,[1] about temptation of being easy with religious alternatives and the dangers of eroding faith for the sake of self-satisfaction. It had learned about the problem of God's transcendence in a place and the possibility that this holy God can and will depart a place that no longer takes him seriously. It had learned about the casual use of power and the consequent loss of land.

Management this time round would avoid every extremity except the extremity of carefulness. And Israel was careful in the extreme. In David's attempt the city was to be used, celebrated, enjoyed. In our current era, the city is to be guarded, protected, kept. The God who leads his people back to Jerusalem and the beginning in the land is disciplined and single-minded, wanting Jerusalem kept and claimed for his exclusive purposes.

---

1. George E. Mendenhall in various articles has characterized monarchic syncretism as "the paganization of Israel."

There is no ambition here beyond the claim of this single, symbolic place (Zech 1:14-17; 8:2-3).

The jealousy of Yahweh for Zion is an appropriate theme under which to understand the new land entry.[2] Yahweh was long identified as jealous that his will be done.[3] But his jealousy had now received a more precise and particular referent, namely, Jerusalem. The jealousy expresses itself for Jerusalem both as threat and as blessing. The land fully under covenant requires his people to be as jealous for covenant as is Yahweh himself (Zech 7:9-10; Mal 3:10-12).[4] The purists had vivid memory and an urgent mission. They were driven to law and order by their passion for the land. And they knew, as the kings had failed to learn, that land is covenantal and will be had on no other terms. As we shall see, in the coming Hellenistic period that view is embarrassingly parochial, as parochial as it sounds to the ones at ease in our own time and place.

In this context the purification and reconstruction under Nehemiah and Ezra can best be understood. In part the return was a political move simply to occupy land and to celebrate the freedom of a particular historical identity there as Jews. It was pragmatic and surely the yearning of any displaced person. But at the same time, it is clear that the didactic and reforming activity of the period was not just to get land. It was to secure a covenantal ordering. It was the attempt to institutionalize a vision. The land, if it was to be retained, would need to be understood, as monarchic Israel had not, in terms of the urgency, precariousness, and graciousness of covenant. The most intentional articulation is found in the prayers of confession in the mouth of Ezra. Ezra traces the pertinent elements:

1. The land is unclean, that is, unacceptable for covenantal life, and must be purged:

---

2. See W. D. Davies, *The Gospel and the Land: Early Christianity and Jewish Territorial Doctrine* (Los Angeles: Univ. of California Press, 1974) 194, ". . . because the Temple and the City are inextricable in Judaism, as we saw, and serve as the quintessence of the land." Compare also 331 and *passim*.

3. On the theme of jealousy, see G. Ernest Wright, *The Old Testament against Its Environment* SBT 1/2 (Chicago: Regnery, 1950) 44–60.

4. Paul D. Hanson, *The Dawn of Apocalyptic: The Historical and Sociological Roots of Jewish Apocalyptic Eschatology*, rev. ed. (Philadelphia: Fortress Press, 1979) 246, agrees that Haggai and Zechariah utilized prophetic themes but only in the interest of their party: "Haggai and Zechariah, by injecting prophetic fervor into the hierocratic program, made that program appealing to the masses, and their accomplishments played no mean role in the ultimate victory of the hierocratic tradition over rival claimants to community leadership." Such a reading seems to me somewhat speculative. It is equally plausible to suggest that the use of prophetic themes served to temper the establishment tendency of their contemporaries.

For we have forsaken thy commandments, which thou didst command by thy servants the prophets, saying, "The land which you are entering, to take possession of it, is a land unclean with the pollutions of the peoples of the lands, with their abominations which have filled it from end to end with their uncleanness. (Ezra 9:10-11)

2. The purification of the land requires an alternative, separatist consciousness:

Therefore give not your daughters to their sons, neither take their daughters for your sons, and never seek their peace or prosperity. . . . (Ezra 9:12; cf. the antithesis in Jer 29:7)

3. The result of such an alternative is land:

. . . that you may be strong, and eat the good of the land, and leave it for an inheritance to your children for ever." (Ezra 9:12)

This is one form of the entire program of Ezra. It is to be noted that the purpose of it all is long life in a secure and prosperous land.

The offenses that most vexed this self-conscious leadership of restoration included several elements:

1. Intermarriage, that is, marriage with nonsectarian Israelites, who did not qualify as "good figs" from Babylon. Thus the urgent call for separatism is in the interest of land retention:

You have trespassed and married foreign women, and so increased the guilt of Israel. Now then make confession to Yahweh the God of your fathers, and do his will; separate yourselves from the peoples of the land and from the foreign wives. . . . All these had married foreign women, and they put them away with their children. (Ezra 10:10-11, 44)

In those days also I saw the Jews who had married women of Ashdod, Ammon, and Moab; and half of their children spoke the language of Ashdod, and they could not speak the language of Judah, but the language of each people. And I contended with them and cursed them and beat some of them and pulled out their hair; and I made them take oath in the name of God, saying, "You shall not give your daughters to their sons, or take their daughters for your sons or for yourselves." (Neh 13:23-25)

And with good reason were they preoccupied with this offense, for the singular model for land-loss was Solomon who "loved many foreign women" (1 Kgs 11:1) and lost the land: "Did not Solomon king of Israel sin on account of such women? . . . Nevertheless foreign women made even him to sin" (Neh 13:26; see Matt 6:29).

2. They did not honor the Sabbath:

> In those days I saw in Judah men treading wine presses on the sabbath, and bringing in heaps of grain and loading them on asses; and also wine, grapes, figs, and all kinds of burdens, which they brought into Jerusalem on the sabbath day; and I warned them on the day when they sold food. . . . Then I remonstrated with the nobles of Judah and said to them, "What is this evil thing which you are doing, profaning the sabbath day? Did not your fathers act in this way, and did not our God bring all this evil on us and on this city? Yet you bring more wrath upon Israel by profaning the sabbath." (Neh 13:15-18)

We have already seen that Sabbath is not only a social arrangement for maintaining humanness but it is a theological affirmation of Yahweh's ownership of the land and of history. And when Israel does not keep Sabbath (see Amos 8:4-6), it acts as though the land is not Yahweh's and can therefore be organized in alternative ways. Thus the call for honoring Sabbath is an insistence upon a right understanding of the continuing source of land.

3. Most peculiarly there emerged—even in this small and intentional community—disparities between the peasants on small farms and the elite who ordered the bureaucracy. One might have thought a community with such a self-conscious vision would have acted differently. But the realities of economic manipulation and political leverage came even here. And it happened that the power class taxed the citizens into debt:

> There were also those who said, "We are mortgaging our fields, our vineyards, and our houses to get grain because of the famine." And there were those who said, "We have borrowed money for the king's tax upon our fields and our vineyards. Now our flesh is as the flesh of our brethren, our children are as their children; yet we are forcing our sons and our daughters to be slaves, and some of our daughters have already been enslaved; but it is not in our power to help." (Neh 5:3-5)

The situation recalls the repeated drama in Israel, of Pharaoh, of Solomon, of Ahab.[5] Each time the voice of indignant poverty cries out

5. Martin Hengel, *Property and Riches in the Early Church: Aspects of a Social History of Early Christianity,* trans. J. Bowden (Philadelphia: Fortress Press, 1974) 15–16, observes the same tension all through Israel's history. That tension also lies behind the conquest theory

(see Exod 22:23-24). And each time land is either lost or another vision of social order displaces the covenantal one. The ultimate immobilization for visionary Israel is here: "for other men have our fields and our vineyards" (Neh 5:5). It is the case that, when others have fields and vineyards, not only is one economically crippled—which was evident—but one has lost the possibility of the promises of Yahweh to Israel. Nothing saving could happen in such a context.

Nehemiah indicts these corruptions of Israel:

> I took counsel with myself, and I brought charges against the nobles and the officials. I said to them, "You are exacting interest, each from his brother." And I held a great assembly against them, and said to them, "We, as far as we are able, have bought back our Jewish brethren who have been sold to the nations; but you even sell your brethren that they may be sold to us!" They were silent, and could not find a word to say. So I said, "The thing that you are doing is not good. Ought you not to walk in the fear of our God to prevent the taunts of the nations our enemies? Moreover I and my brethren and my servants are lending them money and grain. Let us leave off this interest. Return to them this very day their fields, their vineyards, their olive orchards, and their houses, and the hundredth of money, grain, wine, and oil which you have been exacting of them." (Neh 5:7-11)

The program of v. 11 is at the heart of Israelite faith and is a precise refutation of royal confiscation (contrast 1 Samuel 8). A radical reform required return of confiscated good! "They said, 'We will restore these and require nothing from them. We will do as you say'" (v. 12). The encounter is not between honest and dishonest men. There is nothing to suggest illegal exploitation. Rather it is a dispute between two models of community ordering, one conventional after the manner of every highly ordered economic community, the other a radical vision of covenant. The issue is whether the bold vision of the "good figs" can be sustained when the memory of exile cools. It is important to observe in assessing the fanaticism of Ezra that he was rejecting an unexceptional, well-functioning economic arrangement. It was clear that such an arrangement, no matter how pervasive or legitimate, is unacceptable because it denies to the poor "our fields and our vineyards." That is the test of policy! Though cast in different language it is again the dispute of royal prerogative and tribal inheritance in which the limits against legitimated power are firm.

of George E. Mendenhall, "The Hebrew Conquest of Palestine," in *BARead* 3 (Garden City, N.Y.: Doubleday, 1970) 100–120.

The covenantal dimension of the land question is unmistakable in the prayer of Ezra in its concluding statement:

> Behold, we are slaves this day; in the land that thou gavest to our fathers to enjoy its fruit and its good gifts, behold, we are slaves. And its rich yield goes to the kings whom thou has set over us because of our sins; they have power also over our bodies and over our cattle at their pleasure, and we are in great distress. (Neh 9:36-37)

How incongruous! We are slaves in our land. And the alternative is clear: "Because of all this we make a firm covenant and write it, and our princes, our Levites, and our priests set their seal to it" (v. 38).

The verse suggests two appeals to Israel's very oldest tradition. First the Levites are pervasive in the reform of Ezra and Nehemiah. While the Levites are historically obscure and difficult to identify, they surely belong to old traditions that interpret the land covenantly.[6] They provide links between the Ezra-Nehemiah attention to land and that of Deuteronomy. The reform appeals to very ancient convictions in Israel.

Second, if George Mendenhall is right in his bold suggestion about conquest as a covenantal peasant revolt against oppressive Canaanite city-kings, it should not surprise us that covenant with Yahweh is viewed here as a weapon against a hierarchical denial of land and as the radical articulation of an alternative way of understanding, distributing, and managing land.[7] Mendenhall's suggestion locates land distribution as the identifying and most urgent mark of revolutionary Yahwism.[8] Such a connection helps discern the rootage and passion of Nehemiah's insistence.

6. Hanson, *The Dawn,* 209, speaks of the "disenfranchised Levites." In this he follows the reconstruction of the history of the priesthood of Frank Moore Cross, *Canaanite Myth and Hebrew Epic: Essays in the History of the Religion of Israel* (Cambridge: Harvard Univ. Press, 1973) 195–215. On the theological placement of the Levites, see Gerhard von Rad, "The Levitical Sermons in I and II Chronicles," in *The Problem of the Hexateuch and Other Essays,* trans. E. W. T. Dicken (New York: McGraw-Hill, 1966) 267–80, and Jacob M. Myers, "The Kerygma of the Chronicler," *Int* 20 (1960) 259–73.

7. There is an emerging literature concerning a sociological understanding of the traditions about the land. Hanson has done this most effectively by utilizing Mannheim's categories of *Ideology and Utopia.* Especially George E. Mendenhall and Norman K. Gottwald are developing a contrast between the early Mosaic view of a society of liberation and the monarchy. The monarchy echoes the old ideology of Canaanite city-kings and is in turn taken up by the later elite urban priesthood. In addition to the works of Cross, Hanson, and Mendenhall already cited, see especially Gottwald's *The Tribes of Yahweh: A Sociology of the Religion of Liberated Israel, 1250–1050 B.C.E.* (Maryknoll, N.Y.: Orbis, 1976).

8. See Norman K. Gottwald, "Biblical Theology or Biblical Sociology?" *Radical Religion* 2 (1975) 42–57.

The Levites and the notion of Yahweh's land are held together in the covenantal vows of the people. The oath includes:

1. Allegiance to Torah: ". . . join with their brethren, their nobles, and enter into a curse and an oath to walk in God's law which was given by Moses the servant of God, and to observe and do all the commandments of Yahweh our Lord and his ordinances and his statutes" (Neh 10:29).

2. Avoidance of mixed marriages: "We will not give our daughters to the peoples of the land or take their daughters for our sons . . ." (v. 30).

3. Honoring of Sabbath and jubilee: ". . . and if the peoples of the land bring in wares or any grain on the sabbath day to sell, we will not buy from them on the sabbath or on a holy day; and we will forego the crops of the seventh year and the exaction of every debt" (v. 31).

The oath concludes with a vow of offerings, which acknowledges Yahweh's sovereignty over land and Israel's readiness to receive it from him: "We obligate ourselves to bring the first fruits of our ground and the first fruits of all fruit of every tree, year by year, to the house of Yahweh" (v. 35; cf. vv. 36-39).

It is not our intent to confine the reconstruction under Ezra to a concern for land. However, such a consideration invites us to understand the movement in a fresh way. The work of Ezra is often seen as a legalistic, cultic sectarianism, and no doubt it has that dimension. But the data can be differently understood if we consider the powerful memory of land-loss through syncretism and the passion for covenant as a way to survive in history.

The epitome of the movement is no doubt expressed in Nehemiah's last statement: "Thus I cleansed them from everything foreign, and I established the duties of the priests and Levites, each in his work; and I provided for the wood offering, at appointed times, and for the first fruits" (13:30-31). His claim is fully separatist. But the separatism can be understood in ways other than legalistic. The foreigners to be shunned represent an alternative ideology already apparent in the syncretism of Solomon and Ahab. The Levites are teachers who insist on Israel's alternative way in history. The reform is not a desperate moment of parochialism but an attempt to order life, community, and land in covenantal ways and to avoid the Syro-Hittite alternative that denies Israel's holy destiny.[9]

---

9. George E. Mendenhall, "The Monarchy" *Int* 29 (1975), 155–70, has applied the label "Syro-Hittite" to the dominant influences on the United Monarchy that completely contradicted the older covenantal faith of Israel.

For this reason Ezra's program is in part achieved when "the Israelites separated themselves from all foreigners, and stood and confessed their sins" (Neh 9:2). They read Torah and they worshiped. Israel in the new history took seriously Yahweh's jealousy.

Hellenization and Syncretism Revisited

The resetting of Ezra's Judaism in a Hellenistic context of course did not come suddenly. And the precise form and way in which it came are lost to us because of a lack of adequate documentation. But there is little doubt that Hellenization decisively changed the shape of Jewish self-consciousness. Persian toleration can be seen as the fortunate middle way between Babylonian hostility and Hellenistic seduction. And given such alternatives the development of a religiously distinct identity is more likely against overt hostility than it is against an attractive seduction that seems to promise more than it demands. One other feature makes the Hellenistic problem more central for Israel's faith. Whereas Judah was at the periphery of Persian concerns geographically, Jerusalem was positioned unfortunately at the center of imperial disputes after Alexander. There was nowhere to hide.

The development of Hellenization carried with it several features that were to affect post-Ezra Judaism in radical ways.[10] First, its mood and intent were cosmopolitan, denying every historical particularism. It was perhaps especially hostile to Jewish historical particularism not because it was Jewish, but because it was particular and historical. And the contrast is sharp, even total, between that urging and the earlier demands of Ezra.

Second, Hellenization was essentially an urban phenomenon, which focused in the cities and claimed them as vehicles for and expressions of the new vision of universal humanity. Although Alexandria was obviously the model and central temptation against a Jewish consciousness, Jerusalem also appeared to be a likely candidate for the new urbanism. It was the effort to transform an *ethnos* into a *polis*.[11] Obviously such a trans-

---

10. In what follows I am especially dependent on Martin Hengel, *Judaism and Hellenism: Studies in their Encounter in Palestine during the Early Hellenistic Period,* trans. J. Bowden, 2 vols. (Philadelphia: Fortress Press, 1974). Hengel has illuminated the sociological factors related to Hellenistic pressures toward the syncretism of Judaism with an urban, universal consciousness. He speaks of "a changed social consciousness" (136).

11. Hengel writes: "The aim was to *transform* the Jewish *ethnos,* or the temple state of Jerusalem, into a Greek *polis,* with a limited, Greek-educated citizenry" (*Judaism and Hellenism,* 74). Lewis Mumford, *The Myth of the Machine* (New York: Harcourt, Brace and World, 1966) 166, speaks of the same transformation in more general terms as "the passage

formation called into question every claim and effort of Ezra to make Jerusalem the locus of covenant, and to define Jewish sensitivities in terms of Torah and covenantal obedience.[12] The city embodies and suggests another vision of reality, which by definition must deny historical peculiarity.

Third, Hellenization was inevitably a program of cultural and intellectual enlightenment that was antithetical to the unquestioning fideism of Ezra. Here there was no urging about historical remembering and nothing about repentance. In their place came broadness of spirit and tolerant inclusive appreciation for human person, human body, human intellect. The later Jewish period from the Maccabees indicated a careful political program and institutional design whereby cosmopolitanism, urbanization, and cultural enlightenment were championed. The presence of the gymnasium and the accompanying initiation into manhood gave legitimacy to an alternative self-understanding.[13]

Obviously such a radical cultural alternative posed hard questions for Jews. The temptation was not to deny Jewishness as such, but the much more subtle and inevitable tendency to change the nature of Jewishness. The battles fought in this period concerned the extent to which the new possibilities could be embraced as consistent with Judaism. It is clear in a general way how such a change also redefined an understanding of the land according to the old patterns of inheritance, promise, and gift, all of which depend upon (a) historical particularity that now appeared embarrassing if not scandalous, (b) intergenerational identity as land descended with the family, and (c) a notion of inherited right that needed no political legitimacy or defense.[14]

---

to 'civilization.'" On the power and ideological interest in "civilization" and its derived "civility," see John M. Cuddihy, *The Ordeal of Civility: Freud, Marx, Lévi-Strauss, and the Jewish Struggle with Modernity* (New York: Basic, 1974). As Cuddihy observes, for modern Jews in Europe, so for ancient Jews, the civilizing program of Hellenization was an "ordeal."

12. Mumford, *The Myth*, 233, observes that the Jewish community in synagogue and sabbath "found a way of obstructing the megamachine and challenging its inflated claims."

13. Compare Hengel, *Judaism and Hellenism*, 74.

14. Hengel, ibid., in a comment on the alternative understanding of law, writes, "The starting point here was the conception that the whole land was the personal possession (*oikos*) of the king. By far the largest part of the land was the direct possession of the king and was worked by free tenants, the royal peasants, under the strict supervision of royal officials. The royal land also provided those portions of land which were assigned to military settlers or given as gifts to high officials like Apollonius. However, both could be repossessed by the king at any time, as they were his property. The temple land, too, was under strict state control." Hengel contrasts agricultural and urban value systems in a way congenial to Mendenhall's conquest hypothesis (22).

Martin Hengel has shrewdly observed that, while the Hellenistic enlightenment intended to be ideologically neutral (and some no doubt declared it to be the "end of ideology"), in fact it had important class implications. As it valued the sophistication of urban living, the learning of the academy, and the art of political manipulation—all purported by a disinterested vision of the new world of emancipation—it inevitably favored the wealthy urban citizens who had access to and knew how to benefit from the decision-making apparatus. And as it gave its favors, it tended to deny and devalue the old stock of rural peasantry who continued to hold to an Ezra-shaped notion of Jewishness, committed to historical particularity and traditional rights of inheritance.

Concerning our theme of land, the new arrangement worked to make land accessible in bold ways to those who could figure angles to take from those who conversely relied on traditional claims and supports. Thus it is impossible to separate the religious, political, economic, and social dimensions of Hellenization. We have seen that the Ezra movement, often presented simply as religious sectarianism, is in fact a radical statement about a political-economic alternative. In the same way the issues of Hellenization, symbolized by Antiochus, are often discerned simply as issues about the purity of the temple and the maintenance of ritual purity. However they embody important political issues about human worth and economic dignity, about the legitimate claims of traditional rootage and self-understanding. Hellenization gave opening to the possibility of self-seeking by the knowing elite restrained neither by covenant nor by tradition. This matter of alternatives in another form is the same as that expressed in (a) Deut 17:14-20 about "one from the brothers" and one with "lifted" heart, (b) the self-serving power of Solomon, (c) the triangle of Naboth–Jezebel–Elijah, and (d) Jeremiah's neat contrast of Josiah and Jehoiachin, justice and cedar (Jer 22:13-17).[15]

Finally Hellenization raised the issue about whether faith in Yahweh was possible or worth the price. The normative answer, given in Jerusalem and celebrated by the aristocracy who managed the bureaucracy and administered the temple, was that such faith had low priority. Hellenization set a pattern for the knowing, uncaring rich to take advantage of trusting, helpless poor.

The response to such alienated politics and faith came in several forms:

---

15. Morton Smith, *Palestinian Parties and Politics that Shaped the Old Testament* (New York: Columbia Univ. Press, 1971) has attempted to trace these two kinds of opinions through Scripture.

1. It came in the literature and politics of resistance, centering in the Maccabean movement. While that literature lies outside the Old Testament, it is an important element in the history of land theology, for it is the peasantry fighting for land held in covenant (1 Macc 2:19-22, 27 sees the battle in terms of fidelity). This self-understanding is consistent with the ideology of holy war and the old conquest traditions.

2. There is a sapiential, reflective tradition dating from just before the Maccabean uprising.[16] This tradition of wisdom is conservative and not impressed with the new learnings of Hellenization, believing rather that the rules of life ordained by God are not subject to the whims of a new time and place.

Ben Sira approaches the current inventiveness of Hellenization with confidence in the long-held conviction of Judaism that Yahweh has created a world that is coherent and reliable and his will will be done.[17] Ben Sira is a wisdom teacher in the Hellenistic period who presents the teaching of a conservative tradition. His teaching is preserved in an apocryphal book bearing his name. The teaching is conventional and in general urges old sapiential values against Hellenistic alternatives.

In a somewhat understated form, the general reflection of Ben Sira is a rejection of a new mood besetting Jews whose faith now faced hard options. In important ways, his teaching extends the land management concerns of the older wisdom (Ps 37:3, 9, 11, 22; Prov 15:25; 22:28; 23:10-11). He holds to Israel's old conventional notions of responsibility and of reliance upon the purposes of Yahweh. While he teaches individual accountability, he also affirms social solidarity in which the more fortunate must care for the others. Hengel views Ben Sira as a protestor against "Hellenistic liberalism," which was not at all a disinterested program but in fact provided a rationale for the exploitation of class against class.[18] Hengel shows clearly that a reassertion of urgent Jewish

---

16. Compare Hengel, *Judaism and Hellenism,* 52–54.

17. Compare ibid., 131–53; Gerhard von Rad, *Wisdom in Israel,* trans. J. D. Martin (New York: Abingdon, 1972) 240–62.

18. Compare Hengel, *Judaism and Hellenism,* 137, and his comment on Sir 13:2-5, 15-20; 11:10; 31:5; 34:24-37. James L. Crenshaw in "The Functions of Creation Theology in Wisdom Literature" (unpublished), and "The Problem of Theodicy in Sirach," *JBL* 94 (1975) 47–64, has illuminated the relation of theodicy and creation in the tradition of Sirach. One of the important implications of the study of Crenshaw and especially Hengel is that theodicy is never a disinterested, reflective issue. It is always a question for people who are deprived and oppressed. The issue of theodicy is acute in this period because the Hellenistic ordering of life created situations (economic and political) of despair for some to the advantage of others. Hengel has shown that, while Hellenization is a sophisticated cultural and intellectual movement, it also made a decisive difference in the political-economic options open to people. Perhaps the land theme enables us to perceive theodicy in relation to sociopolitical realities.

faith and a protest against the new economic, political arrangement come together and may not be separated. The double focus of land as earth and land as "safe space" is evident.[19] The question of theodicy, which dominates much of the late literature, comes precisely from the disinherited who were betrayed by the new urban arrangements. It is likely that the literature of theodicy is a result precisely of the pathos of this social group.

3. Such a location of an interest in theodicy leads to the third dimension of the response to Hellenization, namely, apocalyptic. It is the special merit of Paul Hanson's study to have placed apocalyptic sociologically among the faithful, even the militantly faithful, who have found their political-economic situation incongruous with the claims and promises of their religious heritage.[20] Apocalyptic is the visionary rage of those victimized by the insanity of the present order. The radical, even desperate yearning for a new age, a new earth, is not likely to surface among those who enjoy all the blessings of this age (thus, "realized eschatology"). Hanson's phrase is pointedly suggestive: "world weariness."[21] Apocalyptic arises precisely among those who have trusted their symbol system to keep its promises and it does not, that is, among those who have obeyed the commandments of covenant blessings but discover that the promises have not been kept.

The response of apocalyptic returned to the most radical, particular tradition in Israel's heritage, to the tradition of holy war, to the memories when Yahweh intervened on behalf of his faithful, helpless people against "unnumbered foes." It is for our purposes adequate to recognize that this tradition was particular, historical and concrete, offensively primitive in its articulation, believingly naïve in its rhetoric. It refused to stay with the rational polite categories of the new urban arrangement, for to do so was to be domesticated by the inclusiveness of Hellenization.[22] And so Hengel's statement is correct: "Thus the picture of history in apocalyptic is above all a fruit of the Jewish struggle for spiritual and religious self-determination against the invasion of Jerusalem by the Hellenistic spirit."[23]

19. See the argument of Robert Ardrey, *The Territorial Imperative: A Personal Inquiry into the Animal Origins of Property and Nations* (New York: Atheneum, 1966) and the comments of Davies, *The Gospel and the Land*, 405–8 on Ardrey.

20. See Hanson, *The Dawn*, 125–34 and *passim*.

21. Paul D. Hanson, "Old Testament Apocalyptic Reexamined," *Int* 25 (1971) 479: "This world-weariness has been the mark of every apocalyptic movement."

22. Hanson has perhaps not fully understood the function of language either as a way of reducing experience to a certain rationality or as a protest against a rationality. More can be made of Hanson's construct of "pragmatist" and "visionary" by paying attention to the language used by each.

23. Hengel, *Judaism and Hellenism*, 196; compare 312.

The Jewish struggle was to recover and foster a set of images that could not be encased by syncretism, to fashion a system of rhetoric that gave standing ground for an alternative identity. Thus the abrasive rhetoric (contrasted to the cool reflection of Ben Sira) already means to construct an alternative world in which intervention is expected and newness is possible.[24] Such a view of the world and therefore of the land is opposed to the managed, closed, reasonable, predictable, explainable world of the aristocracy. At the beginning of any consideration of apocalyptic is the construction of a language that will permit another reading of the experience. As concerns land, the rhetoric rejects seeing land as free space and insists that land is seen as gift, as arena for holy intervention, transformation, and the keeping of promises. The resurrection theme of Ezekiel 37 then is not simply an accidental image but is a basic question about explainable futures and the intrusion of real newness, which in Israel is about land.[25]

Apocalyptic then is concerned for the *land in hope,* which is articulated against *land in possession.*[26] While the new work on apocalyptic has only begun, Hanson's discussion of Zechariah 9 is instructive for our consideration. He locates the "Hymn of the Divine Warrior" in the chapter, which is central to this poetry. The form contains seven or eight elements. The sequence moves through battle, victory, and triumphant celebration. For our purpose the last element should especially be mentioned:[27]

> On that day Yahweh their God will save them
>   for they are the flock of his people;
> for like the jewels of a crown
>   they shall shine *on his land.*

24. For an example of the construction of an alternative world see Eugene Genovese, *Roll Jordan Roll: The World the Slaves Made* (New York: Pantheon, 1974). The subtitle indicates the task of every historically particular community.

25. It is not accidental then that the Sadducees, embodiment of the elite, urban accommodating priesthood, did not affirm hope in a resurrection. If resurrection hope means a sociopolitical hope related to land, that is not the group that could embrace it. On the links between land and the symbol of resurrection, see Davies, *The Gospel and the Land,* 123–24.

26. The "Two Religions of Christianity," articulated by Walter H. Capps, *Time Invades the Cathedral: Tensions in the School of Hope* (Philadelphia: Fortress Press, 1972) 110–26, have ready correlation with the two postures Hanson has identified, although Hanson has been more explicit about the socioeconomic factors.

27. Paul D. Hanson has variously discussed the passage and has given the last element several different labels that are significant for our argument: in "Old Testament Apocalyptic Reexamined," 472, he labeled it "Renewed Fertility in the Land"; in "Zechariah 9 and Ancient Ritual Pattern," *JBL* 92 (1973) 53, he labeled it "Fertility of Restored Order"; and in "Jewish Apocalyptic against Its Near Eastern Environment," *RB* (1971) 55–58, he labeled it simply "Shalom."

> Yea, how good and how fair it shall be!
> Grain shall make the young men flourish,
> and new wine the maidens. (Zech 9:16-17)

The anticipated conclusion of the intervention and triumph of Yahweh is restoration of an idyllic land of security, well-being, and fertility. Israel has no other imagery. The good future is the landed one. This poetry must have served well a world-weary population who watched as their land was consumed and who knew the old system of land arrangements could not keep its promises.

This hope for transformed land, renewed land, new land, became a central point for expectant Israel (which is to be sharply contrasted to possessing, possessive Israel). They were indeed "prisoners of hope" (Zech 9:12). They were enslaved to an expectation that the present arrangement of disinheritance could not endure. And so they waited. They waited with radical confidence because they did not believe that the meek Torah-keepers would finally be denied their land. The Hellenistic world had created a keen sense of alienation. The promise was for luxuriant at-homeness. And they waited. They could neither explain nor understand, but they had a rhetoric that both required and bestowed hope upon them. And it was this promised land that gave them identity and even sanity in a context where everything was denied. They waited for the new land that seemed unlikely and that required the dismantling of everything now so stable. They waited. Jerusalem for some was a present possession to be jealously guarded. For others it was a passionate hope, urgently awaited and surely promised.

10.

"BLESSED ARE THE MEEK"

E VIDENCE ABOUT THE BELIEVING COMMUNITY JUST BEFORE AND INTO
the New Testament period on our theme is sparse and problematic.
Nonetheless an attempt to articulate a theology of land in a Christian
context or in a way that might be useful for the Christian community
requires at least a provisional statement in relation to the faith confessed
in the New Testament.[1]

On Gift and Grasp

Israel had learned that the problem of land and the possibility of land
consisted on the one hand in *grasping with courage* and on the other hand
in *waiting in confidence for the gift.* In the period of the New Testament, as
we have seen, there was a mood of grasping in the form of urbanized syncretism that had oppressive implications. The movement clustering
around Jesus, enigmatic as it is, appears to be a restatement of the theme
of waiting in confidence for the gift. The dominant tendency of the community of biblical faith was oriented to scribalism, an effort to manage
and plan for securing.[2] The Jesus movement, as Ernst Käsemann has
urged most sharply, represents an alternative to the scribal consciousness

1. It will be evident that I regard the interactions between the Old Testament and the
New Testament on this theme as much more dialectical and complex than does W. D.
Davies, *The Gospel and the Land: Early Christianity and Jewish Territorial Doctrine* (Los
Angeles: Univ. of California Press, 1974). It will be equally evident that I have learned much
from his study.

2. Paul D. Hanson, *The Dawn of Apocalyptic: The Historical and Sociological Roots of Jewish Apocalyptic Eschatology,* rev. ed. (Philadelphia: Fortress Press, 1979), has used the term
"pragmatist" for this perspective. It is important that the notion be understood not as
merely an ancient problem but as an inherent temptation of a "management mentality."

because it focused on an apocalyptic perspective.[3] This view believed that a breaking of the ages, a turning of the eons was about to occur. Among other things, those who waited patiently and faithfully would receive the inheritance of the new age, even as those who now held the land according to the norms of the old age would indeed lose it. Thus the Jesus movement is centered on the sharp and radical transformation of the human situation. While the visionary language permits alternative readings, there were no doubt political and economic dimensions to the faith of the Christian movement that were articulated especially by the disinherited.[4]

In trying to assess the Jesus movement in the context of the Judaism of the period, I am aware that this is a particularistic reading of the period, a bold claim that the Jesus movement is indeed the next moment on the way from exile to land. I am compelled by my faith stance and my interpretative decisions to determine where land theology leads if it is understood as moving toward the New Testament.

I am of course aware of alternative Jewish readings and regard them in other contexts and with other interpretative presuppositions as equally appropriate and legitimate.[5] Obviously the land issue of Israel is urgent, given its prominence in any current Jewish understanding of Bible faith. In contemporary thought it is likely that the same question of seizing and waiting is central, and modern Israel is having to decide on it. In contemporary setting these alternatives are perhaps symbolized by the Western Wall (elsewhere the Wailing Wall) and Masada, the latter a powerful symbol laden with energy for resistance and defiance. Even if the conventional account of Jewish resistance of Masada by Josephus is currently under strong challenge, the Western Wall represents and embodies the enduring and resilient conviction that the yearnings of Israel will be honored and fulfilled "when Messiah comes." And while the delay may be long, his coming is not in doubt. The Western Wall is an expression of grieving

3. Compare Ernst Käsemann, "An Apologia for Primitive Christian Eschatology," in *Essays on New Testament Themes,* trans. W. J. Montague (Philadelphia: Fortress Press, 1982). On the more general implications of Käsemann's work, see M. Douglas Meeks, *Origins of the Theology of Hope* (Philadelphia: Fortress Press, 1974) 76–80.

4. Hanson, *Dawn,* is not interested directly in the theme of the land. For that reason it is the more telling how often the theme is central to his work (see 68, 125–27, 131, 146, 241, 250, 254–56, 285, 322, 325).

5. See two important attempts by Christians to deal theologically with the issue of land as a concern common to Christians and Jews: Friedrich-Wilhelm Marquardt, *Die Juden und ihr Land* (Hamburg: Siebenstern Taschenbuch, 1975); and Rolf Rendtorff, *Israel und sein Land: Theologische Überlegungen zu einem politischen Problem,* TEH 188 (Munich: Kaiser, 1975).

hope that never doubts that his purposes will out. Conversely Masada, symbol of resistance, has become a focal point for the passion to resist and to take initiative and so to secure the land.[6] While contemporary Jewish thought honors both, it is unmistakable that they are in tension with each other. On the one hand there is bold waiting, letting the Giver of land work his way at his pace. On the other hand, without doubting, Masada is the bold assertion of human initiative to manage events. The issue may be profoundly theological, but it is expressed very practically and urgently in terms of Israel's yielding for the sake of the promise on the one hand, that is, to try a risky course against conventional military politics, or on the other hand, to use military power to secure that is promised.

While the two symbols of Western Wall and Masada offer the contemporary state of Israel deep options for *waiting in confidence* or *seizing in military assertion,* it is clear that the contemporary state of Israel has opted for the latter, to the complete disregard of the former. As I write this, Israel, under the leadership of Ariel Sharon, is currently undertaking an aggressive, brutalizing assault on the neighboring Palestinian population. That option for brutality against others in the name of the God of Israel is a powerful evidence of the way in which land traditions from the ancient texts are open to a variety of readings and responses, some of which make for war and not for peaceable habitation.[7]

As Christians seek to enter into the pathos of Jewish suffering as a way in history two observations may be made. First, the issue of Western Wall/Masada is not new, but is as old and deep as the awareness that waiting for land secures it and grasping land forfeits it. Second, the issue of grasping/waiting, of Masada/Western Wall, is not one in which a clear Jewish posture can be distinguished from a clear Christian attitude. Things will not be divided that way. Thus there is a community of concern between Jews and Christians about grasping and waiting, about keeping and losing. Because both Christians and Jews are on both sides of the grasping and waiting, this may be an issue about which there can be new dialogue between them. Neither Jews nor Christians have a monopoly on either side of the issue. For both the question is a difficult and urgent one. For both Christians and Jews it is always a question of self-securing and a question of trust. Self-securing seems to work and yet

---

6. On the "Masada complex" and the power it has as a symbol for the land, see Louis H. Feldman, "Masada: A Critique of Recent Scholarship," in *Christianity, Judaism, and Other Greco-Roman Cults,* vol. 3, ed. Jacob Neusner (Leiden: Brill, 1975) 247–48 and *passim.*

7. See Rosemary Radford Ruether and Herman J. Ruether, *The Wrath of Jonah: The Crisis of Religious Nationalism in the Israeli-Palestinian Conflict,* 2d ed. (Minneapolis: Fortress Press, 2002).

leads to death. Trust seems unlikely and yet holds promise. Neither Jews nor Christians can avoid this question. For both it is surely the key question for faith.

Having acknowledged this central and common issue between Christians and Jews, we may now consider it precisely in a Christian context, recognizing that it is parallel to but lacks the urgency of the Jewish question.[8] The theme as it is handled in the New Testament has been reviewed by W. D. Davies.[9] He concludes that in the history of Christianity the land as a central theme has been (a) rejected, (b) spiritualized, (c) treated historically, and (d) presented sacramentally. But the major thrust of Davies's study is to stress that in early Christianity the theme of land was displaced by the person of Jesus Christ.

The present discussion owes much to Davies's work. However, it is here urged that the land theme is more central than Davies believes and that it has not been so fully spiritualized as he concludes. It is more likely that the land theme can be understood in a dialectical way: in contexts of Gnosticism the land theme must be taken in a more physical, historical way; in contexts of politicizing the land theme must be taken in a more symbolic way. In what follows our concern is more deliberately hermeneutical than that of Davies. In order to try to sense the intention of the text, we must note that the promissory language is focused on land and surely cannot be understood apart from it. And no matter how much it has been spiritualized, it is probable that the image is never robbed of its original, historical referent.

1. There is no doubt that the center of the New Testament proclamation is the end of one age, one kingdom, one political-historical arrangement and the announcement of a new age, a new kingdom, a new political-historical arrangement. It is the dynamic of old age/new age that is central to the New Testament, which presents its radicalness, and which embodies the offense of the gospel. The imagery of the primitive preaching is to stress the discontinuity and the contrast between the two arrangements.

2. The most primitive and central image of this contrast is the image of kingdom, Kingdom of God and kingdom of this world. The primary claim is that a new kingdom has come (Mark 1:14-15; see Rev 11:15). The theme of "kingdom" is crucial for our consideration. It clearly includes

8. Davies, *The Gospel and the Land*, 396–404, indicates Christianity has had a history of interpretation that has tended to diverge from Jewish categories. However, as Davies hints, it does not follow that this is necessary. It may well be, as the literature cited indicates, that Christian interpretation of Scripture might more faithfully be done in land categories. I have the impression that Davies himself might have more vigorously pursued such an enterprise.

9. Ibid., 367.

among its nuances the idea of historical, political, physical realm, that is land. It may and surely does mean more than that, but it is never so spiritualized that those elemental nuances are denied or overcome. However rich and complex the imagery may be in its various articulations, the coming of Jesus is understood with reference to new land arrangements.

3. The new land arrangement is sharply contrasted with the old land arrangement. And while one may not be simplistic, the contrast surely includes socioeconomic-political concerns. The contrast between those who have and must lose (see the discussion above on royal history) and those who do not have but who bear the promise (see the history of the landless on the way to land) is clear.

Mary states it in raw and offensive categories:

> He has shown strength with his arm,
> he has scattered the proud in the imagination of their hearts,
> he has put down the mighty from their thrones,
> and exalted those of low degree;
> he has filled the hungry with good things,
> and the rich he has sent empty away.
> He has helped his servant Israel,
> in remembrance of his mercy,
> as he spoke to our fathers,
> to Abraham and to his posterity for ever. (Luke 1:51-55)[10]

Quite clearly this is a vision of land-loss by the graspers of land and land-receipt by those who bear promises but lack power. It cannot be accidental that this "poetry of inversion" parallels the song of Hannah (1 Sam 2:1-10), also out of a context of landless and precarious Israelites. The birth of Jesus presented in this fashion is about the land still being under promise when it seems not to be. Among others, the climactic reference to Abraham leaves no doubt of this.

The theme of radical inversion[11] of landed and landless is presented as the central clue that the messianic age has dawned:

10. José Porfirio Miranda, *Marx and the Bible: A Critique of the Philosophy of Oppression,* trans. J. Eagleson (Maryknoll, N.Y.: Orbis, 1974) 17–18, 217 and *passim* has suggested the abrasive and historical implications of this rhetoric.

11. On the theme of radical reversal see Norman K. Gottwald, *Studies in the Book of Lamentations,* SBT 1/14 (Naperville, Ill.: Allenson, 1954) chap. 3; and Dan O. Via Jr., *Kerygma and Comedy in the New Testament: A Structuralist Approach to Hermeneutic* (Philadelphia: Fortress Press, 1974). We have yet to come to terms with the meaning of the "reversal" as we move from literature to sociology.

> The blind receive their sight,
> the lame walk,
> lepers are cleansed,
> and the deaf hear,
> the dead are raised up,
> the poor have good news preached to them. (Luke 7:22)

See also 4:18-19, which appeals to Isa 61:1-2; the passage announces the end of exile and the inversion of all of life.[12] It is precisely the end of exile, with the inversion of life for those denied turf, which is recognized in the person and preaching of Jesus. This is both celebrated and resisted.

4. The radical inversion of landed–landless arrangements is evidenced in the teaching of Jesus. It is clear in his concise but enigmatic statements that reject the world of grasping and affirm the world of gifts.[13] Thus:

> For whoever would save his life will lose it;
> and whoever loses his life for my sake, he will save it.
> (Luke 9:24)

> And behold, some are last who will be first,
> and some are first who will be last. (13:30)

> For every one who exalts himself will be humbled,
> and he who humbles himself will be exalted. (14:11)

It is no less evident in his more reflective teaching. Thus the narrative of Luke 7:36-50 contrasts the landed and the landless, the Pharisee and the nameless woman. While the narrative makes clear who in fact has turf and who does not, it is precisely the function of the narrative to show that Jesus inverts the situation. By the end of the story, the Pharisee has been dispossessed of any future security and the woman has been in fact secured. The change is wrought by the word and presence of Jesus who is the rearranger of the land.

In a parallel way the story of Luke 16:19-31 makes the same point in the contrast between the rich man and the poor man. And their new situations are precisely inverted. The one who seems to possess all in fact is hopelessly without claim or power. The poor man is now the one "comforted" (see v. 25; Isa 40:1 on the end of exile and "comfort").

---

12. Hanson, *Dawn*, 65–68, has characterized the piece fully. It is clear why Luke has used it.

13. The contrast of Jesus with David on gift and grasp is striking. See David M. Gunn, "David and the Gift of the Kingdom," *Semeia* 3 (1975) 14–45.

5. It is likely that Jesus' actions are also to be understood as the return of the dispossessed to the land from which they had been driven, that is, the rehabilitation of the rejected ones as bearers of the promise.[14] This must in fact be the intent of the action toward Zacchaeus, which ends with a promissory statement: "Today salvation has come to this house, since he also is a son of Abraham" (Luke 19:9). This is not simply a general statement but is in fact a deliberate appeal to the land promise that is now affirmed as effective for this seemingly rejected heir. Jesus' ministry affirms that the land promise is still in effect. And it is operative precisely for those who are without land. His actions serve to fulfill that promise for the seemingly rejected heirs.

The actions of healing and cleansing are in fact actions that rehabilitate. Thus the paralytic is sent home (Mark 2:11). And likewise the demon-possessed man is restored to sanity and sent home (Mark 5:19). He had been living among the tombs, that is, in exile, homeless, among the dead and now he is sent home.[15] Thus the contrast of tomb/home is clear and surely is not unrelated to the theme of exile/land. Jesus' ministry is to restore the rejected to their rightful possession.

6. The radicalness of this ministry is of course in the calling into question those norms and values that serve to enfranchise and disenfranchise.[16] Jesus and his gospel are rightly received as a threat. The new enlandment is a threat to the old arrangements. And he evokes resistance from those who wish to preserve how it had been. A proper understanding requires that we discern the sociopolitical, economic issues in the religious resistance that forms against him. A threat to landholders mobilizes his opponents, land here understood both in literal and symbolic senses.

---

14. Both the actions and parables of Jesus speak about radical reversal. While the work of Crossan and Funk has a somewhat different agenda, the intersection of sociological and literary concerns should not be missed. The radicalness of rehabilitation depends in part on the destruction of the language that legitimates present arrangements. See especially John Dominic Crossan, "Jesus and Pacifism," in *No Famine in the Land: Studies in Honor of John L. McKenzie,* ed. J. W. Flanagan and A. W. Robinson (Missoula, Mont.: Scholars, 1975) 195–208: "Indeed, it is becoming steadily clearer that the *content* of Jesus' message was an attack on *form.* The Kingdom of God comes as the forms of our language are shattered and the world we have created in and by them is shocked into awareness of its relativity" (206).

15. See the exegesis of Jean Starobinski, "The Gerasene Demoniac," in *Structural Analysis and Biblical Exegesis: Interpretational Essays,* PTMS 3 (Pittsburgh: Pickwick, 1974) 57–84.

16. We are only now prepared to face the task of bringing together the radical literary work of Crossan and the sociological concerns expressed by Miranda. Social norms, perceptions, and values are closely dependent on literary forms and categories. They stand or fall together.

Such a threat is evident in the theme of "hardness of heart." Thus the act of "restoration" (*apokathistēmi*, Mark 3:5) is precisely what is resisted. Restoration evokes opposition: "The Pharisees went out, and immediately held counsel with the Herodians against him, how to destroy him" (v. 6).

He came to sheep without shepherd, surely an image of exile (see 6:34). He acted as king and fed them (see Ezek 34), that is, he ended their exile. But the others were "hard hearted" and did not discern the act that ended exile. They were unable to accept or even to recognize the new enlandment (see 8:17).[17]

The resistance Jesus encounters is characteristically among those who possess most and have most to lose. The new possibilities are among those who have least and who welcome what is given. Thus the issue is posed clearly not only between old age and new age, but between haves and have nots, between defenders of old land arrangements and recipients of new land: "The chief priests and the scribes and the principal men of the people sought to destroy him; but they did not find anything they could do, for all the people hung upon his words" (Luke 19:47-48). The action, the preaching, and the person of Jesus all attest to new land now being given. But the land being newly given is land presented in an acutely dialectical way. The way to land is by loss. The way to lose land is to grasp it. The way to life in the land is by death.

Thus at the heart of the reversal of land/landless is a scandal. It is not a new scandal, for it is precisely what the whole history of Israel evidences in terms of gift and grasp. But now that whole dialectic is encompassed in one person. On the one hand it will not do to treat the New Testament as though it is uninterested in the land. On the other hand it will not do to treat the New Testament as though it contains a simple promise of the land, as has been hinted by some liberation theologies informed by Marxist rhetoric.[18] Rather the New Testament has discerned how problematic land is; when the people are landless, the promise comes; but when the land is secured, it seduces and the people are turned toward loss. Thus the proclamation of Jesus is about graspers losing and those open to gifts as receiving.

17. Likely there is a connection between "hardness of heart" and the fear of land-loss. The connection is reflected in the concern of Pharaoh as well as Isa 6:9-12. Jesus meets hardness of heart precisely because he announces such a reversal (see Mark 6:52).

18. Moltmann speaks of the "dialectic of reconciliation." The dialectic is reflected in the titles of his two books *Theology of Hope* and *The Crucified God*. See Meeks, *Origins of the Theology of Hope*, especially chap. 3. Without the cross, a theology of land becomes a theology of glory.

Johannine and Pauline Uses of Land Imagery

Land provides diverse and rich imagery, as Davies noted.[19] In the Fourth Gospel, land = "life in the new age" = "eternal life." More centrally, it surely is not beyond the text to suggest that land-loss = crucifixion and land gift = resurrection. The crucifixion of Jesus is his willing embrace of homelessness or landlessness.[20] The resurrection of Jesus is the amazing restoration of power and turf when they had surely been lost (on this see the clear claim of restoration in Matt 28:19-20). The early church had to reflect long on the crucifixion/resurrection and the enigmatic way they are held together in the experience of Jesus and in the mind of the church. It is likely that the imagery of *land-loss* and *land-gift* became one of the primary ways for understanding and confessing this homeless one who now has been given dominion.

Of course the imagery is powerful and credible because of the church's experience of Jesus. But that experience is not in a vacuum. The church claims that desperate attempts to seize and hold lead to displacement and death, and conversely, gracious risks lead to empowerment and security. That is the central gamble of the Gospel, not simply a gamble in piety or theology, but a gamble in history with valuable turf, with the best worldly wisdom, and with the greatest worldly power.[21]

Nowhere are this gamble and its promissory boldness more evident than in the Beatitudes. They are clues to entry to the new age of enlandment. So the promises:

> the kingdom of God . . .
> shall be satisfied . . .
> shall laugh . . .
> your reward is great in heaven. . . . (Luke 6:20-23)

> kingdom of heaven . . .
> comforted . . .
> inherit the earth . . .
> satisfied . . .
> obtain mercy . . .

19. Compare Davies, *The Gospel and the Land,* 124, 368, who uses the suggestive phrase "Christified holy space."

20. This theme has been especially stressed by Moltmann, *The Crucified God: The Cross of Christ as the Foundation and Criticism of Christian Theology,* trans. R. A. Wilson and J. Bowden (New York: Harper & Row, 1974) 10, 36, 58, on "homelessness."

21. Paul Lehmann, *The Transfiguration of Politics* (New York: Harper & Row, 1975), chaps. 5 and 6, has especially discerned the dialectic of power and suffering in revolution.

> be called sons of God . . .
> theirs is the kingdom of heaven . . .
> your reward is great in heaven. . . . (Matt 5:3-12)

If we take care not to spiritualize or existentialize unmistakably the meaning is a new time in a new land. Meekness leads to turf. Not powerful grasping but trusting receiving. Israel had long known this. But each time the reality lacks credibility. Jesus himself is the meek and homeless one and he has home and land. He is ruler of the new age and invites his people there with him, but on his strange terms (Mark 10:35-45).

An alternative reading of Paul is also possible. Davies denies that Paul has an interest in the land.[22] And on lexical grounds that is so. But some factors hint otherwise:

1. It may well be that the law/gospel theme, especially prominent in Romans and Galatians, can be understood alternatively in terms of grasping land and receiving it freely. If Torah had indeed become problematic for Paul it is significant that Torah has importance only with reference to land. If the law issue is in fact related to having and keeping land, then grace/law becomes a prism for asking about keeping and losing turf.

2. The stress upon Abraham as the paradigm for faith warns us against deciding too quickly that the land motif is absent (see Romans 4; Galatians 3–4). While the Abraham image undoubtedly is transformed, it is inconceivable that it should have been emptied of its reference to land. The Abraham imagery apart from the land promise is an empty form. No matter how spiritualized, transcendentalized, or existentialized, it has its primary focus undeniably on land. That is what is promised, not to the competent deserving or to the dutifully obedient, but freely given (as in the beginning) to one who had no claim and "was as good as dead" (Heb 11:12).[23]

3. It is instructive that the passages that focus on being "heirs" (Rom 8:12-25; Gal 3:27-29; 4:1-7) receive scant attention from Davies.[24] But the assertions are clear:

---

22. Davies, *The Gospel and the Land*, 178.

23. The formula surely reflects resurrection faith. See Miranda, *Marx*, 217, in a fresh perspective on resurrection: "I wonder where there is more faith and hope: in believing in the God who raises the dead (Rom. 4:17) or in believing like Luke in the God who filled the hungry with good things and sent the rich away empty (Luke 1:53)?"

24. In the context of discussing Gal 3:27-29, Davies, *The Gospel and the Land*, 182, concludes, "Pauline eschatology is a-territorial."

The promise to Abraham and his descendants, that they should inherit the world [cosmos], did not come through the law but through the righteousness of faith. If it is the adherents of the law who are to be the heirs, faith is null and the promise is void. (Rom 4:13-14)

. . . and if children, then heirs, heirs of God and fellow heirs with Christ, provided we suffer with him in order that we may also be glorified with him. (Rom 8:17)

. . . that in Christ Jesus the blessing of Abraham might come upon the Gentiles, that we might receive the promise of the Spirit through faith. . . . For if the inheritance is by the law, it is no longer by promise; but God gave it to Abraham by a promise. (Gal 3:14, 18)

So through God you are no longer a slave but a son, and if a son then an heir. . . . Now we, brethren, like Isaac, are children of promise. (Gal 4:7, 28)

Those who gather around Jesus are heirs. Of course Davies is correct that the inheritance has been boldly redefined. But we cannot therefore deny the central and enduring referent, which is land, unless we are to succumb to an otherworldly hermeneutic. The assertions of Paul are about living faithfully in history, about being secure in a world that promises no security, about having a place in a displacing world.

It is central to Paul's argument that the promise endures. The heirs in Christ are not heirs to a new promise, but the one which abides, and that is centrally land. In Rom 8:17 the heirship is suffering and glory, but in light of our argument about crucifixion and resurrection, it surely is possible that suffering = crucifixion = landlessness and glory = resurrection = landedness. So the Pauline question is about "turf" and the gospel answer is that "at-homeness" comes by the homelessness of trusting joyous obedience."[25]

4. One other theme in Paul warrants attention. In 2 Cor 1:3-7 the term "comfort" (*paraklēsis*) is used nine times. Of course the term is open to many meanings, and we must not claim too much in terms of specificity. But we have noted that this term, as for example in Lamentations

25. Especially the Lukan narrative expressed the "dead-come-alive" theme in terms of homecoming. Compare 15:11-32, where v. 31 certainly is about inheritance and 10:1-10 on the promise still functioning. Perhaps it is important that this same Gospel contains the most radical assertion of the reversal contained in the Abraham promise (1:46-55, 68-79). The first refers to Abraham and the second to David. This is more remarkable because, as Davies has seen, Luke apparently is not interested in the land (*The Gospel and the Land,* 247, 271, 273).

and Second Isaiah, frequently is about restoration of exiles. In this passage, we may again note a pair of words, "affliction/comfort," which perhaps correlates with the other pairs we have suggested: crucifixion/resurrection, suffering/glory, landless/landed. Although with a quite different vocabulary, the promissory element here also claims that exile is not the destiny of the church from Yahweh and a reversal will surely come.

As we have seen in the Gospels, it is our contention here that the land theme may simply help us discern dimensions of the text that could otherwise be overlooked, given more conventional categories of interpretation.

Another clear dimension of the land theme in the New Testament is in Hebrews 3-4, which focuses upon the promise of "rest" and the conditions of entry into it. Davies considers this text only in a note.[26] Clearly the message of the text is not concerned with land but with fidelity to the gospel. To that extent the text does not concern our theme.[27] Nonetheless it is clear that, when the text becomes promissory in its affirmation, it has no language to say what must be said except the language of land. And even if we insist that it has been transformed or spiritualized, the persistence of the language itself sets limits to how far the symbol may be removed from its original referent. Obviously the problem here is the problem of every typology, about the relation between the type and the antitype.[28]

But all of that notwithstanding, it is sobering for New Testament exegesis to recognize that the single central symbol for the promise of the gospel is land. That language is evident in 11:13-16 in which the pilgrimage of faith is set in three scenes: (a) a land from which they set out in faith, (b) the present context of exile, and (c) the hoped-for homeland (*patrida*). The last is characterized as "better," "heavenly," "a city."[29] The central movement of faith as understood here is movement from secure

26. Davies, *The Gospel and the Land,* 162 n. 3.

27. Compare Gerhard von Rad, "There Still Remains a Rest for the People of God," *The Problem of the Hexateuch and Other Essays,* trans. E. W. T. Dicken (New York: McGraw-Hill, 1966) 97–98.

28. See the comments of Gerhard von Rad, "Typological Interpretation of the Old Testament," in *Essays on Old Testament Hermeneutics,* ed. C. Westermann, trans. J. L. Mays (Richmond: John Knox, 1963) 17–39. He writes, "Typology, on the contrary, shows itself to be astoundingly free of attachment to the word or to the letter, yet bound to a much greater degree by the historical sense" (21).

29. On the land image here see G. W. Buchanan, "The Present State of Scholarship on Hebrews," in *Christianity, Judaism and Other Greco-Roman Cults: Studies for Morton Smith at Sixty,* vol. 1, ed. Jacob Neusner (Leiden: Brill, 1975). In commenting on this passage, he quotes Delitzsch: "It must be confessed that we nowhere read of the patriarchs, that they expressed a conscious desire for a home in heaven. . . . Even there no desire is expressed for an entrance into the heavenly land, but the promise renewed of future possession of earthly Canaan" (327). See Buchanan's comments on spiritualizing interpretations.

land to gift land and the route from the one to the other is through home-lessness, which is the sojourn of faith. The movement is in close parallel to the movement traced by Jeremiah, for example (2:6-7), from *grasped land* via *exile* to *gift land*. The promised land of course can be interpreted in many ways, and the term *epouranion* hints at a spiritualization, but it is nonetheless still a *country* that is sought. Our interpretation, no matter how we may wish for something less specific and concrete, will have to face that term.

Crucifixion-Resurrection through the Prism of Land

While there is a series of symbols that express our theme, for example, (a) in the Synoptics, "Kingdom of God"; (b) in the Fourth Gospel, "eternal life"; (c) in Paul, "inheritance"; and (d) in Hebrews, "a homeland," it is likely that *crucifixion/resurrection* is the core symbol in every tradition. This symbol is dialectical and is illuminated when linked to land (see Ezek 37:1-14). In such a frame of reference, crucifixion may be understood as a call to leave the old land (see Mark 10:17-22) and to give up power and embrace the risk of powerlessness and turflessness.[30] Or conversely cruci-fixion is land-loss in order that others may receive the same land as gift.

Resurrection is the gift of power to the powerless (see Mark 5:1-20; Luke 19:1-10) and the invitation to the dispossessed to enter new power, freedom, and life, that is, "turf." In the Old Testament the resurrection motif is undoubtedly expressed as the call to exiles to leave exile and return to the land.

Thus crucifixion/resurrection echoes the dialectic of *possessed land lost/exiles en route to the land of promise*. Jesus embodies precisely what Israel has learned about land: being without land makes it possible to trust the promise of it, while grasping land is the sure way to lose it. The powerful are called to dispossession. The powerless are called to power. The landed are called to *homelessness*. The landless are given a *new home*. Both are called to discipleship, to be "in Christ,"[31] to submit to the one

---

30. The term "impossible" (*adunaton*) in 10:27 is the same as that used in Gen 18:14, which is in the context of land. See also Luke 1:37. It may be that the scandal of the good news is that those utterly without power or means are *given* the land.

31. However, "in Christ" may be variously interpreted. Compare Davies, *The Gospel and the Land,* 217–19: "The real center of his interest has moved from 'the land,' concentrated in Jerusalem, to the communities 'in Christ'. . . ecclesiological factors that impinged upon Paul and led him not so much to look away from the land of his fathers as to discover his inheri-tance 'in Christ' = the land of Christians, the new creation, if we may so express the matter." In commenting on Luke 19:11-12, Davies writes: "Christ must first leave his own land (19:12) in order to receive it" (256). And on the Fourth Gospel: "The person of Jesus becomes 'the place' which replaces all holy places" (318).

who has become the embodiment of the new land.[32] In the person of Jesus both histories of Israel are enacted:

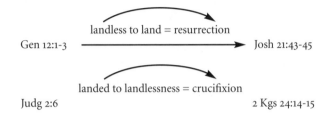

landless to land = resurrection

Gen 12:1-3   Josh 21:43-45

landed to landlessness = crucifixion

Judg 2:6   2 Kgs 24:14-15

It is the third history announced by Jeremiah, Ezekiel, and especially Second Isaiah that comes to dramatic fruition in Jesus, the utterly homeless one who is given dominion.

Three texts may be noted which catch that double understanding of land. In Isa 52:13—53:12, surely a central form of gospel to exiles, we may note the dialectical movement.[33] As Muilenburg has stressed, we must not miss the movement of the poem:[34]

a. the promise:

> Behold, my servant shall prosper,
>   he shall be exalted and lifted up,
>   and shall be very high. (Isa 52:13)

b. the exile:

> . . . his appearance was so marred, beyond human semblance,
>   and his form beyond that of the sons of men. . . .
> He had no form or comeliness that we should look at him,
>   and no beauty that we should desire him.
> He was despised and rejected by men;

32. Davies writes: ". . . the land of Israel in a transformed world, in the Messianic Age or the Age to Come or to recognize that for Matthew, 'inheriting the land' synonymous with entering the Kingdom and that this Kingdom transcends all geographic dimensions and is spiritualized" (*The Gospel and the Land*, 362).

33. The critical problems have been presented by Christopher North, *The Suffering Servant in Deutero-Isaiah: An Historical and Critical Study*, 2d ed. (London: Oxford Univ. Press, 1956). On interpretation see especially Harry M. Orlinsky and Norman H. Snaith, *Studies on the Second Part of the Book of Isaiah*, VTSup 14 (Leiden: Brill, 1967); and Klaus Baltzer, *Deutero-Isaiah*, trans. M. Kohl, Hermeneia (Minneapolis: Fortress Press, 2001).

34. Compare James Muilenburg, "The Book of Isaiah, Chapters 40–66: Introduction and Exegesis," in *Interpreter's Bible*, ed. G. A. Buttrick (New York: Abingdon, 1956) 5.614–31.

> a man of sorrows, and acquainted with grief;
> And as one from whom men hide their faces
>> he was despised, and we esteemed him not. (Isa 52:14—53:3)

c. the new life in the new land:

> He shall see his offspring, he shall prolong his days;
> the will of Yahweh shall prosper in his hand;
>> he shall see the fruit of the travail of his soul and be satisfied.
> (Isa 53:10-11)

The obedient dispossessed one is now newly established in prosperity and luxury. While the passion of Jesus often stresses the barren forlornness of Jesus, the poem in its total structure looks toward landedness.

The uses of Psalm 22 are similar.[35] While there is primary attention to the lament portion, that is, on loss of turf (vv. 1-21), the movement is to well-being and prosperity, that is landedness:

> The afflicted shall eat and be satisfied;[36] . . .
>> and all the families of the nations shall worship before him.
> For dominion belongs to Yahweh,
>> and he rules over the nations.
> Yea, to him shall all the proud of the earth bow down;
>> before him shall bow all who go down to the dust. . . .
> Posterity shall serve him. . . . (Ps 22:26-30)

The text is of course used in the passion of Jesus, and we should not miss the movement from suffering to glory, from landlessness to landedness.

Third, Phil 2:1-11 speaks of the full one (that is, with land) being emptied (that is, sent to exile), only to be enthroned again ruler over the land. Of course land language is not apparent. But the imagery of empty/full (see Luke 1:51-55) clearly refers to people with turf who abandon it, that is, do not grasp but instead have it given.

This central insight and mystery of the gospel—that letting go is to have and keeping is the way to lose—are of special interest to Paul in 2 Corinthians. There he reflects on the possession/dispossession theme concerning Jesus: "For you know the grace of our Lord Jesus Christ, that though he was rich, yet for your sake he became poor, so that by his poverty you

---

35. On the use of the psalm in the New Testament see especially Hartmut Gese, "Psalm 22 und das Neue Testament," *ZTK* 65 (1968) 1–22; as well as Loren R. Fisher, "Betrayed by Friends," *Int* 18 (1964) 20–38, for a somewhat different reading.

36. Note the same term in Isa 53:11.

might become rich" (2 Cor 8:9). And just before, he notes the state of the church after the manner of Jesus: ". . . as sorrowful, yet always rejoicing; as poor, yet making many rich; as having nothing, and yet possessing everything" (2 Cor 6:10). The ones who possess do not. And the ones who have nothing do possess.

To argue that land is or is not a New Testament concern, literally or spiritually, misses the point. It is rather the history of *gift and grasp* that concerns the church. It is a radical affirmation in the New Testament, but an affirmation that Israel surely learned: "Kings who grasp lose. Pilgrims who risk are given." And Paul affirms what the whole history of land is finally about: "What have you that you did not receive? If then you received it, why do you boast as if it were not a gift?" (1 Cor 4:7). It is not what one would expect. It is not how it seems with land. But it is the case nevertheless. Coveting yields nothing but anxiety. The meek, the ones claiming no home and living with homelessness, do indeed inherit the land.[37] That scandal announces the absurdity of all alternative ways in the land, even if they seduce us.

---

37. Compare Davies, *The Gospel and the Land*, 359–63. While Davies may be correct in interpreting the text as having been spiritualized away from the meaning of Ps 37:11, that must be done only with a troubled conscience. Compare the strictures of Miranda concerning spiritualizing the text (*Marx*, 36, 104, 217).

11.

LAND: FERTILITY AND JUSTICE

HUMAN CONNECTEDNESS TO THE LAND IS SUGGESTED IN BIBLICAL
language by a play on words. '*Adam*, that is, humankind, has as partner and mate, '*adamah* (land).[1] Humankind and land are thus linked in a
covenantal relationship, analogous to the covenantal relationship between
man and woman.[2] A sound theology requires honoring covenantal relationship. The operating land ethic in our society denies that relationship
at enormous cost not only to land but to our common humanity.

Women and Land

I begin with a most suggestive statement from Wendell Berry, who has
reflected on land as much as anyone I know. He writes:

> I do not know how exact a case might be made, but it seems to me
> that there is an historical parallel, in white American history,
> between the treatment of the land and the treatment of women. The
> frontier, for instance, was notoriously exploitative of both, and I
> believe for largely the same reasons. Many of the early farmers seem
> to have worn out farms and wives with equal regardlessness, inter-
> ested in both mainly for what they would produce, crops and dol-
> lars, labor and sons; they clambered upon their fields and upon their

1. Phyllis Trible shrewdly names '*adam* as "the earth creature" in order to underscore the
relation to earth in *God and the Rhetoric of Sexuality,* OBT (Philadelphia: Fortress Press,
1978) 78. Moreover, Trible rightly sees that '*adamah* has priority over '*adam* in the creation
narrative.

2. The relation of covenant and creation is not without problem in current Old Testament theology. Nonetheless, Karl Barth, *Church Dogmatics* III/1 (Edinburgh: T. & T. Clark,
1958) has wisely seen that the two themes are integrally related to each other. The juxtaposition of the two is necessary to see that humankind has a covenantal relation with creation.

wives, struggling for an economic foothold, the having and holding that cannot come until both fields and wives are properly cherished. And today there seems to me a distinct connection between our nomadism (our "social mobility") and the nearly universal disintegration of marriages and families.[3]

On the land theme, he comments:

> The rural community—that is, the land and the people—is being degraded in complementary fashion by the specialists' tendency to regard the land as a factory and the people as spare parts. Or, to put it another way, the rural community is being degraded by the fashionable premise that the exclusive function of the farmer is production and that his major discipline is economics.[4]

The relation between women and land, between sexuality and economics, is the theme I want to pursue, to suggest that sexuality (which here includes fertility and production) and economics (which here includes the question of justice) cannot be separated. Sexuality and economics are the two great spheres of our life, the ones about which we most trouble, over which we most quarrel, and toward which we most hope. When sexuality is connected to fertility, and when economics is connected to justice, we are close to the core of all biblical ethics, for the Bible insists that fertility is impossible without justice; that is, economics cannot be separated from sexuality, nor sexuality from economics. We treat the land the way we treat women; "we" being dominant males who are historically owners of both.

My articulation of the parallel between issues of land and sexuality is cast in masculine terms and I regret that, but I hope you can translate. I leave the argument in masculine terms because that is the biblical casting of the problem, and because I believe the contemporary problem is still largely machismo. A serious relationship between a man and a woman requires attention to two temptations.[5] On the one hand, there is the

---

3. Wendell Berry, *Recollected Essays, 1965–1980* (San Francisco: North Point, 1981) 215.

4. Berry, *Recollected,* 191. See also the British anthropologist Jack Goody's important study, *Production and Reproduction: A Comparative Study of the Domestic Domain,* Cambridge Studies in Social Anthropology 17 (Cambridge: Cambridge Univ. Press, 1976); and the promises of land and children in Genesis discussed in Claus Westermann, *The Promises to the Fathers: Studies on the Patriarchal Narratives,* trans. D. E. Green (Philadelphia: Fortress Press, 1980).

5. Abraham Heschel has characterized human life when there is a loss of transcendence, *Who Is Man?* (Stanford: Stanford Univ. Press, 1965). Everyone then is a tool to be used and is reduced to usefulness. Phyllis Trible has explicated in a most discerning way biblical texts in

temptation to *promiscuity,* so that the woman is used by the man and discarded for the sake of another, i.e., reduced to a commodity. The relation is held casually, and there is no abiding or serious relationship, but only a momentary convenience. On the other hand, there is the temptation to *domination,* so that the woman is held by the man with such an intense commitment that she is owned, controlled, without rights, and so reduced in a different way to a commodity. There are women who are discarded, and there are women who are helplessly and legally dominated, so that they will never be discarded. So also with the land. It can be regarded promiscuously as though it had no significance, and it can be bought, sold, traded, used, discarded as a convenient commodity. Or the land can be held so closely and so tightly, dominated as though it had no rights, until the life is squeezed out of it. In either case, it is as though the land exists for the one who possesses it.

The mystery of an adequate relation with a woman (which we do not often realize) is to hold so loyally as to preclude promiscuity, but to hold so freely as to respect her rights. It is the same with the land. The mystery of faithfulness is to hold the land loyally so as not to reduce it to a commodity, but to hold so freely as to honor its rights as partner and not as possession.

In our society we have terribly distorted relations between men and women, between *'adam* and *'adamah,* distortions that combine promiscuity and domination, precluding in both cases loyal, freely held covenantal commitments. Likely we shall not correct one of these deathly distortions unless we correct both of them. We shall not have a new land ethic until we have a new sexual ethic, free of both promiscuity and domination. Applied to the land, we shall not have fertility until we have justice toward the land and toward those who depend on the land for life, which means all the brothers and sisters.

Sexuality and Economics

The linking of sexuality and economics, of fertility and justice, is evident at many places in the Bible. I will mention two such passages in this preliminary statement, and then a more contemporary observation.

Ezekiel 18:6-8
This passage provides a succinct catalog on what constitutes moral responsibility, that is, the practice of righteousness that leads to life.

which women are subjected to promiscuity and domination in *Texts of Terror: Literary-Feminist Readings of Biblical Narratives,* OBT (Philadelphia: Fortress Press, 1984).

Righteousness, according to this catalog, consists in only three elements. The first is to shun idolatry. The God-questions must be truly discerned so that absolute loyalty is not assigned to any other. Luke Timothy Johnson has usefully grasped the economic spin-offs from idolatry, because oppression regularly derives from idolatry.[6] Second, right sexuality is required, so that there is no defilement. The righteous man "does not defile his neighbor's wife or approach a woman in her time of impurity." Third, the most extended statement concerns economics. The righteous man "does not oppress anyone, but restores to the debtor his pledge, commits no robbery, gives his bread to the hungry and covers the naked with a garment, does not lend at interest or take any increase." I find it telling that this ethical summary of Ezekiel 18 derives from idolatry the two decisive ethical questions of sexuality and economics. The first of these is as clear as any conservative could desire, and the second is as extended as any liberal may wish. It would be health-giving in the church if we agree that every statement on sexuality must be accompanied by one on economics, and conversely. The two are the arenas in which idolatry usually becomes visible. In the language of Wendell Berry, the first concerns how women are treated; the second concerns the treatment of land.

Ezekiel 16:46-50
A second remarkable statement related to our theme appears in Ezekiel 16. The Sodom story of Genesis 18–19 is commonly regarded as a statement about homosexuality or gang rape or some such social aberration. The narrative is clearly about violence in sexual relations. But the Ezekiel text handles this narrative memory with remarkable freedom and imagination. Ezekiel 16 is a long recital of Israel's history, only now it is not a recital of God's mighty deeds. It is rather a recital of sin, betrayal, and distortion on the part of Israel. It is predictable that the Sodom story might occur in such a recital, but its use by Ezekiel is most surprising. The distortion is now handled in this way:

> This was the guilt of your sister Sodom: she and her daughters had pride, surfeit of food, and prosperous ease, but did not aid the poor and needy. They were haughty, and did abominable things before me; therefore I removed them, when I saw it. (Ezek 16:49-50)

The narrative on sexuality has been recast now as an indictment on economic distortions. The prophet is no doubt inventive. But the prophet is

6. Luke T. Johnson has a remarkable analysis of the interrelation between idolatry, possessiveness, and oppression in *Sharing Possessions: Mandate and Symbol of Life*, OBT (Philadelphia: Fortress Press, 1981) 84–95 and *passim*.

also discerning, for he has seen that sexuality and economic justice are of a piece. The treatments of women and of land are closely paralleled.

Freud and Marx

The third preliminary reference is simply to observe that the great themes of sexuality and economics require us in the contemporary world to pay attention to the insights of Sigmund Freud and Karl Marx and the interrelatedness of the two. Freud understood that, concerning the mystery of sexuality, we have an endless capacity for distortion and deception. And Marx understood that in economics, self-interest is readily passed off as reality. Marx and Freud were in the end speaking of the same social reality. They understood that modern civilization is grounded in an extraordinary self-deception that distorts both sexuality and economics, and that ends in deep alienation from self, from neighbor, from land.[7]

It is clear that we have become, in all kinds of popular ways, fascinated with Freud. It is equally clear that we are terribly intimidated by the insights of Marx. I submit that in terms of modern categories of criticism, it is the interface of Marx and Freud that will be necessary, urgent, and decisive for the large public problem of sexuality and economics, of productivity and justice. Trying to have Freud without Marx, sexuality without economics, as we mostly do, is an attempt to deal with part of an issue that in fact cannot be separated from its other part. In the end it means we imagine we can have productivity without justice. As long as we entertain that deception, we will not understand how or why Ezekiel transformed the Genesis narrative of sexual violence into a statement about economic abuse. And if we cannot understand that, we shall not have a land policy that avoids both promiscuity and domination.

Against that background, I now want to explore three biblical themes that occur at the interface between sexuality and economics, and that ask about the relation of productivity and justice.

The Right of Enclosure

Israel's theory of land, as it is portrayed in the conquest traditions and in the Torah provisions, is that the land is assigned to the entire community as a trust from Yahweh. Within the community, clans and "houses" held

---

7. Erich Fromm has most discerningly reflected on the interrelatedness of the themes of Marx and Freud in *Escape from Freedom* (New York: Farrar and Rinehart, 1941), and *The Anatomy of Human Destructiveness* (New York: Holt, Rinehart and Winston, 1973). For a suggestion on the common rootage of their concern, see John M. Cuddihy, *The Ordeal of Civility: Freud, Marx, Lévi-Strauss, and the Jewish Struggle with Modernity* (New York: Basic, 1974).

certain land as entities in the community. This land is regularly designated not as possession but as "inheritance"; that is, the connection
between the social unit and the land is inalienable and endures to perpe-
tuity. It need not concern us whether this notion of land was imple-
mented in detail or if it is an imaginative social contract that existed only
in theory. What matters is that this is the land theory appropriate to this
community, which regarded the land as a gift of God.[8]

Israel's theory of land, deeply rooted in the liberation traditions,
clashed with alternative theories and practices that regarded the land as a
tradable commodity, not as a gift or trust or inheritance. This alternative
land theory[9] (which comes to powerful expression in the tale of Naboth's
vineyard in 1 Kings 21) meant that in the real world nobody's land was safe
or secure, but that land became an arena for commercialism and all the
social problems that emerge when the strong are aligned against the weak.
That social relationship of conflict ended, as in the tradition of Amos,
with some having a monopoly and others being systematically reduced to
poverty, dependence, and despair.[10] The fundamental dream of Israel is
about land.[11] Israel is a social, theological experiment in alternative land
management. The God of Israel is a God who gives land, and Israel is a
people that holds land in alternative ways. The core tradition is intended
to promote an alternative to the imperial system of land known both in
the Egyptian empire and in the Canaanite city-states.[12]

Israel's theory of land as inheritance is practically designed to resist
monopoly and the corresponding social displacement that is caused by
monopoly. In both the Torah and in the wisdom instruction, land boundaries are to be maintained as a fundamental anchor of social policy. Thus
in the Torah:

8. Norman K. Gottwald has most sharply articulated the socioeconomic foundations
and implications of this alternative notion of land in *The Tribes of Yahweh: A Sociology of the
Religion of Liberated Israel, 1250–1050 B.C.E.* (Maryknoll, N.Y.: Orbis, 1979). Clearly there is
nothing romantic in such a view of land, but it has profound and serious social implications
that can only be regarded as subversive.

9. See Robert B. Coote, *Amos among the Prophets* (Philadelphia: Fortress Press, 1981)
24–25.

10. On the intentional management of such poverty, see Bernhard Lang, "The Social
Organization of Peasant Poverty in Biblical Israel," *JSOT* 24 (1982) 47–63.

11. On my own exposition of the theme, see esp. chap. 1; and Norman C. Habel, *The Land
Is Mine: Six Biblical Land Ideologies,* OBT (Minneapolis: Fortress Press, 1995).

12. On the "core tradition" see Walter Harrelson, "Life, Faith, and the Emergence of Tra-
dition," in *Tradition and Theology in the Old Testament,* ed. D. A. Knight (Philadelphia:
Fortress Press, 1977) 11–30; and Norman K. Gottwald, *The Hebrew Bible: A Socio-Literary
Introduction* (Philadelphia: Fortress Press, 1985) 144.

> In the inheritance which you will hold in the land that Yahweh your
> God gives you to possess, you shall not remove your neighbor's
> landmark, which the men of old have set. (Deut 19:14)

The language of inheritance is important,[13] but even more important is
the theological grounding of social practice and social guarantees in Yahweh's will and gift. Social arrangements are legitimated in theological
terms.

In wisdom instruction, the prohibition is the same:

> Remove not the ancient landmark which your fathers have set. Do
> you see a man skilful in his work? He will stand before kings; he will
> not stand before obscure men. (Prov 22:28-29)

> Do not remove an ancient landmark or enter the fields of the father-
> less; for their Redeemer is strong; he will plead their cause against
> you. (Prov 23:10-11)

In the first of these two sayings, it is not clear that v. 29 ought to be taken
with v. 28; but they are placed together in the text. Taken that way, the
connection between the verses is interesting, because v. 29 observes that
technical skills are always in the service of the powerful.[14] Applied to v. 28
and with reference to boundary stones, this suggests that moving boundary stones is not done as a thief in the night, nor is it a random social
practice that anyone may undertake; rather, it is done through sharp
legal practice, shrewd economics, or cunning court action, whereby the
shrewd can deprive the simple of their patrimony. The practice involves
social "know-how" that is a monopoly of the wise, who are characteristically on the side of the "haves."[15] Their work is systemic and legal, even
though socially destructive. Common people, or as v. 28 says, "obscure

---

13. See particularly the NEB translation of this passage. The term here rendered "inheritance" is there rendered as "patrimony," a term more telling for a theory of land possession.

14. The text contrasts kings with "hidden" (ḥk) people. The RSV renders as "obscure," the
NEB as "common." In this context, the contrast suggests people who have no public visibil-
ity, no social power, and so who have no chance for "the pursuit of happiness."

15. On the interplay of technical wisdom and established political interest, see Glendon
E. Bryce, *A Legacy of Wisdom: The Egyptian Contribution to the Wisdom of Israel* (Lewisburg,
Pa.: Bucknell Univ. Press, 1979) chaps. 6–7; and George E. Mendenhall, "The Shady Side of
Wisdom: The Date and Purpose of Genesis 3," in *A Light Unto My Path: Old Testament Stud-
ies in Honor of Jacob M. Myers,* edited by H. N. Bream et al., Gettysburg Theological Studies
4 (Philadelphia: Temple Univ. Press, 1974) 319–34.

people," are helpless in the face of such a concentrated, determined technical knowledge.[16]

In the second sapiential prohibition quoted above, the problem of social equality is more obvious because it warns against taking land from orphans, that is, from socially marginal people who have no connections, means, or "know-how" to protect their own interests. Indeed, this is why the prophets regularly inveigh against the leadership who "pervert justice" (Isa 5:7; Amos 5:7; 6:12). When the socially powerful pervert justice through legal channels, the "have-nots" who are socially disadvantaged have no recourse. Proverbs 23:11 is somewhat enigmatic, but the "powerful guardian" (NEB), that is, an avenger, may indeed be a reference to God, who will not tolerate such violation of land rights, especially if done to the marginal, even if done in socially, legally approved ways. It is striking that on a mundane matter like land boundaries in the literature of Proverbs, such a role is assigned to God.[17]

The most dramatic case of such usurpation is the self-indictment placed in the mouth of the arrogant Assyrian Sennacherib:

> By my own might I have acted, and in my wisdom I have laid my schemes; I have removed the frontiers of nations, and plundered their treasuries. (Isa 10:13; see Deut 32:8; translation mine)

Sennacherib is condemned for violation of fixed property boundaries on an international scale. It is probable that the prohibitions in Deuteronomy and Proverbs concern local transactions, but the problem is the same. Now whole nations are cast in the role of the marginal in the face of the Great Power. Seizure of the land of another is an act of exploitative greed and violates God's intent for social order, whether it is local or international. The prohibitions intend to protect the weak against the strong. The development of large landholdings by the rich and powerful is condemned as a betrayal of Israel's most elemental social dream.

These three prohibitions against moving boundaries contain three interesting notes. The first (Deut 19:14) mentions patrimony (Heb.

---

16. F. C. Fensham has summarized the data on curses related to the movement of boundaries in "Common Trends in Curses of the Near Eastern Treaties and *Kudurru* Inscriptions Compared with Maledictions of Amos and Isaiah," *ZAW* 75 (1963) 155–75. The use of curse formulas suggests that such religious sanction is the only force available to those who have no real social power.

17. It is instructive that the RSV capitalizes "Redeemer," thus interpreting unambiguously with reference to God. That the text speaks so of God may suggest a connection to Job 19:25 and the appeal there to a redeemer. Both texts, in very different contexts, raise the question of theodicy.

naḥalah), which bespeaks a certain theory of land and property. The second reference (Prov 22:28-29) addresses a contrast between the king and common people, indicating that these innocent-sounding prohibitions are quite discerning statements of social criticism. And the third (Prov 23:10-11) refers specifically to orphans. Taken together, the three articulate a theory of land division that assumes inheritance and the right to hold land, as in the case of an orphan without social power, simply because one is entitled as a member of the community. This view of the land is explicitly contrasted with "royal service" (Prov 22:28), that is, service in the interest of another theory of land that ignores such entitlements and believes that if there is a concentration of power formidable enough, which can claim legitimacy, moving land markers is simply a legal transaction to secure land for the strong against the weak. This is the theory that operates in the narrative of Naboth's vineyard. Jezebel is unhindered by Israel's dream of family-owned farms and freedom from monarchic tyranny.

The three prohibitions are stated in absolute terms. F. C. Fensham has studied curse provisions in other cultures that concern moving land markers (see n. 16 above). The recurrence of this concern suggests that the matter is foundational for a society. The fact that they are stated as curses indicates that these societies attached to the prohibition the harshest, weightiest religious sanctions available. Society cannot survive when some seize land to which others are entitled simply by being a part of the community, even if the seizure is legally sanctioned.

I want to relate this biblical prohibition on moving land markers to the modern practice of enclosure. By enclosure I mean the legal capacity of more powerful parties to claim exclusive right to a land to the exclusion of the others so that the land can be legally enclosed. Karl Polanyi has studied the dramatic emergence of a theory of market that is related to theories of land.[18] Until the eighteenth century, the market was to held to be autonomous in its operations, but was an aspect of social policy; that is, economic transactions were regarded as part of a larger social network. In that larger network, it was assumed that all parts were related to each other and must in some sense take each other into account. But the emergence of a new theory of autonomous market meant that each party in society was free to do any economic act with respect to neighbors. "Enclosure" is a formidable act that images the land and one's possession of it to be unattached to and unconcerned for other social relations. The right of enclosure meant that some could legally keep others off the land. The

18. Karl Polanyi, *The Great Transformation* (New York: Farrar & Reinhart, 1944).

ones excluded were characteristically the weak and the poor. The policy of enclosure was a radical social change that separated land policy from social interconnectedness and had the effect of further denigrating some to the benefit of others.[19] Polanyi presents the Tudor rulers of England as defenders of the poor against the practice of enclosure. But in the end it was the practice of enclosure that prevailed. That practice embodies the notion that land is privately held without reference to the community.[20]

In a recent, alarming book, Richard Rubenstein judges the policy of land enclosure to be in effect a practice of triage, that is, the intentional elimination of those who are judged to be superfluous, marginal, and not of sufficient value to sustain.[21] Rubenstein then traces the practice of triage into the modern world to more dramatic and obvious matters of social policy and practice. It is crucial to his argument that land enclosure, which excludes some from the land, is in effect triage. Rubenstein's passionate conclusion agrees with the judgment I would make that the Bible in its central social vision opposes policies of land enclosure precisely because they have implicit in them the seeds of triage.

The linkage between enclosure (that denies land to some) and triage is based on the conviction that one cannot live without land. Everyone must have access to land. (In a mass urban society, everyone must have the social, economic equivalent of land.) It behooves us to recognize that all free-market theory that seeks to separate economic transactions from social relations is destructive, so that the poor (parallel in Berry's reference to women and land) are used and thrown away. The church must make the case out of its text that such land practice and economic theory—which blatantly serve certain vested interests—are not value-free "laws," but are the practice of visibly destructive values. The reason land markers cannot be moved is because land markers enact and assert social relations that include inalienable guaranteed rights of the weak in the face of the strong, of the poor in the face of the economically powerful.

In Proverbs 22 the inalienable right of the poor to have land is presented by a warning that is pertinent to our argument:

19. Polanyi, *Great*, 78. He cites a key decision made at Speenhamland, England, one that was pivotal in repositioning the poor in the network of social relations. This particular case cited by Polanyi indicates that the issue of theodicy is not a general speculative issue, but relates to quite concrete questions of social policy and practice.

20. One may regard Deut 24:19-22 as an Israelite articulation against the practice of enclosure. The land must be left open for those not "in possession."

21. Richard L. Rubenstein, *The Age of Triage: Fear and Hope in an Overcrowded World* (Boston: Beacon, 1983).

> Do not rob the poor, because he is poor, or crush the afflicted at the gate; for Yahweh will plead their cause and despoil the life of those who despoil them. (Prov 22:22)

It is clear that "robbery" here is not breaking and entering, but is a legal transaction "at the gate."[22] The response of Yahweh to such victimization is that Yahweh will "go to court" on behalf of the poor. This same warning is evident in Prov 23:11: "for their Redeemer is strong; he will plead their cause." Yahweh is allied with the poor and will engage in legal defense. It remains in our interpretation to see what this means for contemporary social practice, but the Israelite commitment against rapacious confiscation seems clear enough. Israel well understood the costs of such policy and practice.

You Shall Not Covet

The second central biblical motif I will explicate is the familiar tenth commandment "You shall not covet" (Exod 20:17; Deut 5:21).[23] That commandment has been largely trivialized into a psychological matter concerning jealousy and envy. Marvin L. Chaney has most persuasively argued that the commandment does not refer to such matters that may vex "the introspective conscience of the West," but is to be understood in terms of public policy and social practice.[24] Chaney concludes that the commandment concerns especially land policy: "Do not covet your neighbor's field." In terms of our governing parallel between land and women, it is worth noting that the second most important matter is, "You shall not covet your neighbor's wife." It is wife and land that are crucial to the ordering of the community. Moreover, it is plausible to suggest that this tenth commandment corresponds in a special way to the first commandment, "You shall have no other gods." Yahweh, unlike other gods in the Near East, is holy, and therefore beyond location, and acts in freedom.[25] The

---

22. On the "gate" as a social institution, see Ludwig Köhler, *Hebrew Man,* trans. P. R. Ackroyd (New York: Abingdon, 1956) 127–50; References to "the gate" show that the act against the poor is systematic and institutional.

23. On this commandment, see the fine introduction by Walter Harrelson, *The Ten Commandments and Human Rights,* OBT (Philadelphia: Fortress Press, 1980) 148–54.

24. Marvin L. Chaney, "You Shall Not Covet Your Neighbor's House," *Pacific Theological Review* 15 (1982) 3–13. The formula on "introspective conscience" is from Krister Stendahl, "The Apostle Paul and the Introspective Conscience of the West," *HTR* 56 (1963) 199–215.

25. Cyrus H. Gordon has suggested that the tenth commandment is derived from the character of Yahweh, because Yahweh is unlike the other gods of Canaan who covet; "A Note on the Tenth Commandment," *JBR* 31 (1963) 208–9. Such a theological contrast with other gods helps link the commandment to the fundamental claims of Yahwism.

counterpart to that radical character of God who may not be reduced in idolatrous ways is the dignity and worth of the neighbor. That respect for neighbor comes to its climactic expression in the maintenance of and respect for land and house. Insofar as the tenth commandment is related to the first, we have a structure not unlike Ezek 18:6-9, which moves from idolatry into matters of sexuality and economics. Chaney concludes that this prohibition on coveting concerns land management and land owner-ship. The rapacious land policies of the monarchy (as in 1 Kings 21) per-mitted and legitimated confiscation of a most greedy and destructive kind.[26] The Israelite vision of social organization, articulated by this com-mandment, is to prevent such confiscation that takes from the defenseless poor who have no economic or legal means to protect themselves against the economically powerful.

Perhaps the two most important exegetical comments on this com-mandment are in prophetic oracles from Micah and Isaiah. These two prophets most consistently critique the royal apparatus in Jerusalem, which is to be understood, among other things, as an embodiment of land surplus, if not monopoly.[27]

Micah 2:1-5 begins in vv. 1-2 as a sapiential statement simply observing the predictable consequences of land seizure. But then in vv. 3-5 the poetry takes a more severe prophetic tone with a double "therefore," lay-ing out the consequences of such land seizure:

> Therefore thus says Yahweh: Behold, against this family I am devis-ing evil, from which you cannot remove your necks; and you shall not walk haughtily, for it will be an evil time. In that day they shall take up a taunt song against you, and wail with bitter lamentation, and say, "We are utterly ruined; he changes the portion of my peo-ple; how he removes it from me! Among our captors he divides our fields." Therefore you will have none to cast the line by lot in the assembly of Yahweh. (Mic 2:3-5)

The first two verses concern scheming and calculation that amount to sharp, exploitative business dealing. The "woe" asserts that those who

---

26. On this dimension of monarchy, note that Gottwald refers to the monarchy as "Israel's Counterrevolutionary Establishment" (*The Hebrew Bible,* 293). Clearly, Gottwald intends that "counterrevolutionary" apply to socioeconomic matters such as land policy. In parallel fashion, George E. Mendenhall refers to the monarchy as the "paganization" and "Canaanization" of Israel in "The Monarchy," *Int* 29 (1975) 155-70. This also applies to ques-tions of egalitarianism in economic relations.

27. See Mendenhall, "Shady," on the monopoly of knowledge that supports a monopoly of technology, which soon leads to a monopoly of wealth.

manage to grab land from others will surely come to death.[28] That in itself is a remarkable statement. Then the "therefore" statements of threat correspond to the violations.[29] Those who devised evil now have Yahweh devise evil against them. Now there is a reaping of what has been sown.

Finally, according to Israelite faith, Yahweh must be reckoned with and answered to for the way land is managed. There is no escape from this accountability. Those who have so much land that is not rightly theirs, even if legally secured, will come to destruction. Others will come and divide their fields. In context the poetry presumably refers to the Assyrians. The Bible insists that undisciplined and unneighborly land practice finally leads to a reckoning. The extreme case among us was the land in Nicaragua controlled by the Somoza family. President Anastasio Somoza Debayle was forced out of office in 1979 by the Sandinistas and assassinated in Paraguay in 1980. Even in the late 1990s, the land confiscated and redistributed to peasants by the Sandinista government was contested by the wealthy families and property rights remained unclear.[30] But we would do well to think through the social dynamics closer to home. The Bible articulates a remarkable theory of how the historical process works, because Yahweh governs that process. In our postmodern culture, we must see if these same realities must still be heeded.

The end result in v. 5 says simply, "Therefore you will have none to cast the line by lot in the assembly of Yahweh." Albrecht Alt has argued that this poetic statement anticipates that there will come a time when the adherents of Yahweh, the ones blessed by Yahweh (perhaps the meek), will meet in public assembly to redistribute the land.[31] That assembly, in the name of the liberating, covenanting God, will be a meeting of peasants entitled to their patrimony.[32] The big land-grabbers will not be present

28. See Klaus Koch, "Is There a Doctrine of Retribution in the Old Testament?" in *Theodicy in the Old Testament,* ed. J. L. Crenshaw, IRT (Philadelphia: Fortress Press, 1983) 57–87, on the certitude with which consequences follow deeds. The "woe" form does not assert an active agent in punishment, but only that such outcomes inexorably follow such actions. Thus land-grabbing does not depend on the action of God for retribution, but yields its own destructive consequences. One cannot grab land, so the poem argues, with impunity.

29. On this correspondence, see Patrick D. Miller, *Sin and Judgment in the Prophets,* SBLMS 27 (Chico, Calif.: Scholars, 1982), and specifically on this text, 29–31.

30. On the inevitability of this social movement, see Walter LaFeber, *Inevitable Revolutions: The United States in Central America,* 2d ed. (New York: Norton, 1993). On land and insurgency, see Jan L. Flores, "The Roots of Insurgency," *Latin American Issues* 5 (2001) (on the web at http://webpub.alleg.edu/group/LAS/LatinAmIssues/Articles/Vol5/LAI_vol_5.htm).

31. Albrecht Alt, "Micah 2:1-5 Ges Anadasmos in Judah," in *Kleine Schriften zur Geschichte des Volkes Israel,* vol. 3 (Munich: Beck, 1959) 373–81.

32. On the sociology of Micah, see Hans Walter Wolff, *Micah the Prophet,* trans. R. D. Gehrke (Philadelphia: Fortress Press, 1981).

when the boundary lines are redrawn. Indeed, the land-grabbers will not even be admitted to the meeting and so will end up landless. Now this may sound like an extreme social vision, but it is the vision that is being acted out in revolutionary ways in many parts of our world. This is a vision of a complete inversion, in which coveting as social policy comes to its sorry end. In a quite concrete way, the first will become last and the last will finally be first. That terse formula is, among others things, a theory of land distribution (see Mark 10:31 in context).

Isaiah 5:8-10 closely parallels the Micah passage. This text also begins with "woe":[33]

> Woe to those who join house to house, who add field to field, until there is no more room, and you are made to dwell alone in the midst of the land. Yahweh of hosts has sworn in my hearing: "Surely many houses shall be desolate, large and beautiful houses, without inhabitant. For ten acres of vineyard shall yield but one bath, and a homer of seed shall yield but an ephah."

The warning is against buying up large tracts of land and therefore displacing peasants who have lived on the land. Verse 9 departs from the "woe" form (as did Mic 2:3-4) in order to announce Yahweh's immediate engagement on the side of the dispossessed. This great concentration of wealth will come to a sorry end, because it cannot be sustained against the intent of Yahweh, who opposes monopoly and is inclined toward egalitarianism. Thus the large houses will be terminated.

And finally, in v. 10 we have a consequence that is of interest for our juxtaposition of justice and fertility. Ten acres will yield only a little. The land will not yield as it is expected to do. Land that is handled unjustly will finally not be productive. "Bath" and "ephah" are measures of grain. This land will be short on produce. Because the Bible does not speak in terms of secondary causation, it does not comment on or explain the reasoning that leads to this conclusion. We are not told why or in what way injustice works against productivity. But in broad sweep, it is sufficient to know that where there is injustice, there will sooner or later be infertility. The connection between justice and fertility is invisible and never well-explicated. But it must be noted that for ancient Israel, just social relations are foundational and prerequisite for productive land.

---

33. On this passage and the "woe" form, see J. William Whedbee, *Isaiah and Wisdom* (Nashville: Abingdon, 1971) 93–98; and K. C. Hanson, "How Honorable! How Shameful! A Cultural Analysis of Matthew's Makarisms and Reproaches," *Semeia* 68 (1994[96]) 81–111.

This latter point is dramatically stated in Hos 4:1-3. Every part of this brief poetic unit concerns land. It begins with a summons to court concerning the inhabitants of the land (v. 1a). It indicts the community for violating Torah, because there is no knowledge of God in the land (vv. 1b-2). It concludes with an announcement that the land has severe drought until the reliable structures and systems of life are destroyed. It is astonishing that the poet dares to say that failure to keep Torah leads to life-destroying drought. Failure to practice justice makes fertility impossible.

I wish to cite only one other text that may illuminate the matter of coveting as a systemic practice of the strong against the weak. In the well-known narrative of 2 Samuel 11, David covets Bathsheba, wife of Uriah, and takes possession of her. He covets and seizes. He regards this woman as something to use and abuse. The connection to our theme is in the prophetic parable of Nathan in 2 Sam 12:1-4. Nathan's parable gives a close reading of David's "conquest" [sic]. It is a rich man and a poor man, one who had much and one who had little. The parable is pliable. It can, as Nathan intends, be linked to sexual conquests. But it could as easily refer to land, concerning those who have little and those who have much. The operational verb is "take" (laqaḥ; see 11:4 and Nathan's indictment in 12:9). In 1 Kgs 21:19, the verbs are different (raṣaḥ, yara'), but the questions concerning land are the same. Thus the parable mediates between land and sexuality, between field (Naboth, Ahab, Jezebel) and wife (Bathsheba, Uriah, David). Both forms of coveting will finally destroy.[34]

Defilement of the Land

The third theme I will pursue is more radical and more difficult to handle. It is defilement of the land. The reason this is such a difficult theme is that ritual defilement is a notion quite alien to us. Now we are in the sphere of shame and contamination that is much more elemental than guilt and morality.[35] Such defilement renders its object impure, unavailable for religious use. The holy God of Israel will not and cannot stay in a place that is defiled.

---

34. Gottwald offers an exposition of the commandment, which relates it to land policy (*Hebrew Bible*, 210).

35. On the elemental character of shame that is more foundational than guilt, see Erik Erikson, *Identity and the Life Cycle* (New York: International Universities Press, 1959) 65–82; and Paul Ricoeur, *The Symbolism of Evil*, trans. E. Buchanan, Religious Perspectives 17 (New York: Harper, 1967).

Deuteronomy 24

The text that is my point of reference is Deut 24:1-4. This law concerns marital relations. It is about a situation in which a man divorces a wife. She goes to a second husband. But the second marriage also ends. Then she wants to return to the first husband and resume that relation. The point of the legal prohibition is that the first husband, even if he wants to, may not take the woman back again. Notice that in v. 4 we again have the word "take" (*laqaḥ*). The reason that such a return is prohibited is that she is "defiled" (*time'*). That is, she was intended for this singular "use" of the first husband. But having been put to other use, that is, the second husband, she is no longer suitable for the first, proper relation. Now this may strike us as primitive and severely sexist, for matters are clearly not symmetrical for the man and the woman. But on its own terms, one may consider this defilement. The prohibition refers to improper use that renders proper use impossible. The improper use is to be engaged for something other than intended us.

The Deuteronomic theological commentary on this prohibition makes an important move in interpretation:

> for that is an abomination before Yahweh, and you shall not bring guilt upon the land which Yahweh your God gives you for an inheritance. (Deut 24:4)

First, the commentary labels the second relationship an abomination, which means a distortion that endangers the entire community.[36] We may say such marital maneuvering may threaten social solidarity and order, but the usage attributes an almost material notion of abomination, as though a substance of destruction is thereby introduced into the community.

The other theological comment interests us most directly. Such an act will bring guilt on the land of inheritance. The distorted marital relation causes distortion of the land. Moreover, the land is *naḥalah*, that is, land that is a trust made according to the promise of Yahweh. Distorted marriage relation leads to distorted land. The ritual language of contamination makes the land less than productive—under curse—a place where God will not grant fertility.

Jeremiah 3

It is a matter of great interest that this text is utilized by Jeremiah in 3:1-5.[37] Jeremiah lived at a moment when Judah was to be exiled and lose its land.

---

36. On the meaning of "abomination" in Deuteronomy, see Jean L'Hour, "Les Interdits *toéba* dans le Deuteronome," *RB* 71 (1964) 481–503.

37. For one proposal concerning the relation of these texts, see T. R. Hobbs, "Jeremiah 3:1-5 and Deuteronomy 24:1-4," *ZAW* 86 (1974) 23–29.

Jeremiah is preoccupied with the matter of land and land loss, and presents an argument about how land is lost.[38] In this poetry the prophet takes the law of Deut 24:1-4 as a metaphor. In this usage Yahweh is the first husband who has been violated by the wife, Judah. Judah the wife has been rejected in infidelity, and so she goes to a second husband, presumably Egyptian alliance (Jer 2:36) and Canaanite religion. But those connections do not work, so Judah wishes to return to Yahweh, to reestablish the covenant relation with Yahweh. The Torah precludes that resumption of relation, however. Yahweh is prevented by the Torah from taking Judah back, even if Yahweh had chosen or wished to do so.

Two points interest us here. First, Yahweh is willing to violate the Torah prohibition for the sake of the relation. Against the Torah, Yahweh yearns for a restoration. Against the Torah, Yahweh urges Israel to repent and come home (Jer 3:12, 14; 4:1-2). Notice that in Jer 4:3-4, agricultural images are used for criteria of return as in Hos 10:12.

The second item that concerns us is that Jeremiah uses the language of defilement, as in the old teaching of Deuteronomy:

> Would not that land be greatly polluted? (Jer 3:1; see 2:7, 23)

> You have polluted the land with your vile harlotry. (3:2)

The language of defilement is used to portray distorted covenant. That language concerns the relation with Yahweh. But at the same time, that language is used to characterize the situation of the land and its social organization. The land has now been treated so that it is not productive. And this in turn is because Yahweh refuses to stay in such a place or to grant blessings of fertility in such a context.

The language of *ritual contamination* is an important one for speaking about land abuse.[39] I suggest four dimensions of the problem vis-à-vis a holy God and holy ground.

1. The language of defilement and contamination is probably what is operative in much of the current conversation about sexuality, with particular reference to homosexuality, escalated even more with the panic about AIDS, particularly in the first decade of the pandemic.

---

38. On the motif of land in the tradition of Jeremiah, see Walter Brueggemann, "Israel's Sense of Place in Jeremiah," in *Rhetorical Criticism: Essays in Honor of James Muilenburg,* ed. J. J. Jackson and M. Kessler, PTMS 1 (Pittsburgh: Pickwick, 1974) 149–65; and John M. Bracke, "The Coherence and Theology of Jeremiah 30–31" (Ph.D. diss., Union Theological Seminary, 1983) esp. chap. 3.

39. On land and its contamination as a religious-cultural problem, see Mary Douglas, *Purity and Danger: An Analysis of the Concepts of Pollution and Taboo* (New York: Routledge & Kegan Paul, 1966).

That is, the enormous passion against acceptance of homosexuality and fear of it appear to be a sense of uncleanness that endangers the entire community and "pollutes the land," endangering everyone. The reaction indicates that something more profound and elemental than guilt or moral outrage is at work. The response is of a depth to show that this social phenomenon is perceived as endangering the entire community. The disproportionately negative response to homosexuality is an indication that what is at issue is something deeper than holding homosexuals guilty. That deeper feeling expressed as rejection and anger is, I suggest, a sense that homosexuality is a profound impurity that jeopardizes the entire community in a way that moral affront does not. Thus the response is a pre-rational response congruent with an inchoate, completely unarticulated sense that the community is placed in jeopardy by "pollution." Such thinking is, I believe characteristic of the holiness traditions.

2. Environmentally, there is no doubt that chemicals (particularly fertilizers) contaminate the land, threaten the water table, and eventually endanger the productivity of the soil.

3. It is striking that we refer to nuclear fallout as "pollution" and contamination, and that we speak of "dirty bombs" that so defile the earth as to make life impossible except in its lowest forms. The 2002 congressional debate about the advisability of relocating all nuclear waste in the depths of Yucca Mountain, Nevada, raises all sorts of questions about the production, transportation, disposal, and long-term effects of these materials. The citizens of Nevada certainly have vocalized opposition to bearing the brunt of a national failure to make plans on the front-end of this problem.

4. Taken all together, the technology of contamination may create a moral situation in which the possibility of life is jeopardized. That, in fact, is what the priestly tradition in the Old Testament is about.[40] An ethic of "use, abuse, discard" is evident in every area of life. In terms of land and sexuality, matters of wrong use (injustice) threaten fertility and productivity. In our secular mode we would not speak of it so, but such a practice eventually will make the earth a place where God cannot and will not abide. At least we might say that the "power of life"

---

40. See Fernando Belo, *A Materialist Reading of the Gospel of Mark,* trans. M. J. O'Connell (Maryknoll, N.Y.: Orbis, 1981) for a consideration of the sociology of purity; see also Jerome H. Neyrey, "Pure/Polluted and Holy/Profane: The Idea and System of Purity," in *The Social Sciences and the New Testament,* ed. R. L. Rohrbaugh (Peabody, Mass.: Hendrickson, 1996).

may be withdrawn. And where that happens, productivity ends. It is clear that a land ethic that uses, abuses, and discards is a practice of pollution and fickleness. It creates a fundamental cleavage between a Creator who wills life and a creation that squanders and finally rejects life.

These three themes together—*moving boundaries,* which translates into the practice of enclosure; *coveting,* which we understand as rapacious land policy; and *defilement,* which we understand as pollution of the ecosystem of life—are ways in which the Bible speaks about land management. These three themes respectively concern geographic, economic, and ritual dimensions of life. All of them together articulate policies that end in death. Death is caused where boundary markers abuse the poor and God's vengeance is evoked. Death is caused where coveting becomes policy and the poor are displaced and despoiled. Death is caused when defilement is practiced that causes the power for life to be withdrawn. The conversation in ancient Israel (which we must continue) is whether the way we relate to the land is a way of death. The staggering discernment is that death comes not only to the weak and poor who are victims of such policies and values, but eventually death reaches even into the life of the powerful and affluent who are not immune to death when it comes to the community (see, for example, Exod 11:4-6).

Land Management

Finally, the Bible affirms that land can be managed in ways that give life. It does not need to be handled toward death. The Bible is not a warning or a threat, but an invitation to another way. It is, however, an invitation that requires a break with the death systems that encompass us. Let me review briefly three texts that are related our three themes.

Boundaries

Against moving boundaries and enclosure systems, the Bible celebrates the old land theory of *inalienable patrimony.* The text I cite is Jer 32:1-15. In that text (which is commonly regarded as having a historical connection to the prophet), the prophet is summoned directly by God to purchase the land. The occasion of the summons is that the Babylonian armies are invading and the economic system is collapsing. But the summons from Yahweh is based on the conviction that the old inheritance rights finally will prevail. Even the great empire is not free to move boundaries and claim land against those old tribal claims. The careful language of the mandate is to exercise the "right of redemption by purchase" (*mi'paṭ haggᵉulah liqᵉnôth*;

v. 7) and "right of possession and redemption" (*mi'paṭ hay'ru'ah . . . hagg'ulah*; v. 8). The transaction is done in precise legal terms, with great care to secure clear title. Even the mandate from Yahweh is expressed in those categories.[41] But the theological claim of the narrative is the oracle in v. 15: "Houses and fields and vineyards shall again be bought (*qanah*) in this land." The economy will be reestablished. And when the economy is reestablished after the current debacle, the old rights will prevail. (The argument is parallel to that in Mic 2:5. In both cases, the old tribal basis of land will endure after the current imperial rapaciousness.) Those who violate those old rights in the interest of land speculation and land seizure will not prevail. The text seems to assume an economic retribalization against the more recent concentration of wealth in the hands of the few, either foreign or Israel's own elite.

Coveting

Against coveting, Israel celebrates land redistribution, which breaks up monopolies and gives back land to those who should properly have it. In Joshua 13–19, care is taken that tribal groups receive their proper entitlements. In Joshua 7–8, the text knowingly observes that this practice of patrimonial land is threatened by Achan's sin, which holds goods apart from the community. But the narrative of Achan's sin is only a candid footnote to the main textual tradition of land division. According to the stylized claims of the tradition, the land is held in alternative ways.[42]

That land division from the Joshua text was obliterated by royal patterns that violated such covenantal guarantees. The Davidic house ignored and destroyed old tribal land arrangements. In the later anticipation of Ezek 47:13—48:29, the land memory of Joshua 13–19 becomes a prototype for the land apportionment to come. The way the land was remembered in Joshua becomes the way it is expected in Ezekiel. Micah

---

41. On the relation of this passage to the issue of theodicy as a social problem, see Walter Brueggemann, "Theodicy in a Social Dimension," in *A Social Reading of the Old Testament: Prophetic Approaches to Israel's Communal Life*, ed. P. D. Miller (Minneapolis: Fortress Press, 1994) 174–96.

42. It is telling that in the Book of Joshua, it is Rahab the harlot who is instrumental in the well-being of Israel and the downfall of Jericho. Jericho is clearly a walled city that embodies the "Canaanite" monopoly against which Israel is mobilized. It is therefore expected that such a marginal person should be on the side of those who assault the monopoly. A great deal will be discerned in such narratives when we read with sociological sensitivity. Gottwald, in speaking of the social location of Rahab, says that the narrative "never ceases to emphasize how much of the 'outside,' both communally and territorially, is 'inside' Israel" (*Hebrew Bible*, 258–59).

2:1-5 had anticipated a new land division. And now Ezekiel speaks after the long generations of the monarchal system, after the failure of that system of 587, and after the exile without land. Ezekiel 47–48 shows the old memories coming to fresh fruition. The report of this anticipation in Ezekiel is obviously much too stylized and artificial to be regarded in terms of an actual policy action. But the text does show that Israel believes present land arrangements are unfortunate developments that are not secure in the future. In the coming time, the land will be reapportioned according to the old, enduring promises. The promises speak authoritatively against current practice.

The land will indeed be redistributed. This relates to the practice of the Jubilee Year, which consists of returning land to its rightful owner (Leviticus 25). The land is not managed according to calculating economic transactions. There may be such transactions, but they happen in contexts of promise and inheritance, which finally override such transactions. It is worth noting that that powerful tradition of land redistribution can be understood as the center of Luke's presentation of Jesus.[43] Jesus is a threat to vested interests in his time because he proposed to give land and dignity back to those who had lost it. I judge such matters to be important among us because the great revolutions of our time against colonial power are in fact an effort to redistribute land according to tribal conventions that have been gravely distorted in the interest of concentrated surplus. It will not do to dismiss as terrorist or communist those who insist on implementing the old promissory land management in the face of present settlements based on seizure.

Defilement

Against defilement and abomination, the Bible anticipates a time when the land is free of such contamination so that production can be full and the blessings of life abundantly available. Two prophetic texts may be cited. Hosea 2:21-23 is an answer to Hos 5:3 and 6:10. In 5:3 and 6:10 Israel's covenantal violations have polluted the land:

> For now, O Ephraim, you have played the harlot, Israel is defiled. (5:3)

> In the house of Israel I have seen a horrible thing; Ephraim's harlotry is there, Israel is defiled. (6:10)

---

43. See Sharon H. Ringe, *Jesus, Liberation, and the Jubilee Year: Images for Ethics and Christology*, OBT (Philadelphia: Fortress Press, 1985).

In both cases, land defilement is expressed in the metaphors of fickleness and harlotry.

In the great poems of Hos 2:2-23 (Heb. 2:4-25), the land will function again, after it has ceased to function.[44] And then, in a lyrical portrayal of new creation, the poet says:

> In that day, says Yahweh, I will answer the heavens and they shall answer the earth; and the earth shall answer the grain, the wine, and the oil, and they shall answer Jezreel and I will sow him for myself in the land. (Hos 2:21-23)

The restored land is a conversation of productivity in which all parts will gladly respond to each other, and the land will bear an abundance of grain, wine, and oil. But that will happen only where the defilements and harlotries are overcome by a season of exile-landlessness. It is after exile that this faithful God will say,

> And I will have pity on Not pitied, and I will say to Not my people, "You are my people"; and he shall say, "Thou art my God." (2:23b-d)

The other text related to defilement and restoration is Isa 62:4-5, which is an answer to Isa 6:5. In that first familiar text, the prophet says, "I am defiled and I live among defiled people" (6:5). The book of Isaiah asserts that judgment comes against such massive defilement. But then in 62:4-5, after the judgment and exile and loss of land, the lyrics again assert the coming fullness of productivity:

> You shall no more be termed Forsaken, and your land shall no more be termed Desolate; but you shall be called My delight is in her, and your land Married; for Yahweh delights in you, and your land shall be married. For as a young man marries a virgin, so shall your sons marry you, and as a bridegroom rejoices over the bride, so shall your God rejoice over you. (62:4-5)

It is amazing that in v. 4 land is referred to three times: "Your land shall no more be termed Desolate . . . your land Married . . . your land shall be married." The term "married" is *be'ulah,* which is derived from *ba'al* and means "fructified," "made productive." The statements about land are sur-

---

44. On the structural reversal in this poem, see David J. A. Clines, "Hosea 2: Structure and Interpretation," in *Studia Biblica 1978,* ed. E. A. Livingstone, JSOTSup 11 (Sheffield: Univ. of Sheffield, 1979) 83–103.

rounded in vv. 4a and 5 with marriage images: You will no more be divorced, abandoned. In v. 5 the metaphor concerns human marriage (twice), and then offers joy as the joy of a wedding.

In all these cases the power is overcome. The laws of patrimony prevail against moving boundaries (Jer 32:1-15). Land redistribution overcomes coveting, which leads to inequality (Ezek 47:13—48:29). Productivity recurs in a land marked by defilement (Hos 2:21-23). The land will again be home. It does not happen simply by divine fiat, but only by historical activity that is risky and costly.

I suggest that this analysis provides a grid of three pairs of themes:

Enclosure	————	Inalienable patrimony (Jer 32:1-15)
Coveting	————	Redistribution (Ezek 47:13—48:29)
Defilement	————	Restored fertility (Hos 2:21-23; Isa 62:4-5)

These are ways of life and death. We must ponder that the ways of enclosure, coveting, and contamination have become acceptable policy among us. Now we are at a crisis point. The text reintroduces to us the nonnegotiable conditions of life in the land. We hold a view of land that we know has pertinence to public conversation. We are at a place in our society when we must re-ask foundational questions about use, abuse, and discarding. The alternative mediated in these texts is to "tend and care," to caress and cherish (Gen 2:15). But that work requires a break with an ethic of monopoly and surplus value. It is a costly repentance. So the prophet Jeremiah can say:

> "If you return, O Israel, says Yahweh, to me you should return. If you remove your abominations from my presence, and do not waver, and if you swear, 'As Yahweh lives,' in truth, in justice, and in uprightness, then nations shall bless themselves in him, and in him they shall glory." For thus says Yahweh to the men of Judah and to the inhabitants of Jerusalem: "Break up your fallow ground, and sow not among thorns. Circumcise yourselves to Yahweh, remove the foreskin of your hearts, O men of Judah and inhabitants of Jerusalem; lest my wrath go forth like fire, and burn with none to quench it, because of the evil of your doings." (Jer 4:1-4)

There is in this poem a massive condition of "if–then," and it is presented as an agricultural metaphor. The poet invites Judah to a repentant life in the land in order to avoid the fire. The human, covenantal issues do not admit of technical solution. Land management must be restored to its place in the fabric of social relations. Productivity requires attention to justice. Fertility causes us to rethink economics. Sexuality raises questions of righteousness. Without righteousness and justice in land management, there may come a destroyer who will "make your land a waste" (Jer 4:7). It need not be so. But it can happen, and is indeed happening before our very eyes.

12.

CONCLUDING
HERMENEUTICAL
REFLECTIONS

THIS EXPLORATION OF THE LAND MOTIF IS NOT INTENDED SIMPLY TO add yet another theme to the rich arsenal of biblical materials. Rather it is intended to contribute to the current hermeneutical discussion, that is, to reflect upon our categories and presuppositions in interpretation, to probe the shape of the expectations we have of the text and therefore our discernment of what we find in the text. It is the argument of these statements that if land is indeed a prism through which biblical faith can be understood, not only will specific texts take on different nuances and tones, but we shall find that the Bible in its entirety is about another agenda that calls into question our conventional presuppositions and our settled conclusions.

Land and Our Hermeneutical Categories

Such a hermeneutical discussion may serve in two important ways. First it may require us to review the categories in which we interpret Scripture, both to be alert to fresh possibilities and to critique our usual ones. Out of this come several observations:

Scripture interpretation has thrived on the antitheses of space/time and nature/history. In each case scholars have often regarded the latter as peculiarly Hebrew.[1] It is implicit in the foregoing argument that such

1. See especially the critique of James Barr, *The Semantics of Biblical Language* (Oxford: Oxford Univ. Press, 1961); idem, *Biblical Words for Time*, SBT 1/33 (Naperville, Ill.: Allenson, 1962).

antitheses or at least polarities misrepresent the data. In the Old Testament there is no timeless space, but there also is no spaceless time. There is rather *storied place*, that is, a place that has meaning because of the history lodged there.[2] There are stories that have authority because they are located in a place. This means that biblical faith cannot be presented simply as a historical movement indifferent to place that could have happened in one setting as well as another, because it is undeniably fixed in this place with this meaning. And for all its apparent "spiritualizing," the New Testament does not escape this rootage. The Christian tradition has been very clear in locating the story in Bethlehem, Nazareth, Jerusalem, and Galilee.

Of the God of the Bible then, it is likely that we can no longer settle for the antithesis of the God of history versus the gods of the land.[3] As Yahweh is Lord of events so he is also fructifier of the land. As he comes "in that day," so also he watched over the land. He not only intrudes to do saving deeds, but he also governs in ways to assure abiding blessings.[4] Harrelson is surely correct that Yahweh is indeed a fertility god who gives life as well as a historical god who saves and judges.[5] He is Lord of places as well as times.

This questioning of categories raises important issues with an existentialist hermeneutic especially associated with Rudolf Bultmann. It makes a vigorous attack on the notion of individualism, which presumes there are only individuals in pursuit of private and/or personal meanings through instantaneous and radical decisions of obedience. In the latter perspective the Old Testament must be rejected so that the New Testament may be taken away from history in land or history toward land.

2. Jonathan Z. Smith correctly concludes: "It is, briefly, history that makes a land mine," "Earth and Gods," *JR* 49 (1969) 109. On the distinction between space and place, compare F. W. Dillistone, *Traditional Symbols and the Contemporary World* (London: Epworth, 1973) chap. 6.

3. See Patrick D. Miller, Jr., "God and the Gods," *Affirmation* 1 (1973) 37–62, and Bertil Albrektson, *History and the Gods: An Essay on the Idea of Historical Events as Divine Manifestations in the Ancient Near East and in Israel*, CBOT 1 (Lund: Gleerup, 1967).

4. On the distinction between blessing and salvation as modes of biblical faith, see Claus Westermann, "Creation and History in the Old Testament," in *The Gospel and Human Destiny*, ed. V. Vajta (Minneapolis: Augsburg, 1971) 11–38; and Patrick D. Miller, Jr., "The Blessing of God," *Int* 29 (1975) 240–51.

5. Walter Harrelson, *From Fertility Cult to Worship* (Garden City, N.Y.: Doubleday, 1969) chap. 1.

There are, of course, long-standing criticisms of such an approach,[6] but the issues are sharpened by attention to land.[7] It is clear that the land emphasis, which concerns transmission of the inheritance from generation to generation, places the faithful believer in the flow of the generations. A focus on "now" decisions of faith is untenable because land must be cared for in sustained ways. It is equally the case that the land possessed or the land promised is by definition a communal concern. It will not do to make the individual person the unit of decision-making because in both Testaments the land possessed or promised concerns the whole people. Radical decisions in obedience are of course the stuff of biblical faith, but now it cannot be radical decisions in a private world without brothers and sisters, without pasts and futures, without turf to be managed and cherished as a partner in the decisions. The unit of decision-making is the community and that always with reference to the land.

But the issues may be pressed deeper to ask about what is the central human yearning and vocation. The existentialist perspective in response to a comprehensive and containing idealism saw *emancipation* as the central human agenda, "freedom to be me," in self-assertion apart from a larger totality. In more popular form, the human agenda, in postwar romanticism, has been a pursuit of *meaning* that is peculiarly appropriate to the individual. This hermeneutic then in romantic terms, in response to the terrors and failures of Western ideologies, located the possibility of faith in the realm of private decision-making, which placed enormous burdens on the individual and articulated promises, if there were any, in private terms.[8]

Our study of land suggests that such an approach is a misunderstanding of biblical categories. The central problem is not emancipation but *rootage,* not meaning but *belonging,* not separation from community but

6. See G. Ernest Wright, *The Old Testament and Theology* (New York: Harper & Row, 1969); B. W. Anderson, ed., *The Old Testament and Christian Faith: A Theological Discussion* (New York: Harper & Row, 1963); and the articles by Hans Walter Wolff and Claus Westermann in *Essays on Old Testament Hermeneutics,* ed. C. Westermann, trans. J. L. Mays (Richmond: John Knox, 1963).

7. The issue is articulated from many sides: by Dorothee Soelle, *Political Theology* (Philadelphia: Fortress Press, 1974) from within Bultmann's categories; John MacQuarrie, *Thinking About God* (New York: Harper & Row, 1975) 227, in distinguishing two hermeneutical perspectives; and from José Porfirio Miranda, *Marx and the Bible: A Critique of the Philosophy of Oppression,* trans. J. Eagleson (Maryknoll, N.Y.: Orbis, 1974), in terms of radical sociological criticism.

8. Compare Philip Rieff, *The Triumph of the Therapeutic: Uses of Faith after Freud* (New York: Harper & Row, 1966); and most fundamentally Paul Tillich, *The Courage to Be* (New Haven: Yale Univ. Press, 1952), especially 40–63.

location within it, not isolation from others but *placement* deliberately between the generations of promise and fulfillment. The Bible is addressed to the central human problem of homelessness *(anomie)* and seeks to respond to that agenda in terms of grasp and gift. The author is aware that the current effort is not unlike Bultmann's; interest in land may well be the result of the rootlessness *of our situation.* Nonetheless, it is also clear that such an approach stays close to the categories of the Bible itself, as an existentialist approach has not.

It is much more difficult for this writer, but equally important, to see that a study of the land motif also provides a critique of the "mighty deeds of God in history" approach articulated especially by Gerhard von Rad and G. Ernest Wright.[9] This perspective focused singularly on the great events of God's intrusive action from time to time that reversed historical circumstance and destiny. This approach was concerned to establish the distinctiveness of Israel's faith, the free sovereignty of Yahweh, and the historical character of biblical faith, to all of which I agree.

But in making the case and in overstating the sharp discontinuities from Canaanite factors, this view has tended to fall into the space/time, nature/history antithesis in a one-sided way. Moreover, the category of history has often been presented as though these events that happened between Yahweh and his people could have happened anywhere since only these two parties were involved and it was a covenantal relation without reference to context or place. An inordinate stress on *covenant* to the neglect of *land* is a peculiarly Christian temptation and yields to a space/time antithesis.

I wish in no way to caricature a view that I largely share. Because of zeal to make the case for a covenantal/historical understanding, the inter-actions of biblical faith have been treated as though only Yahweh and Israel were involved. It is clear, I hope, from the discussion above that covenant never concerned only Israel and Yahweh or church and Yahweh, but the land is always present to the interaction and is very much a deci-sive factor. The covenant of Yahweh and Israel is of course "historical" and not "natural." But it is characteristically about land, about promise of land not yet given, about retention of land now possessed, and about land-loss because of covenant-breaking. Israel never had a desire for a relation with Yahweh in a vacuum, but only in land. In the New Testament the crisis of exile/crucifixion is ultimately dealt with in the same categories.

9. Compare Brevard S. Childs, *Biblical Theology in Crisis* (Philadelphia: Westminster, 1970) 13–147, who has given the most comprehensive critique. It is likely that Gerhard von Rad, *Wisdom in Israel*, trans. J. D. Martin (Nashville: Abingdon, 1972), was himself beginning to explore alternative modes of biblical theology, distinct from the historical traditions approach which he himself had established.

It is ironic that, while a "mighty deeds of God in history" approach delivered harsh criticisms of an existentialist perspective, this view also came to be largely expressed in existentialist categories of event to the disregard of *structure*, of history to the denial of *nature*, act to the disregard of *abiding continuities*, distinct deliverances to unawareness of *enduring blessings*.[10] It seems clear that in the zeal to be freed from nineteenth-century evolutionary approaches the posture of "againstness" has caused an imbalance of categories. Our theme reasserts faith in Yahweh as land-governor and -maintainer, and creation not simply as innovative act but as resilient sustenance. Israel is to be discerned not as people waiting only for occasional intrusions but as living always with gifts that are entrusted and grasping that seduces.

Such a notion of *placed history* may be an important affirmation about the character of human life, about the strange struggle of homelessness and home,[11] about the God who both leads out and brings in,[12] about the Messiah who has no place and yet who is the very one with authority to give a place (Luke 9:58).[13]

10. See. Walter Brueggemann, *In Man We Trust: The Neglected Side of Biblical Faith* (Richmond: John Knox, 1972) and the statements of Westermann and von Rad, cited in notes 4 and 9. Clearly the "mighty deeds of God in history" perspective could not permit this polarity, characterized as it was with a firm over-againstness toward whatever gave stability to cultural forms. It is obvious that, for all the polemics against Bultmann, the existentialist and "mighty deeds of God" hermeneutics are in essential agreement on this point. Both must stress *event* to the neglect of *structure*, and on such a basis, an appreciation of land as a central theological motif is impossible.

11. Paul Tournier, *A Place for You: Psychology and Religion* (New York: Harper & Row, 1968) has articulated this dialectic in psychological terms. On the psychological dimensions of land, see John H. Snow, *On Pilgrimage: Marriage in the '70s* (New York: Seabury, 1971) 38; James Luther Adams, "The Geography and Organization of Social Responsibility," *USQR* 29 (1974) 245–60; and Edward Tiryakian, "Phenomenology and Sociology," in *Phenomenology and the Social Sciences I,* ed. M. Natanson (Evanston: Northwestern Univ. Press, 1973) 218–21.

12. Friedrich-Wilhelm Marquardt, *Die Juden und ihr Land* (Hamburg: Siebenstern Taschenbuch, 1975) 75, has made the point that Yahweh not only leads out of land and brings in, but he himself is with his people in every circumstance: "Das ist Solidarität Gottes zu Jerusalem! Er bleibt heimatlos, solange Israel heimatlos ist, er hat selbst im Himmel keine feste, bleibende Stadt zu betreten, solange nicht das 'wohlgefugte' Jerusalem auf Erden (Psalm 122:3) für die Jüden wieder aufgebaut und betretbar ist."

13. Hans W. Frei, *The Identity of Jesus Christ: The Hermeneutical Bases of Dogmatic Theology* (Philadelphia: Fortress Press, 1975) 29–30, develops the theme: "Jesus is the archetypal man, or the pattern for authentic humanity. He is the *stranger*—as we all are—in this harsh and hostile universe. . . . In just this wandering estrangement, Jesus is our embodiment or representative. . . . In Jesus, the typical human situation finds its most early progenitor to establish his identity on earth. As early as the moment of his conception and birth, it is symbolically the case that he has no place to lay his head."

The Prospect for New Interfaces

The second possible contribution of such hermeneutical reflections is to identify new interfaces or to discern old interfaces in new ways as biblical faith engages a series of dialogue partners. The central learning about the land motif that has come out of this study is that grasping for home leads to homelessness and risking homelessness yields the gift of home. We yearn deeply for home but we live in ways that surely will result in homelessness.

We can thus understand the land histories of Israel. The first is a history of risking homelessness that yields the gift of home. The second is the deep yearning for home, but in ways that result in homelessness. And in the third history, from exile to Jesus, we learn that Jesus' embrace of homelessness (crucifixion) is finally the awesome, amazing gift of home (resurrection). The learning is radically dialectical. It will not do, as one might be inclined to do with a theology of glory, to say that God's history is simply a story of coming to the land promised.[14] Nor will it do, as one might be tempted in a theology of the cross, to say God's history is a story of homelessness. Either statement misses the main affirmation of the unexpected way in which land and landlessness are linked to each other.

Although that insight has been taken up by many voices, perhaps it is appropriately the peculiar stress of biblical theology in various interactions. Among them are these:

1. It is clear that, since the recent wars of the state of Israel, Christians cannot speak seriously to Jews unless we acknowledge land to be the central agenda.[15] While the Arabs surely have rights and legitimate

---

14. Some forms of liberation theology are expressions of theology of glory. They affirm a singular theme of reception of land and have lost the dialectic of land as gift that cannot be had as grasp. Thus Moltmann in his more recent *The Crucified God* has corrected any tendency to a theology of glory in theology of hope.

15. Concluding his study, Peter Diepold writes: ". . . das Wohnen im Land konstitutiv für Israels Existenz ist" (*Israels Land,* BWANT 95 [Stuttgart: Kohlhammer, 1972] 187). On the relation of Jewishness to land see Isaac H. Jacob, "Israel, History and the Church," *CCI Notebook* 8 (1972) 1–6; *Judisches Volk-gelobtes Land,* ed. W. Eckert, et al. (Munich: Kaiser, 1970); Abraham Heschel, *Israel: An Echo of Eternity* (New York: Farrar, Straus and Geroux, 1969); Hans Ruedi Weber, "The Promise of the Land," *Study Encounter* 7 (1971) 1–16; Hans Eberhard von Waldow, "Israel and Her Land," in *A Light unto My Path: Old Testament Studies in Honor of Jacob M. Myers,* ed. H. N. Bream, et al. (Philadelphia: Temple Univ. Press, 1974) 493–508; Marquardt, *Die Juden und ihr Land;* Rolf Rendtorff, *Israel und sein Land,* TEH 188 (Munich: Kaiser, 1975); and Jacob Neusner, *American Judaism: Adventure in Modernity* (Englewood Cliffs, N.J.: Prentice-Hall, 1972) chap. 4. Neusner asserts, "One cannot divide the Jewish people into two parts, the 'enlandised' and the 'disenlandised.' Those in the land look outward. Those outside look toward the land. Those in the land identify with the normal peoples.

grievances, the Jewish people are peculiarly the pained voice of the land in the history of humanity, grieved Rachel weeping (Jer 31:15). And unless we address the land question with Jews, we shall not likely understand the locus of meaning or the issue of identity. The Jewish community—in all its long, tortuous history—has never forgotten that its roots and its hopes are in storied earth, and that is the central driving force of its uncompromising ethical faith.[16]

Obviously Christians have failed to understand that immense and costly stance. Not only have we misunderstood Jewish perspective, but I should argue, we have misunderstood our own Scripture that is also about the land of promise. If Christians could be clear that the gospel entrusted to Christians is also about land, perhaps a new conversation could emerge, but it will not so long as we misunderstand our faith in categories either existentialist or spiritual-transcendental.

But we have not only new understandings to embrace. It may be that we have also an important role to play vis-à-vis the Jewish land question. It is clear that the question of land allotment in the "Holy Land" is a deeply complex matter. Not only does the contemporary state of Israel appeal to old traditions as a basis of entitlement, but that appeal is, of course, reinforced by the abomination of the twentieth-century Shoah. That claim of entitlement, however, cannot now be permitted to go uncontested, and Christians who appeal to the same authoritative land traditions must be deeply engaged in that contestation.

While the urgency of the security of the contemporary state of Israel is readily acknowledged, it is acknowledged with equal urgency that the Palestinian community also has a profound claim upon the land. Many Palestinians, moreover, are Christians, and therefore Christian people in the West must care intensely about the Palestinian population and its land entitlement. Christian appeal to biblical land traditions must insist that land possession is held, according to that tradition, only as land practices are under the discipline of neighbor practices grounded in the Torah. Any claim of land apart from that Torah tradition is deeply suspect and open to profound critique.

But perhaps it is important to assert the dialectic of land and land-lessness, that grasping leads to homelessness and gift leads to home. That is what our common history has taught. But we seem always to

---

Those abroad see in the land what it means to be extraordinary" (14). See the various essays in *Speaking of God Today: Jews and Lutherans in Conversation*, ed. P. D. Opsahl and M. Tanenbaum (Philadelphia: Fortress Press, 1974).

16. See James A. Sanders, "Torah and Christ," *Int* 29 (1975) 372–90.

need to relearn. Such an affirmation is not transparently applicable to the political realities, but it is equally clear that it does relate to them. Perhaps the dialectic of home/homelessness could be taken seriously in the public arena.

2. Focus upon the land may be an important resource for further Marxist-Christian conversations. It is clear in what I have urged that the land motif requires that (a) land be handled always as a gift not to be presumed upon and (b) land be managed as an arena for justice and freedom. This concern for a material, physical promise gives credibility to Christianity as a religion of materialism. When Christianity went spiritual and denied its proper focus on land it rightly earned the critique of Marx.[17]

Thus Marxism and Christianity share the vision of a new land commonly and rightly held. But it is clear that a need in Marxism for some recognition of transcendence is essential. It may be that Christianity can contribute to the conversation. The understanding of land we have discerned in the Bible is never just about land, never only land possessed and managed. It is always a land of gift and promise, a gift given when it could never be taken or grasped or seized, a promise by a Promiser who stands outside history but has been found faithful in history. We have negatively to affirm that the Promiser can never be reduced to or contained by our best explanations or structures. But positively we affirm he has been found faithful when his purposes are honored. Land is both held and fruitful. When his vision of justice is ignored, the land is endangered.

But at the same time, the land is not only gift from God, transcendent Promiser. It is also land in history, land not usurped or simply mastered, but a land with its own history. Therefore this people does not own the land but also belongs to the land. In that way, we are warned about presuming upon it, upon controlling it in scientific and rational ways, so that its own claim, indeed its own voice, is not heard or is disregarded.

This could be the time when Christians and Marxists can discern again their common origins. In such an exploration of commonality, perhaps Marxism can be corrected of an ordinate materialism in which land is only turf to be managed, while Christianity can be corrected of

17. See Miranda, *Marx*, for a protest against a Christian tendency to spiritualize. Although Paul Hanson is not concerned with a Marxist perspective, his utilization of Mannheim's *Ideology and Utopia* is instructive. Our analysis suggests a dialectic that neither Christian spiritualism nor Marxist materialism has effectively maintained.

its temptation to spiritualism in which we focus on the transcendent Promiser without taking responsibility for the gift given. The transcendence in the midst of materialism that Israel knew is the Holy Voice of the Promiser in the land, a voice of gift and of demand. Perhaps we are required to face that even modern society will not be viable until that voice in the land leads us away from grasping to gift.

3. Closely related to the previous point is the interface of biblical faith with the cause of the dispossessed—the young, the black, the poor, and women. It is striking that an important word for their commonality is *dispossessed,* that is, those denied land, denied power, denied place or voice in history. The essential restlessness of our world is the voice of the dispossessed demanding a share of the land. And that restlessness is a precise echo of the biblical voice of the poor (see Exod 2:23-25; 1 Kgs 12:4).[18] The indignant voice of the prophets announces Yahweh's alliance with the poor against the landed.[19] In our time the voices of the dispossessed seem only threatening and boisterous, but biblical faith is the reminder to us that those boisterous voices may well be the voice of God himself allied always with the dispossessed against the landed.

While the issues are complex, few things have contributed more to our wrong understandings of theology than our false spiritual interpretation of Scripture that has made landlessness a virtue instead of a condition for receiving land. And from that interpretation has come the notion of poverty (landlessness) as virtue.[20] We have so interpreted the Bible away from its agenda and so focused on spiritual matters that we have not caught the power of its claim or the richness of its dialectic. Not only have we failed to hear the gospel with its staggering promise but we have, perhaps unwittingly, embraced the status quo inequities of landlessness and landedness. Spiritual Christianity, by refusing to face the land question, has served to sanction existing inequities.

18. See George E. Mendenhall, "The Hebrew Conquest of Palestine," *BA* 25 (1962), reprinted in *BARead* 3 (Garden City, N.Y.: Doubleday, 1970) 100–120. On the land belonging to the poor see Moshe Weinfeld, *Deuteronomy and the Deuteronomic School* (Oxford: Clarendon, 1972) 313–16. See the programmatic statement of Frederick Herzog, "Liberation Hermeneutic as Ideology Critique?" *Int* 28 (1974) 387–403.

19. See James H. Cone, *God of the Oppressed* (New York: Seabury, 1975); Preston N. Williams, "Toward a Sociological Understanding of the Black Religious Community," *Soundings* 54 (1971) 260–70.

20. See the summary of the twists and turns in the history of the church on poverty and property, Martin Hengel, *Property and Riches in the Early Church,* trans. J. Bowden (Philadelphia: Fortress Press, 1974).

The church is immobilized by phony polarizations, as though the issue was liberal/conservative, revolutionary/reactionary, when in fact the real radicalness is the agenda of land that undercuts all other postures.[21] We have yet to face how odd and discomforting is the biblical affirmation that God wills land for his people and he will take it from others for the sake of the poor.[22] We have failed to maintain the land/landless dialectic, so that we are immobilized on the issue without power to invite the landed to landlessness or to include the landless in the land. The good news is not that the poor are blessed for being poor, but that to them belongs the kingdom, that is, the new land. Similarly the meek are not simply blessed but are identified as heirs of the land.

It is likely that our theological problem in the church is that our gospel is a story believed, shaped, and transmitted by the dispossessed; and we are now a church of possessions for whom the rhetoric of the dispossessed is offensive and their promise is irrelevant. And we are left to see if it is possible for us again to embrace solidarity with the dispossessed.

4. Finally the land then is pertinent to our interface with the claims of urban technocratic values in America. It may be that it can call us away from total accommodation so that we are aware in new ways of an interface with unresolved and perhaps unresolvable issues.

What we have learned of the dialectic of landlessness/landedness, of gift/grasp, of crucifixion/resurrection, suggests some alternatives among us:

a. The grasped land of the kings has important points of contact with a production-consumption set of values in which it is assumed that *more* leads to well-being and security. It is dawning in some quarters

---

21. In addition to the article of Herzog cited in note 18, see the remarkable article by Roy Sano, "Neo-Orthodoxy and Ethnic: Liberation Theology," *Christianity and Crisis* 35 (1975) 258–64.

22. See the abrasiveness of the Song of Hannah and Mary's Magnificat. Robert McAfee Brown, in addressing the Nairobi World Council of Churches Assembly, stressed the bad news aspects of the good news. If land is to be given to some, others will surely lose it. Compare "WCC Assembly: A Sober Celebration," *ChrCent* 92 (December 10, 1975) 1123. Krister Stendahl writes: "To the oppressed, the suppressed, and the repressed, there is no message of more comfort than to know that all flesh is grass and all the powers that lord it over them are passing away. The message of comfort is the downfall of the 'haves,' the downfall of the powerful. There is little comfort or no comfort at all for the comfortable. The comfort consists in the announcement of the revolution of the change of crew, of the leveling of the fact that those who hunger and thirst for justice are finally going to be satisfied," in "Judgment and Mercy," in *The Context of Contemporary Theology: Essays in Honor of Paul Lehmann*, ed. A. J. McKelway and E. D. Willis (Atlanta: John Knox, 1974) 148.

that we have gone as far as we can with that line of effort, and it has not kept its promise. The theme of land on the way to exile raises the hard question about the relation of production-consumption to the issues of justice and righteousness.

b. The production-consumption values inevitably place a central priority upon utility, upon reward for people who can perform useful tasks. Such values tend to discard people without utility. And Jesus, the center of land history, announced and embodied the conviction that in the new land (the kingdom) the issue of utility as a means of entry was not pertinent (see Luke 14:12-14, 21-24). How staggering it could yet be if we are driven to the unthinkable possibility that land cannot be arranged on the basis of utility. The articulation of the gift/grasp issue is a warning against utility as a norm for land.

c. If utility for production and consumption is not a norm for landedness, then we are given new pause about urban development and "progress" that claims the right to relocate and reassign people, to move them from storied place to history-less space. And in new ways urbanization will need to focus on the presence of stories for humanness and the difference between trusted place and coerced space.[23]

d. Related to this is of course the crunch of pollution and energy. After an interlude, we have regressed to believe that pollution problems will not endure and hopefully will solve themselves. We are left to reflect on biblical understanding of pollution that leads to exile (see Jer 3:1-5).

All of these issues revolve around our values that make us insatiable (see Lev 26:26; Hos 4:10). We are consumed by aliens—alien values and alien loyalties—and we eat our way into exile (see Hos 7:9).

It may be that John Steinbeck has put the issue most eloquently. He has presented two stories of the dispossessed. In *Of Mice and Men*, Lennie holds to a vision that keeps him functioning: "We could live offa the fatta the lan.'"[24] He lives while he holds to that hope. When that hope is gone, he is a despairing exile. More fully, *Grapes of Wrath* is a story, as true today, about dispossessed exiles.[25] Two lines can serve as our conclusion. First, as they set off from Oklahoma, Pa is sick atop the truck that holds all their belongings. (Exiles travel light.) Pa cannot bear to leave the land because

---

23. See Peter L. Berger, *Pyramids of Sacrifice* (New York: Basic, 1974) 23–24, 167–75, and his harsh critique of modernity as the loss of place.

24. John Steinbeck, *Of Mice and Men* (New York: Viking, 1937, 1965). Perhaps one must be as "God damned dumb" as Lennie to believe the land will be given as promised.

25. John Steinbeck, *The Grapes of Wrath* (New York: Viking, 1939). For a suggestion on the relation between Steinbeck and Deuteronomy, see H. Kelly Crockett, "The Bible and the Grapes of Wrath," *College English* 24 (1962) 197–99.

"Pa is the land." And land-loss is crucifixion, because not many days out, Pa is dead, unable to live apart from his storied place. Second, when they arrive in California, they seek a place to settle. Like Israelites come to Canaan, they find that all the land is occupied. "Everything is tractored." And when it is tractored, the dispossessed count for nothing. The Steinbeck picture parallels the tractored land of Pharaoh and Solomon in which there is enormous prosperity but the dispossessed never enter history and never share in the prosperity.[26] They die and they disappear. But the ones who tractor the land stay anxious (see Matt 6:25ff.).

The gospel is about the coming of the new age, the new kingdom, the new land. In that context there is no anxiety, no sorrow (John 16:20). There is only trust in the promise of a land of rest and joy. But surely such a gift is a scandal!

---

26. On the hard interface between political freedom and economic well-being, see Berger, *Pyramids of Sacrifice*, particularly his comments on the calculus of pain and meaning, chaps. 5 and 6.

SELECT BIBLIOGRAPHY
ON THE BIBLE AND THE LAND

Ahituv, Shmuel. "Land and Justice." In *Justice and Righteousness: Biblical Themes and Their Influence,* edited by H. G. Reventlow and Y. Hoffmann, 11–28. JSOTSup 137. Sheffield: JSOT Press, 1992.

Barstad, H. M. *The Myth of the Empty Land: A Study in the History and Archaeology of Judah during the "Exilic" Period.* Symbolae Osloensis 28. Oslo: Scandinavian Univ. Press, 1996.

Boorer, Suzanne. "The Importance of a Diachronic Approach: The Case of Genesis–Kings." *CBQ* 51 (1989) 195–208.

Brueggemann, Walter. *Hopeful Imagination: Prophetic Voices in Exile.* Philadelphia: Fortress Press, 1986.

———. "Hunger, Food and the Land in the Biblical Witness." *Lutheran Theological Seminary Bulletin* 66.4 (1986) 48–61.

———. "Israel's Sense of Place in Jeremiah." In *Rhetorical Criticism: Essays in Honor of James Muilenburg,* edited by Jared J. Jackson and Martin Kessler, 149–65. PTMS 1. Pittsburgh: Pickwick, 1974.

———. "The Kerygma of the Deuteronomistic Historian." *Int* 22 (1968) 387–402.

———. "The Land and Our Urban Appetites." *Perspectives: A Journal of Reformed Thought* 4.2 (1989) 9–13.

———. "Land: Fertility and Justice." In *Theology of the Land,* edited by Bernard F. Evans and Gregory D. Cusack, 41–68. Collegeville, Minn.: Liturgical, 1987.

———. "On Land-losing and Land-receiving." *Dialog* 19 (1980) 166–73.

———. "'Placed' between Promise and Command." In *The Covenanted Self: Explorations in Law and Covenant,* edited by Patrick D. Miller, 99–107. Minneapolis: Fortress Press, 1999.

———. "The Practice of Homefulness." *Journal of Preachers* 15:4 (1992) 7–22.

————. "Theses on Land in the Bible." In *Erets, Land: The Church and Appalachian Land Issues,* 4–13. Ames, Ohio: Coalition for Appalachian Ministry, 1984.

————. "Weariness, Exile and Chaos (A Motif in Royal Theology)." *CBQ* 34 (1972) 19–38.

Carroll, Robert P. "The Myth of the Empty Land." *Semeia* 59 (1992) 79–93.

Davies, E. W. "Land: Its Rights and Privileges." In *The World of Ancient Israel: Sociological, Anthropological, and Political Perspectives,* edited by R. E. Clements, 349–69. Cambridge: Cambridge Univ. Press, 1989.

Davies, W. D. *The Gospel and the Land.* Berkeley: Univ. of California Press, 1974.

————. *The Territorial Dimension of Judaism: Early Christianity and Jewish Territorial Doctrine.* Berkeley: Univ. of California Press, 1982.

Diepold, Peter. *Israels Land.* BWANT 95. Stuttgart: Kohlhammer, 1972.

Elliott, John H. *A Home for the Homeless: A Social-Scientific Criticism of 1 Peter, Its Situation and Strategy.* 2d ed. Minneapolis: Fortress Press, 1990.

Glass, Zipporah G. "Land, Slave Labor and Law: Engaging Ancient Israel's Economy." *JSOT* 91 (2000) 27–39.

Gnuse, Robert K. *You Shall Not Steal: Community and Property in the Biblical Tradition.* Maryknoll, N.Y.: Orbis, 1985.

Gunn, David M. "David and the Gift of the Kingdom." *Semeia* 3 (1975) 14–45.

Habel, Norman C. *The Land Is Mine: Six Biblical Land Ideologies.* OBT. Minneapolis: Fortress Press, 1995.

Hopkins, David C. *The Highlands of Canaan: Agricultural Life in the Early Iron Age.* SWBA 3. Sheffield: Almond, 1985.

Janzen, Waldemar. "Land." In *ABD* 4.143–54.

Japhet, Sara. "People and Land in the Restoration Period." In *Das Land Israel in biblischer Zeit,* edited by Georg Strecker, 103–25. Göttinger theologische Arbeiten 25. Göttingen: Vandenhoeck & Ruprecht, 1983.

Klein, Ralph W. *Israel in Exile: A Theological Interpretation.* OBT. Philadelphia: Fortress Press, 1979.

Knierim, Rolf P. "Food, Land, and Justice." In *The Task of Old Testament Theology: Substance, Method, and Cases,* 225–43. Grand Rapids: Eerdmans, 1995.

———. "Israel and the Nations in the Land of Palestine in the Old Testament." In *The Task of Old Testament Theology,* 309–21.

Lang, Bernhard. "The Social Organisation of Peasant Poverty in Biblical Israel." *JSOT* 24 (1983) 47–63.
Lemche, Niels Peter. *The Canaanites and Their Land: The Tradition of the Canaanites.* JSOTSup 110. Sheffield: JSOT Press, 1991.

March, W. Eugene. *Israel and the Politics of Land: A Theological Case Study.* Louisville: Westminster John Knox, 1994.
Miller, Patrick D. "The Gift of God: The Deuteronomic Theology of the Land." *Int* 23 (1969) 451–69.

Oakman, Douglas E. "The Countryside in Luke-Acts." In *The Social World of Luke-Acts: Models for Interpretation,* edited by Jerome H. Neyrey, 151–79. Peabody, Mass.: Hendrickson, 1991.
Orlinsky, Harry M. "The Biblical Concept of the Land of Israel: Cornerstone of the Covenant between God and Israel." In *The Land of Israel: Jewish Perspectives,* edited by L. A. Hoffman, 27–64. Notre Dame, Ind.: Univ. of Notre Dame Press, 1986.

Pastor, Jack. *Land and Economy in Ancient Palestine.* London: Routledge, 1997.
Premnath, D. N. *Eighth Century Prophets: A Social Analysis.* St. Louis: Chalice, 2002.
———. "Latifundialization and Isaiah 5:8-10." *JSOT* 40 (1988) 49–60.

Rad, Gerhard von. "The Promised Land and Yahweh's Land in the Hexateuch." In *The Problem of the Hexateuch and Other Essays,* 79–93. Translated by E. W. T. Dicken. New York: McGraw-Hill, 1966.
Rendtorff, Rolf. "Das Land Israel im Wandel der alttestamentlichen Geschichte." In *Judisches Volk—gelobtes Land,* edited by W. P. Eckert et al., 153–68. Munich: Kaiser, 1970.
Rost, Leonhard. "Die Beziechnungen für Land und Volk, im Alten Testament." In *Festschrift Otto Prockch zum sechzigsten Geburtstag am 9. August 1934 überreicht,* edited by Albrecht Alt et al., 124–48. Leipzig: Hinrichs, 1934.
Ruether, Rosemary Radford, and Herman J. Ruether. *The Wrath of Jonah: The Crisis of Religious Nationalism in the Israeli-Palestinian Conflict.* 2d ed. Minneapolis: Fortress Press, 2002.

Smith, Daniel L. *The Religion of the Landless: The Social Context of the Babylonian Exile.* Bloomington, Ind.: Meyer & Stone, 1989.

Smith, Jonathan Z. "Earth and the Gods." *JR* 49 (1969) 108–27.

Smith-Christopher, Daniel L. *A Biblical Theology of Exile.* OBT. Minneapolis: Fortress Press, 2002.

Steck, Odil Hannes. *World and Environment.* Biblical Encounter Series. Nashville: Abingdon, 1980.

Waldow, Hans Eberhard von. "Israel and Her Land: Some Theological Considerations." In *A Light Unto My Path: Old Testament Studies in Honor of Jacob M. Myers,* edited by Howard N. Bream et al., 493–508. Philadelphia: Temple Univ. Press, 1974.

Westermann, Claus. *The Promises to the Fathers: Studies on the Patriarchal Narratives.* Translated by D. E. Green. Philadelphia: Fortress Press, 1980.

Whitelam, Keith. "Israel's Traditions of Origin: Reclaiming the Land." *JSOT* 44 (1989) 19–42.

Zimmerli, Walther. "Land and Possession." In *The Old Testament and the World,* 67–79. Translated by J. J. Scullion. Atlanta: John Knox, 1976.

———. "The 'Land' in the Pre-Exilic and Early Post-Exilic Prophets." In *Understanding the Word: Essays in Honour of Bernhard W. Anderson,* edited by J. T. Butler et al., 247–62. JSOTSup 37. Sheffield: JSOT Press, 1985.

———. "Plans for Rebuilding after the Catastrophe of 587." In *I Am Yahweh,* edited by Walter Brueggemann, translated by D. W. Stott, 111–33. Atlanta: John Knox, 1982.

INDEX OF ANCIENT SOURCES

Apocrypha

INDEX OF AUTHORS